SPECTRUM OF DESIRE

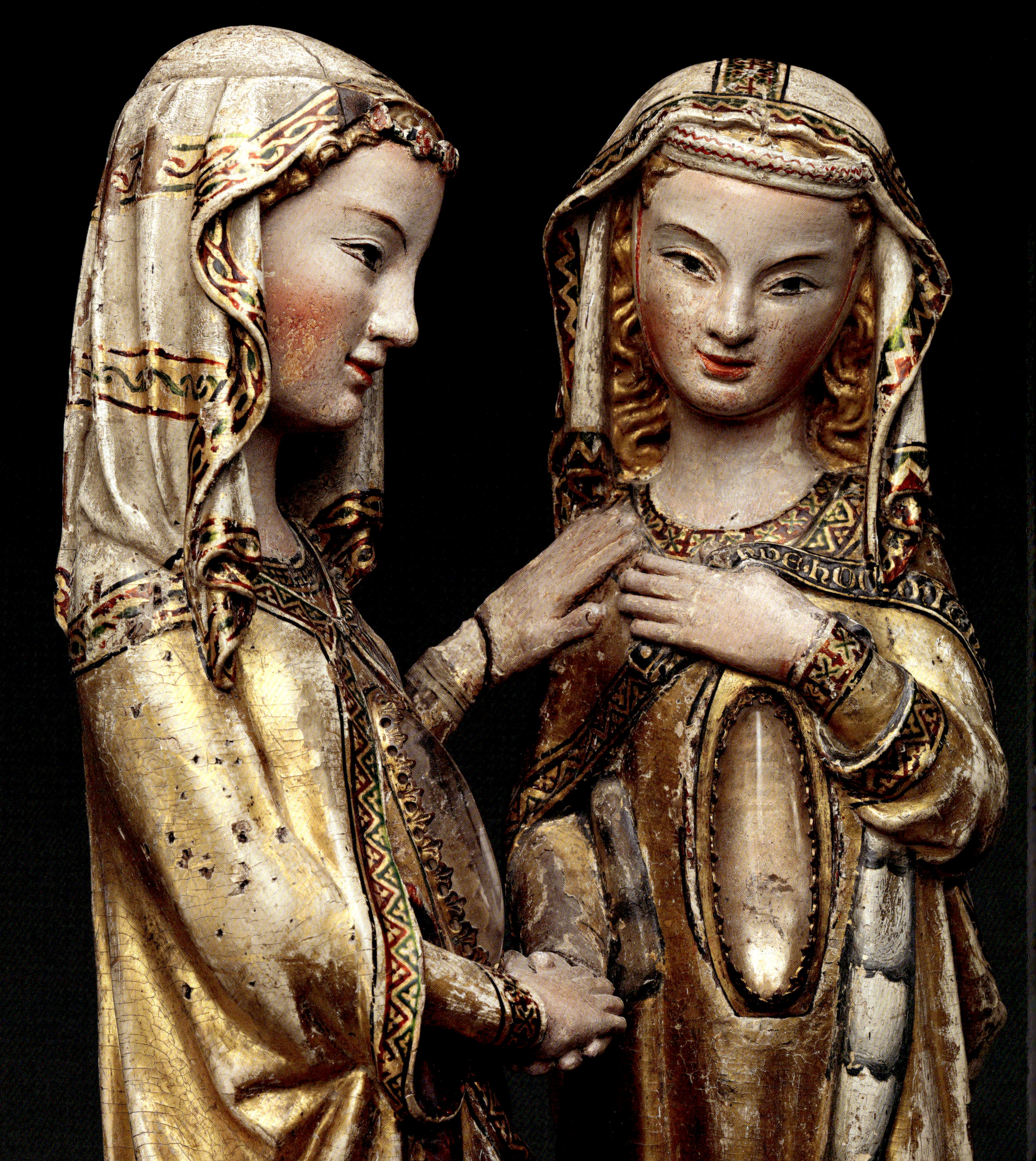

Melanie Holcomb
and Nancy Thebaut

SPECTRUM OF DESIRE

LOVE, SEX, AND GENDER IN THE MIDDLE AGES

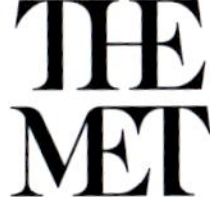

The Metropolitan Museum of Art
NEW YORK

Distributed by Yale University Press
NEW HAVEN AND LONDON

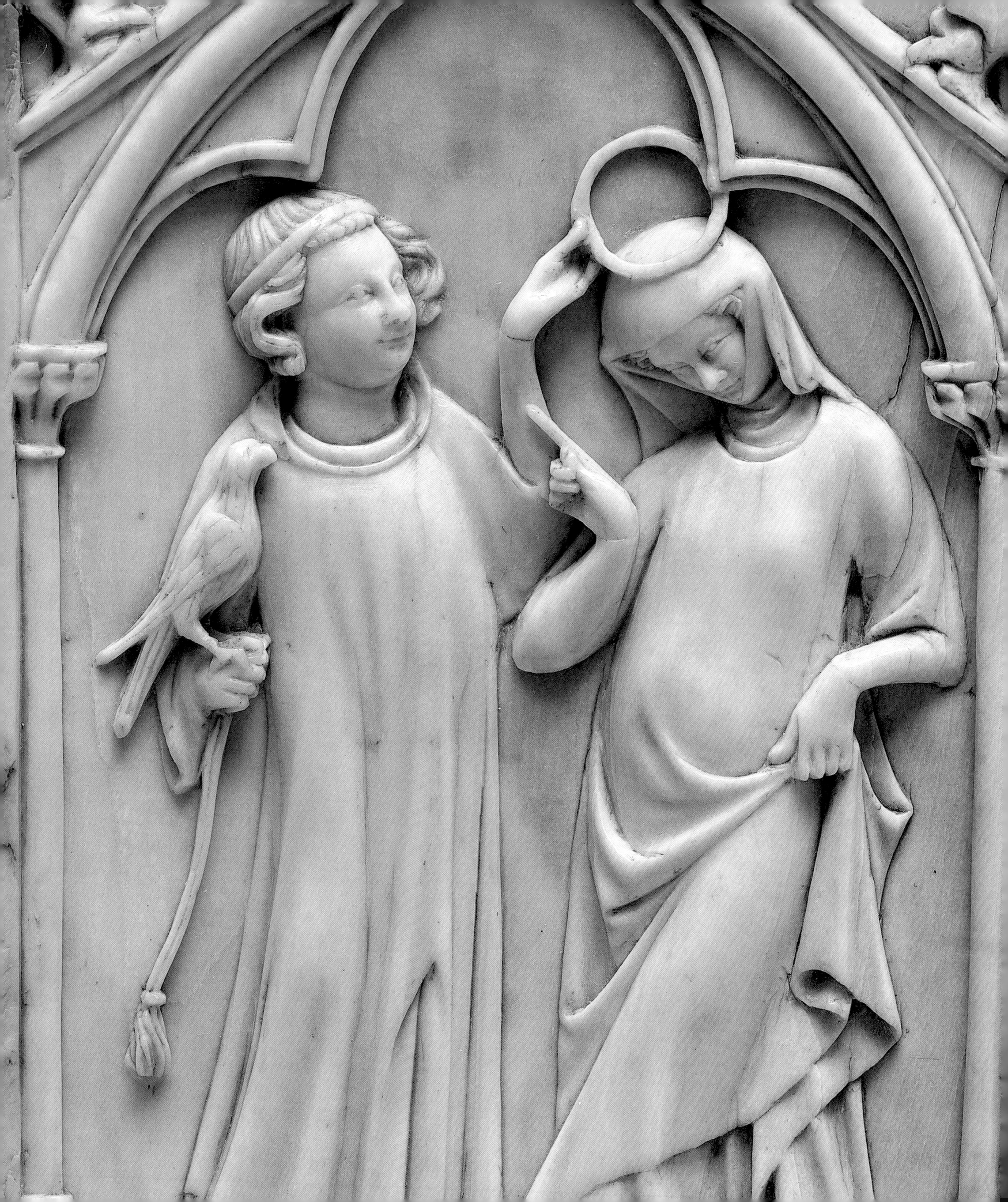

DIRECTOR'S FOREWORD

THE METROPOLITAN MUSEUM OF ART IS FORTUNATE to have one of the richest collections of medieval art in the world. *Spectrum of Desire: Love, Sex, and Gender in the Middle Ages* asks visitors to look anew at some of our most beloved works—alongside some exceptional loans—to consider their meaning and reception through the lens of desire. In so doing, it shows how desire, whether in the context of courtly love, spiritual quests, or carnal lust, and the visual arts were deeply entwined in medieval art and thought. Feelings, fantasies, and longings were at once shaped by and in turn actively shaped art in poignant, even surprising ways.

Firmly grounded in decades of scholarship, the exhibition and catalogue focus on panel paintings, sculptures, stained glass, and illuminated manuscripts made across western Europe between the fourteenth and sixteenth centuries, a period that saw ideas of love, sex, and gender expanding in certain contexts and narrowing in others. Though it does not skirt the bigotry of the period, the catalogue showcases the diversity of ways that medieval people imagined how to live and to love. Readers will invariably find themselves making connections between past and present. While medieval identities and norms are not those of the twenty-first century, they nonetheless invite us to reflect on the manner in which sex, gender, and relationships structure our own identities and lives. At the same time, *Spectrum of Desire* shows the important role that art history itself can play now: it can expand our perspective, if we let it, and help us consider how we today choose to cite, erase, or mobilize the past, for better or worse.

The exhibition and catalogue were conceived and organized by Melanie Holcomb, Curator and Manager of Collection Strategy in the Department of Medieval Art and The Cloisters, at The Met and Nancy Thebaut, Associate Professor in the Department of History of Art, St. Catherine's College, at the University of Oxford. This project is based on their thorough research and deep commitment to sharing this work, and the outcome is a powerful, engaging, and important exhibition.

Although the exhibition has only a few loans, they are all critical to its success. We are thus exceedingly grateful to the museums and libraries that have entrusted us with their treasures: Beinecke Rare Book & Manuscript Library, Yale University, New Haven; The Cleveland Museum of Art; The Morgan Library & Museum, New York; Princeton University Library, Princeton, New Jersey; and The Walters Art Museum, Baltimore. The catalogue and exhibition have benefited from generous donations by established and new supporters of the Department of Medieval Art and The Cloisters. We appreciate the important financial support provided by the Michel David-Weill Fund, which made both the exhibition and this publication possible. Kathryn A. Ploss and Museo Mexico offered meaningful gifts that helped make possible the installation, while Nellie and Robert Gipson, and Wendy A. Stein and Bart Friedman generously championed the publication. Together, their commitments to this project ensure that the catalogue will remain a valued resource for years to come.

Max Hollein
Marina Kellen French Director and CEO
The Metropolitan Museum of Art, New York

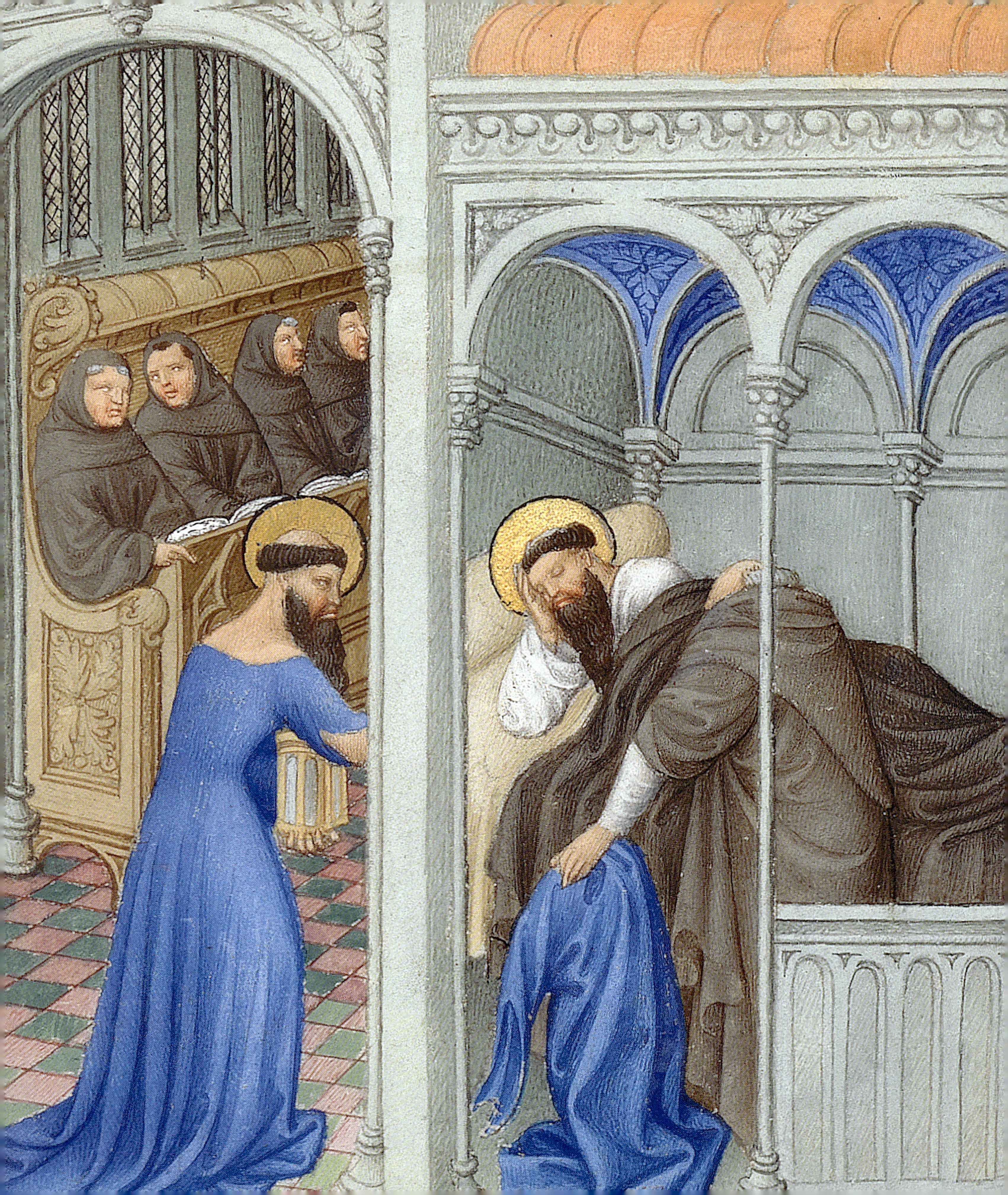

ACKNOWLEDGMENTS

FROM ITS INCEPTION, *SPECTRUM OF DESIRE: LOVE, Sex, and Gender in the Middle Ages* has been a collaboration benefiting from the care, counsel, and expertise of dear colleagues and friends. We are grateful for their immense generosity, all the more valuable for an exhibition and catalogue that explores sensitive material in a challenging political climate.

Profound thanks are due to Max Hollein, Marina Kellen French Director and CEO of The Metropolitan Museum of Art, who encouraged the exploration of these ideas from the very beginning. His support has never wavered, and we count ourselves lucky to look toward his leadership. Quincy Houghton, Deputy Director for Exhibitions and International Initiatives, has been a steadfast champion, thoughtfully considering myriad details for the successful presentation of the exhibition. We extend our deep appreciation to the Departments of European Sculpture and Decorative Arts, Drawings and Prints, European Paintings, and the Robert Lehman Collection for their willingness to send important works from their holdings to The Met Cloisters for the exhibition.

Our community partners have been key allies in the formulation of *Spectrum of Desire*. With significant support from our colleagues in the Met's Education Department, we formed a Community Advisory Group that met several times over the course of exhibition planning. Working with these inspiring local leaders was among the most enriching aspects of bringing the exhibition and catalogue to fruition. Together, we contemplated how best to present challenging objects and ideas, while considering the experiences of people of the past and of today. The group's members were Mariel de la Cruz, Leah DeVun, Martha Easton, Rev. Dr. Marian Edmonds-Allen, Natalie Espino, Trevon Mayers, Victoria Munro, Fr. Paul Rospond, Sebastian Stafford, Elisabet Velasquez, and Memphis Washington. The depth of our gratitude is impossible to express. The Met's Education Department has been a crucial partner from the moment we shared this project. Heidi Holder, Frederick P. and Sandra P. Rose Chair of Education, wholeheartedly supported the work, generously committing resources and members of her talented staff to the endeavor. We thank Clara Maria Apostolatos, Aminah James, Denia Lara, Martina Lentino, Marty Preciado, Christina Westpheling, and Sherri Williams.

We are indebted to other scholars and colleagues at The Met, at the University of Oxford, and beyond. For providing generous feedback in early days and contributing to the ongoing development of the exhi bition, we thank Roland Betancourt, Bryan C. Keene, Clare Kemmerer, Aden Kumler, Sarah E. Lawrence, Iris and B. Gerald Cantor Curator in Charge of the Department of European Sculpture and Decorative Arts, Rachel Seligman, and Karl Whittington. For preliminary conversations about specific objects and themes, we are grateful to Mathilde Arnau, Jess Bailey, Barbara Boehm (Curator Emerita, Department of Medieval Art and The Cloisters at The Met), Daisy Delogu, Charlotte Denoël, Evangeline Giaconia, Samuel Grassin, Sarah-Grace Heller, Marine Kisiel, Anna Klosowska, Rotem Linial, Gerhard Lutz, Jesse Lockard, Meekyung MacMurdie, Scott Miller, the deeply missed Will Noel, Joshua O'Driscoll, Nicole Pulichene, Donna Sadler, Cécile Voyer, Jacqueline Victor, Roger Wieck, and Kelso Wyeth. Several colleagues read drafts of our essays and graciously shared their advice: Meg Bernstein, Carly Boxer, Kristopher Driggers, Emma Le Pouésard, Clovis Maillet, Eric Palazzo, Christopher T. Richards, Martin Schwarz, and Kristine Tanton, as well as colleagues in the Department of Medieval Art and The Cloisters: Andrea Myers Achi, Mary and Michael Jaharis Associate Curator of Byzantine Art; Julia Perratore, Associate Curator; and Shirin Fozi, Paul and Jill Ruddock Associate Curator.

We are also grateful to those who invited us to speak about the exhibition at various venues and thus benefit from the feedback of others: Maeve Doyle and Gerry Guest at the International Congress of Medieval Studies, Kalamazoo, Michigan; students at the Centre d'études supérieures de civilisation médiévale, Université de Poitiers; Department of History of Art, University of Oxford; Centre for Women's, Gender and Queer Histories, University of Oxford; University of Utah, Salt Lake City; Queen Mary University of London; Colby College, Waterville, Maine; International Center of Medieval Art, New York; and Bard High School Early College, Manhattan. Students have also played a key role in refining this project: at Skidmore College, Saratoga Springs, New York, undergraduate students in the art history course "Queering the Middle Ages" invited us to see objects in new ways. The research of Helen Branch and Thomas Myhill proved especially fruitful. We thank the staff at the Alice Austen House, Staten Island, New York, for their warm welcome and their willingness to share ideas and experiences. We are also appreciative of the members of The Met's Exhibition Advisory Committee for their wise guidance.

Many colleagues at The Met provided valuable counsel. We thank Lavita McMath Turner, Chief Diversity Officer; Joanna Sheers Seidenstein and Elizabeth Zanis in Drawings and Prints; Rebecca Capua and Yana van Dyke in Paper Conservation; Drew Anderson, Linda Borsch, Marina Kastan, Jennifer Schnitker, and Karen Stamm in Objects Conservation; Kathrin Colburn in Textile Conservation; Kristin Holder in Paintings Conservation; Gretchen Scott, Head of Marketing; Ann Bailis, Head of Communications, and Publicist Stella Kim; Becky Bacheller and Elsie Alonso in the Registrar's Office; and Kate Thompson in Development. Lucretia Kargère in Objects Conservation deserves special commendation for her splendid conservation of the late fifteenth-century St. Sebastian sculpture. At The Cloisters, we thank Andreas Burckhardt in Visitor Experience; Chris Dunbrack and Jason Quinones in Buildings; Sheryl Esardial in Retail; and Brandi Watson in Security; Michael Carter at The Cloisters Library; Robyn Fleming, Amy Hamilton, Ren Murrell, Jessica Ranne Cardona, and Fredy Rivera in the Thomas J. Watson Library all possess magic powers when it comes to tracking down books and articles. The creativity of Alicia Cheng, Head of Design, and Ezra Wu, Harrison Carter, Jourdan Ferguson, and Sarah Parke in the Design Department never ceased to amaze us.

The Publications and Editorial Department continuously encouraged the creation of this beautiful book. Mark Polizzotti, Publisher and Editor in Chief, Michael Sittenfeld, Associate Publisher for Editorial, and Peter Antony, Associate Publisher for Production, seized upon the promise of this publication right away and provided critical early steering. Elizabeth L. Block, our superb editor, reviewed our text dozens of times, improving it with every read. We feel exceptionally lucky to work with someone who brings such intelligence, experience, and nuance to book editing. The inviting design is due to the creativity of designer Beverly Joel and production manager Christina Grillo. We thank Margaret Aspinwall for bibliographic editing, Jenn Sherman for acquiring the images and clearing rights, and Alison Tretter for editing the exhibition texts. We also thank Peter Zeray of the Imaging Department for his expert photography of many of the works of art.

It is a privilege to organize any project that involves The Department of Medieval Art and The Cloisters. C. Griffith Mann, Michel David-Weill Curator in Charge, has been a stalwart supporter at every juncture. We are grateful to Farhan Ali, Christina Alphonso, Carly Amarant, Christine Brennan, Jeff Elliott, Amelia Roche Hyde, Stephanie Pace, and Carly Still. We owe a special debt of gratitude to Sophia Figuereo and Andrew Winslow, who patiently and expertly managed endless details for the exhibition and catalogue. Their instinct is to say "yes" warmly, even when we ask the impossible. The same is true of Aileen Marcantonio, Senior Exhibitions Project Manager in the Exhibitions Office, whom we consider an honorary member of the department.

Our dedicated donors and friends are owed sincere thanks for their investment in this project. The Michel David-Weill Fund provided key support for both the exhibition and this beautiful publication. We are grateful to Kathryn A. Ploss and Museo Mexico for their great generosity toward the presentation. The publication also benefited from wonderful gifts from dear friends Nellie and Robert Gipson, and Wendy A. Stein and Bart Friedman.

On a more personal note, there are several individuals who provided emotional sustenance and support throughout this undertaking and to whom we are indebted: Josh Feldstein, Ann, Emily, and Stephen Thebaut, Pauline Blaise, Ida Holcomb, Sophie Shapiro, Amelia Holcomb, Evan Palmer, Linda Carlyle, and Douglas Shapiro.

Melanie Holcomb and Nancy Thebaut

LENDERS TO THE EXHIBITION

Beinecke Rare Book & Manuscript Library, Yale University, New Haven

The Cleveland Museum of Art, Ohio

Griffin Collection

The Metropolitan Museum of Art, New York

The Morgan Library & Museum, New York

Princeton University Library, Princeton, New Jersey

The Walters Art Museum, Baltimore

CONTRIBUTORS

MELANIE HOLCOMB (she/her), Curator and Manager of Collection Strategy, Department of Medieval Art and The Cloisters, The Metropolitan Museum of Art, New York

BRYAN C. KEENE (he/él/they/elle), Associate Professor, Department of Art and Art History and Department of Theatre Arts, Riverside City College, Riverside, California

EMMA LE POUÉSARD (she/her), Arts Coordinator, Koestler Arts, London

CLOVIS MAILLET (he/him/they/them), Historian, Lecturer, and Artist, Haute école d'art et de design, Geneva / Fellow of the French Academy in Rome – Villa Medici

SCOTT D. MILLER (he/him), Assistant Curator of European Art, Princeton University Art Museum, Princeton, New Jersey

NANCY THEBAUT (she/her), Associate Professor in the Department of History of Art, St. Catherine's College, University of Oxford

KARL WHITTINGTON (he/him), Professor and Chair of the Department of History of Art, Ohio State University, Columbus

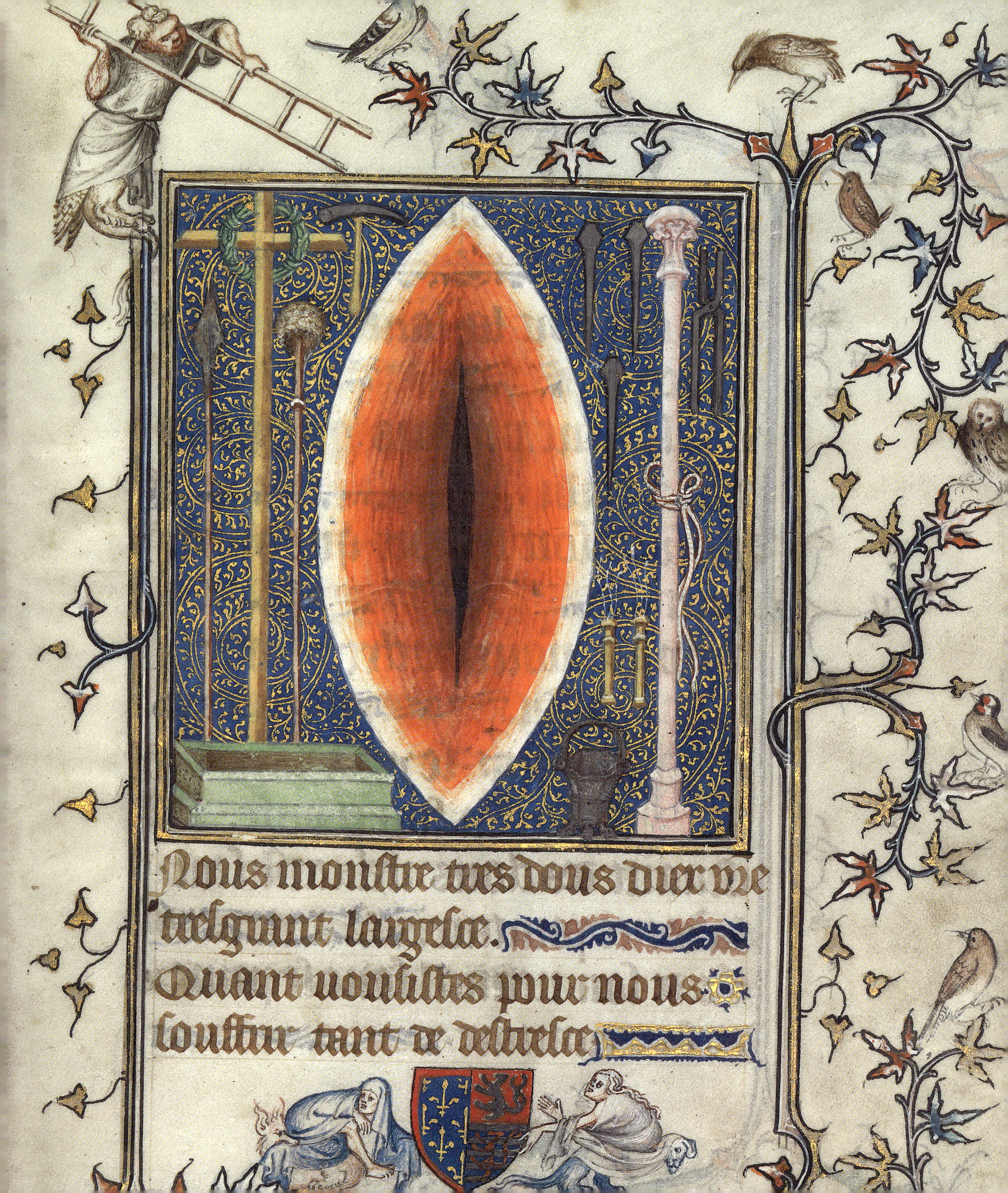
Nous monstre tres dous dieux vre
tresgrant largesce.
Quant vousistes pour nous
souffrir tant de destresce

MELANIE HOLCOMB AND
NANCY THEBAUT

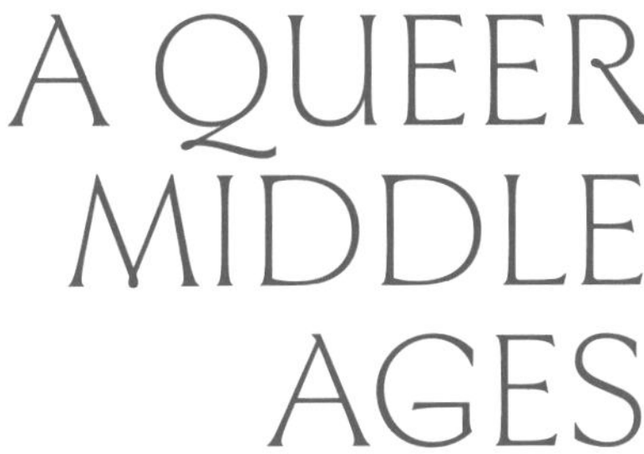

A QUEER MIDDLE AGES

A striking image of the side wound of Christ fills a framed field of blue and gold in a devotional manuscript made for Bonne of Luxembourg (1315–1349), princess of Bohemia and wife of John II of France. Flanked by the whipping post and cross, along with the instruments of Christ's torture and death, the disembodied gash with its inscrutable black interior offered a powerful point of meditation (PL. 1). The likely painter Jean le Noir (perhaps working with his daughter Burgot) created a picture of mesmerizing tactility and depth. It beckoned the eye to penetrate the wound as if a lance, allowing Bonne to imagine and enter the abyss of Christ's suffering.

But was a wound ever just a wound? The painting is strange, perhaps even shocking for many modern viewers, not least because its orientation, colors, and shape strongly suggest a vulva. Medieval artists and viewers also noted, even exploited, the resemblance.[1] A less elegant version of the form surrounded by a curtain of blood appears on a scroll used by women for protection during childbirth (FIG. 1). The text indicates that the evocative lozenge is the exact height of Christ's actual wound and includes a charm for a quick and painless delivery.[2] The wound's worn and abraded center implies that women touched it to activate its devotional and amuletic properties. Medieval writers consistently encouraged Christian devotees to imagine probing the wound and to find refuge in Christ's side as if it were a womb.[3] Some even compared his suffering on the Cross to the pangs of birth.[4] Although we do not know whether Bonne relied on an amulet to see her through labor, we do know she had given birth to nine children by the age of thirty-four when she died of the bubonic plague.[5] A representation of Christ's wound in her private prayer book would call to mind his body and her own, with their shared susceptibility to penetration, pain, and parturition. A man's wound could be a woman's vagina, an aperture sexed and sexualized. The gender instability that the image endorsed only enhanced its efficacy as a devotional object.

A similar almond shape with a central opening appears on a humble pilgrim's badge, a cheap trinket of medieval tourism, where it is crowned and carried on a litter by three phalluses, mimicking the reliquaries or statues of the Virgin or Christ that were paraded

1. **The wound of Christ from the Prayer Book of Bonne of Luxembourg, Duchess of Normandy, before 1349. Attributed to Jean Le Noir and workshop. Opaque watercolor, silver, gold, and iron gall ink on parchment**

Fig. 1. **Side wound. Detail from a birth girdle. English, ca. 1450–1500. Opaque watercolor and ink on parchment, complete roll, 48 × 3⅜ in. (112.5 × 8.5 cm). The British Library, London (Harley Roll T.11)**

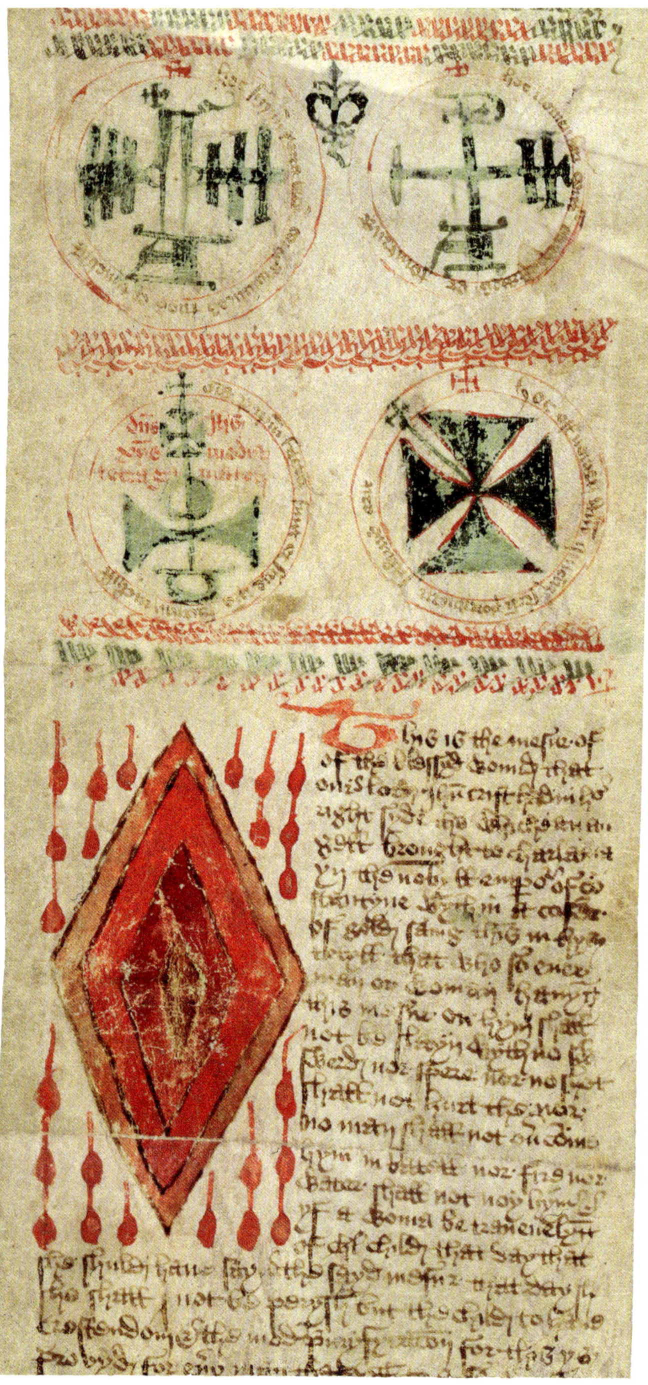

through city streets on feast days (FIG. 2). The work belongs to a category of badges, fairly significant in number, that show anthropomorphized genitalia engaged in a variety of activities from gardening to pilgrimage to relic processions.[6] The satire takes aim at public displays of piety and the pomp of religious ceremonial, but perhaps also the object of devotion itself. Held aloft by a crew of lanky penises, the noble wound has been stripped of its solemnity. In the spirit of carnival, the badge may well be mocking medieval devotion to the wound and the elaborate theological paradigm that practice required. Dress it up all you want, it seems to say with a wink, but sometimes genitalia is just that.

These visual discourses around wounds and wombs—at times deeply serious, at others enjoyably ludicrous—transpired across a range of media and social classes. They demonstrate that medieval artists inventively experimented with signs of sex and gender, making claims and counterclaims about their meaning. If one artist could use the yonic motif to create an image so lush in its associations that the essence of God himself seemed to lay within, another found it perfect for a sly jab at such endeavors. The two approaches might appear in the same work, as in the bawdy humor that made its way into Bonne's painting. There, to the left of her coat of arms, a fox-like creature noses under the skirt of the veiled woman who straddles it, a not-so-subtle nod to the sexual implications of the framed orifice above.

As representations of the wound make clear, medieval images imply more flexible boundaries in the spheres of love, sexuality, and gender than we might initially suspect. Historians have argued that the thirteenth through fifteenth centuries in western Europe saw increasingly restrictive definitions and tighter regulations of sex, marriage, and the family, particularly through Christian canon law.[7] Works of art tell a more complex story: this was also a period of surprising creativity, with even a degree of openness in these domains. Manuscript paintings, wood sculptures, woven textiles, ivory boxes, gold jewelry, and other kinds of visual art provided generative settings for the expansion of ideas about gender expression, erotic union, and loving kinship. Desire, both physical and spiritual, fueled these explorations. Images in turn helped to shape and reimagine the possibilities of desire, often revealing a queer sensibility and operating at an angle to prevailing norms.

THE CONTOURS OF DESIRE

Desire takes many forms, and medieval writers inherited from Latin a rich and nuanced vocabulary with which to discuss it.[8] *Appetitus* derived from the idea of striving toward or making an assault on something. As such, it conveyed desire in a broad sense as a strong propensity. *Libido* linked desire to pleasure, usually tainted by the lack of restraint during its pursuit. *Cupiditas* too could carry connotations of desire gone amok, whether in the sense of avarice or lust. That *concupiscentia,* which was used exclusively to mean consuming sexual desire, arrived in the language late, only in the first millennium, is a function of many early Christian thinkers' obsession with the virtues of continence. A sense of urgency was inherent to all these terms, but *desiderium* colored zeal with hints of pain. It communicated the pang of longing that arose from absence, lack, or loss. While all these shades of meaning overlapped and contributed to medieval understandings of desire, this last sense most especially animated stories of courtly love as well as the spiritual pursuits of the devout.

As opposed to say a simple wish, desire presumed a physical dimension. Its power lay in its essential irrationality, in the way it could take hold of the senses and propel a bodily response. Its causes therefore intrigued medieval thinkers, whose disciplines led them to different explanations. Theologians focused their inquiries specifically on sexual desire and located its origin in the Fall, the moment when Adam and Eve ate the forbidden fruit from the Tree of Knowledge. Sexual urges were thus tinged from the outset with the contemptible attributes of shame and sin. Medical doctors and natural philosophers took a more disinterested approach. They understood human appetites in physiological terms. Using medical theories drawn

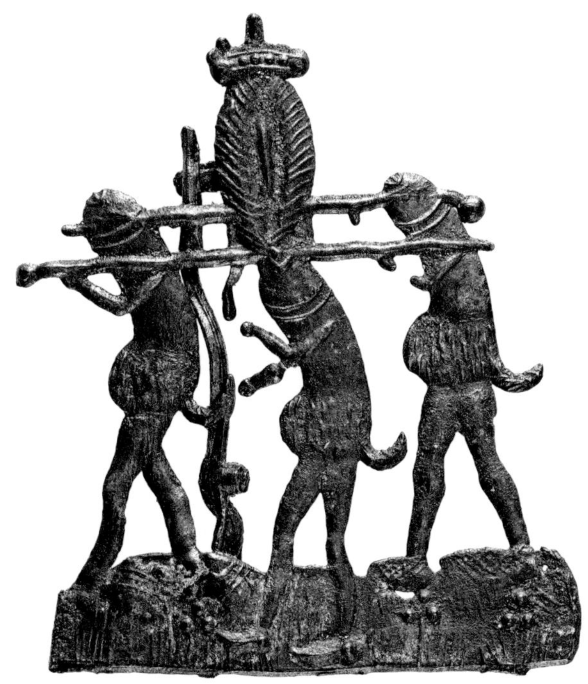

Fig. 2. **Pilgrim's badge showing phalluses carrying a vagina on a litter. Found in Bruges. Late 14th century. Pewter, 2¼ × 1¾ in. (5.6 × 4.5 cm). Van Beuningen Family Collection (inv. 0967)**

from antiquity, they spoke of the body's need for release from a buildup of bodily fluids and heat.[9] As such, coitus provided relief and thus promoted good health. The ardor that we associate with passionate love drew the attention of poets and storytellers, along with Christian exegetes (interpreters of the Bible), clerics, and mystics, who saw it as stemming from outside the body. Prompted by the sight or sound of the beloved, a literal or figurative arrow pricks the heart, and body and soul are lost in their quest to unite with the object of their yearnings. A fourteenth-century ivory tablet shows the moment just before the god of love strikes a young woman and man with his fateful arrow (PL. 2). In his study of German courtly romance, James Schultz underscores the passivity and powerlessness of someone thus stricken: "Desire does not well up within the lover and seek an object. Something about the object assaults the lover and takes him or

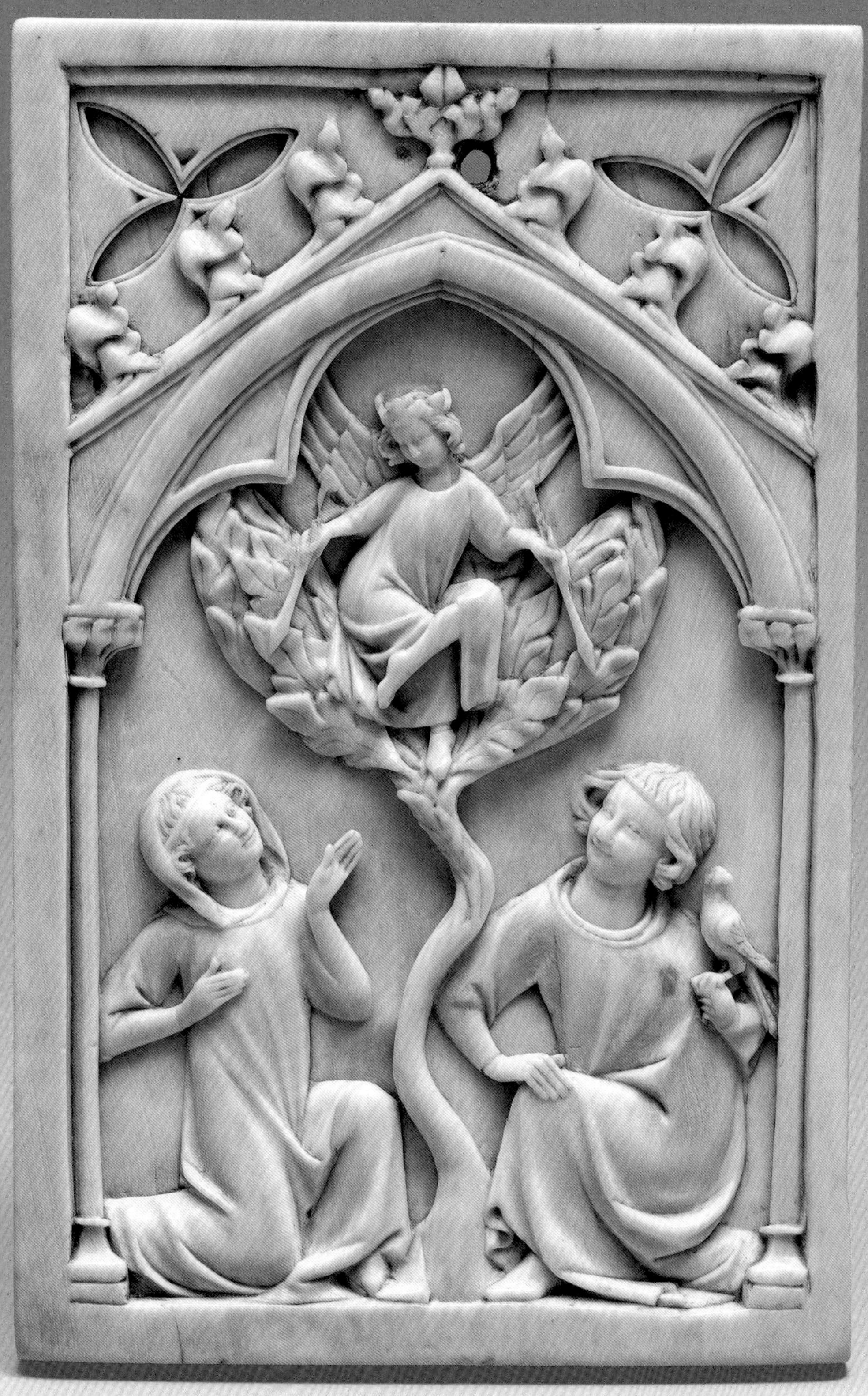

2. **Cover of a writing tablet with lovers and the god of love. French, ca. 1325–50. Elephant ivory**

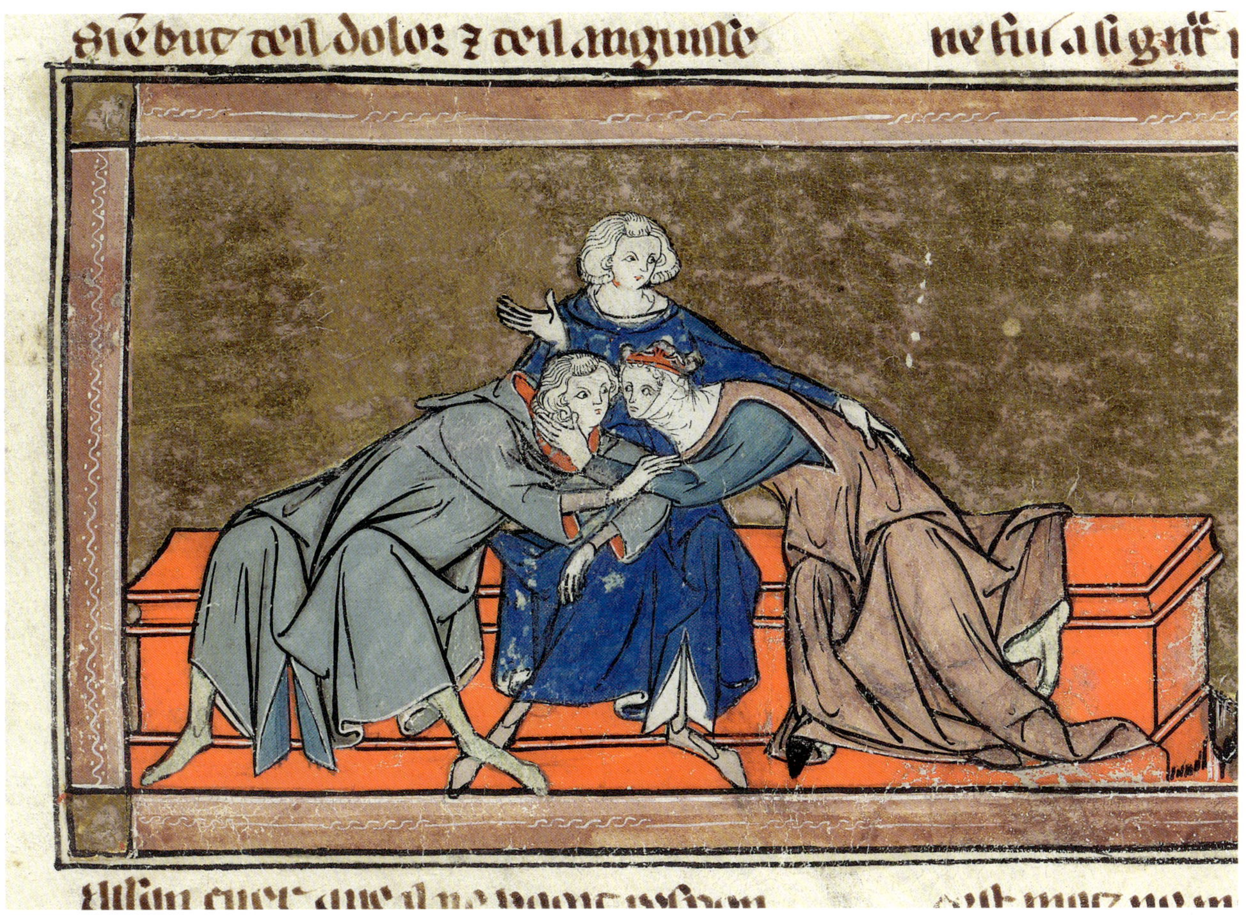

Fig. 3. **The first kiss of Lancelot and Guinevere from *Lancelot du Lac*. Northeastern France, perhaps Saint-Quentin or Laon, between 1310 and 1315. Opaque watercolor, gold leaf, and iron gall ink on parchment. The Morgan Library & Museum, New York, Purchased on the Lewis Cass Ledyard Fund, 1938 (MS M.805 fol. 67r)**

her captive."[10] There is no defense against *desiderium*, what local vernaculars expressed as *dezire, desir, desyr*, or *begern*.[11]

Such desire assumed a complete intertwining of the emotional and the physical. Medieval artists were adept at showing that connection by enlisting the body to express both the torments of longing and the ecstasy of its fulfillment. A painting from an early fourteenth-century manuscript devoted to the story of Lancelot of the Lake makes this point plain (FIG. 3).[12] Lancelot is the most famous of all the Arthurian knights and his forbidden romance with Arthur's queen, Guinevere, exemplifies the courtly love tradition, which plumbed the deep anguish of impossible love. The miniature depicts the first tryst between the two. Lancelot's obsession with Guinevere has been so severe that he soaks his blanket with tears each night, and the knight Galehot has arranged the meeting to relieve the suffering of his friend. Silhouetted against a gold backdrop, the two lovers stretch across Galehot

3. **Saint Catherine of Siena in the throes of rapture receiving the stigmata, ca. 1447–65. Giovanni di Paolo (Giovanni di Paolo di Grazia). Tempera and gold on wood**

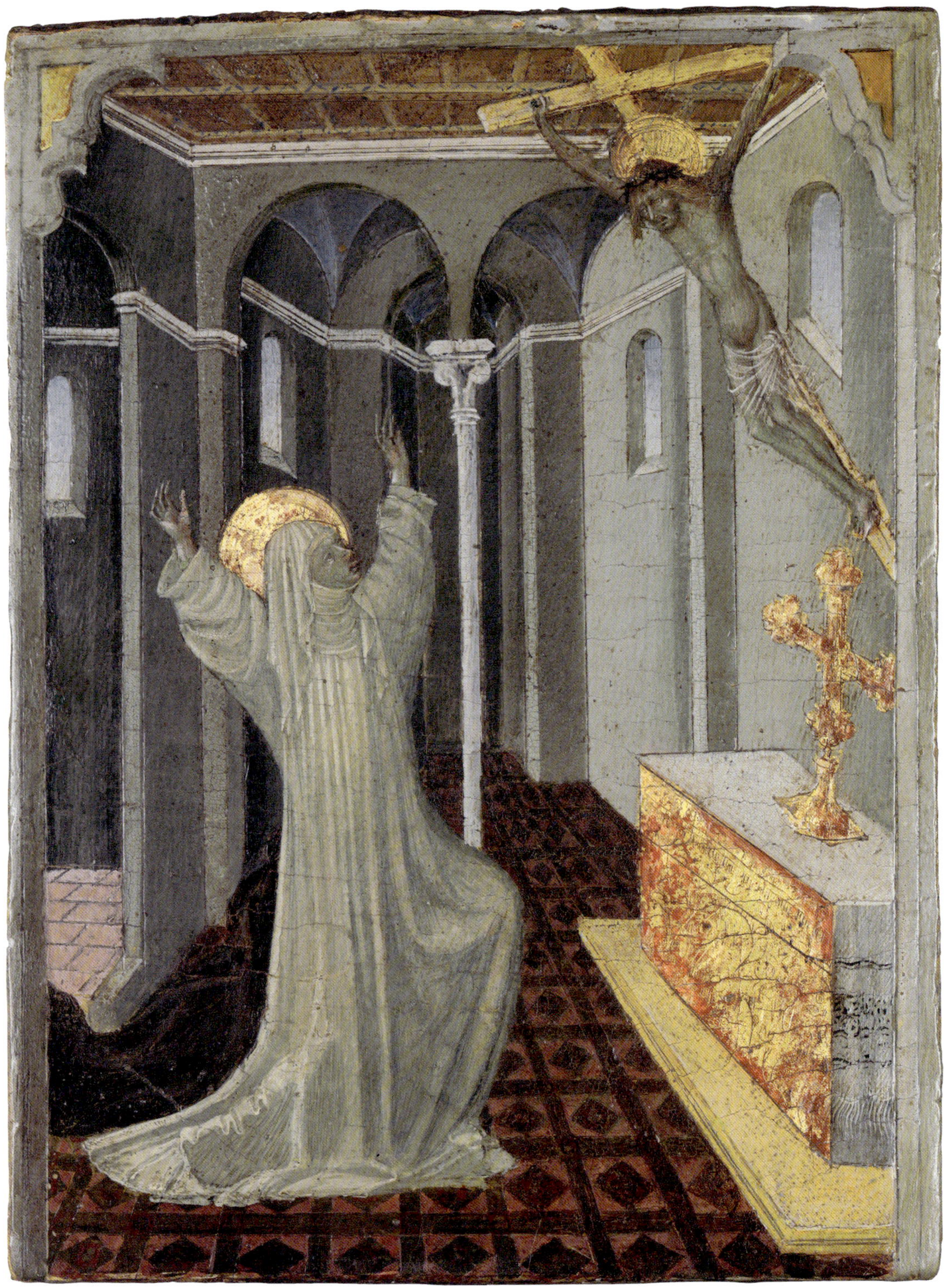

to kiss for the first time. Eyes lock, while outstretched arms fall into a loose braid. Their impossibly elongated torsos embody their protracted wait for this moment and the hunger for one another the meeting has unleashed.

The love of God could provoke no less passionate a response. A panel painting of Catherine of Siena highlights her complete bodily submission to her heavenly spouse (PL. 3). Born in 1347, Catherine began to have holy visions when still a young child. At the age of twenty-one, she experienced a mystical marriage with Jesus, in which he placed a ring on her finger as his pledge. (One biographer describes it as gold with precious gems while her own account declares it the ring of Christ's foreskin!)[13] This painting, part of a set devoted to her life story, portrays her receiving the stigmata, the marks corresponding to the five wounds of the crucified Christ. In the throes of rapture, Catherine's body mirrors that of Christ. Their wide-open eyes, directed unremittingly toward one another, convey the intensity of their connection. The small gold crucifixion on the altar locates the event in a church. It also clarifies that the crucified Christ overhead is not a sculpture but revelation, no mere symbol but a sentient partner.

The shared physicality of this episode cannot be overemphasized. In her ecstasy, Catherine becomes like Christ by replicating his body, taking on the specific pains of his wounds. Yet her stigmata are invisible. At her own insistence, she did not retain the telling scars. The painting documents the refusal by not depicting the rays which emanated from Christ's wounds to her body and which her biographer describes at length.[14] The merest hint of blood on her hand and a tiny nail in her left palm provide the only visible verification of this miraculous joining of bodies. While this minimalist approach vouches for her unassuming character in refusing physical marks that others might note, it also masterfully communicates the rich mystery of mystical union. It is an intense corporeal experience that others generally cannot see. As is so often the case with medieval portrayals of desire, the image insists that viewers take a leap of faith.

EMBRACING QUEERNESS

Because desire is an unpredictable force, its legibility is never a given. To see it in works of art can require untangling the forms of love, sexuality, and relationality that attend it and even then, ambiguity will often prevail. Accordingly, Galehot's prominence in the scene of Lancelot and Guinevere's first assignation demands explanation. In the text he serves as intermediary, and many illuminations simply show him to the side looking on as the two lovers come together. Here, he is the apex of the triangle formed by the three bodies. He sits squarely in the center, suggesting he is both an enabler of their meeting and an obstacle they must overcome. His blue robe provides a vivid backdrop against which hands and lips come together. His left hand gently nudges the queen toward her admirer, while his right foot crosses underneath his fellow knight's left foot. Through gesture and pose, the painting acknowledges a network of complex intimacies.

Lancelot loves Guinevere. Galehot, the text recounts, loves Lancelot. Once Galehot saw Lancelot's magnificence in battle, he doggedly pursued him, suppressing his own ambitions to gain his affection. He gives him his armor. He watches him sleep. He devotes his "heart and body" to him.[15] In one scene, the two men "lay down in one bed and talked all night long of that which made their hearts content."[16] When it comes to Lancelot, one character notes, Galehot is as jealous as any knight in love with a beautiful lady.[17] Ultimately, Galehot declares that he will die without him, and he does, out of grief, when he receives a false report of Lancelot's death.

Many scholars have noted that Galehot's behavior toward Lancelot follows the model of the male courtly lover in pursuit of a lady. They have argued over the nature of the men's relationship.[18] Is it sexual? Or does their bond epitomize the passionate, but chaste, friendship revered by medieval comrades-in-arms? The story is reticent and so is the painting. Are they hinting at a secret or luxuriating in the equivocations and overlaps of medieval love and friendship? Negotiations around Lancelot's and Guinevere's first kiss underscore how messily entangled desire can be. Galehot commands that Guinevere kiss Lancelot in front of him, and, in turn, Guinevere gives Lancelot to Galehot except, she qualifies, "for what I have already."[19] The text goes on to convey that Lancelot is torn between the man whom he loves "more than all the men in the world" and his queen.[20] Later musicals and movies aside, the great love triangle in this most famous of all Arthurian tales has little to do with King Arthur. The image succinctly illustrates what the text also suggests—the dramatic tension of this romance depends upon a queer dimension.

The ambiguity of Galehot and Lancelot's relationship reminds us of the difficulty in assigning contemporary labels to people and stories of the past. Whereas sex acts are often considered a defining feature of sexual orientation today, this was almost never the case for medieval people. Identity categories like lesbian, gay, bisexual, or straight would not have made sense to them; no one used terms like *heterosexual* or *homosexual*. *Queer* is a useful term here, not as a substitution for homosexual, gay, or lesbian, but because of its capacity to operate against the presumption of modern heterosexuality. It embraces a range of gender identities, sexual practices, and refusals. Queer can also be a powerful means to uncover meaning in an expansive way, seeing anew (or even for the first time) people, identities, feelings, and ways of being that do not neatly fit into predetermined categories, either medieval or modern. As a noun, an adjective, or a verb, *queer* offers a way to think more broadly about people, their relationships, and the artworks they produce.[21]

To acknowledge the queerness of medieval art is to call out the ways that gender and sexuality figure in images of desire, even outside the genre of romance. An unnamed monk once lived with a poignant, fifteenth-century painting of the Crucifixion that orchestrates a fully immersive devotional experience (PL. 4). One of twenty such paintings commissioned for individual cells at the Carthusian monastery of Champmol, the work provided a point of focus for private contemplation within the practice of shared solitude that was and is characteristic of the order.[22] In the work, a Carthusian monk in his distinctive white habit witnesses the Crucifixion of Jesus at Calvary alongside Jesus's mother Mary, who has collapsed in grief, and John the Evangelist behind. The painting presumes a cross-temporal cohabitation between the pictured monk and the biblical figures. The gold backdrop embellished with delicate punchwork ensures there is no defined spatial reality, no window to look through, but rather an undetermined shared space that extends into the monk's own cell.

The blood pouring from Christ's side wound is but one feature that invites a slow perusal of the dead body, as it traces the contours of his torso and flows downward between his legs before tapering off at his calf. So masterfully painted is the diaphanous loincloth that it invites scrutiny rather than providing cover. We can imagine this painting as the kind that prompted another Carthusian writing a century later at a monastery near Basel, Switzerland, to warn against looking at images of the naked Christ for the impure thoughts they could arouse.[23] The anonymous writer pointedly notes how such images direct the eye to Christ's loins in a way that tempts not only women but also men, even those sworn to the monastic life. Written on the eve of the Reformation, with a heightening suspicion of images, the text is a world away from the aesthetic and spiritual milieu that produced the painting. In the Champmol image, the sensuousness of looking is not sublimated but harnessed. The monk lunges dramatically toward the crucified body in a rush of affective devotion. The desire for God is staged as a wholly physical encounter. Cross-gender identification sanctions this mobilizing of bodily sensation, with the swooning Virgin providing a model of empathetic suffering and corporeal engagement. The monk-viewer is thus presented as a fully sensing subject. The gendered and sexualized aspects of the viewing experience only enhance the devotional practice that the painting models.

Sometimes devotion extended beyond the ocular. In the case of an ivory plaque of the Crucifixion, the faithful were encouraged not only to look at, but also kiss an image of the crucified Christ (PL. 5). This depiction of the Crucifixion visualizes the transfer of Christ's pain to Mary's body as a sword emerging from

4. **Crucifixion scene with a Carthusian monk gazing at the body of Christ, 14th century. Jean de Beaumetz. Oil on oak panel**

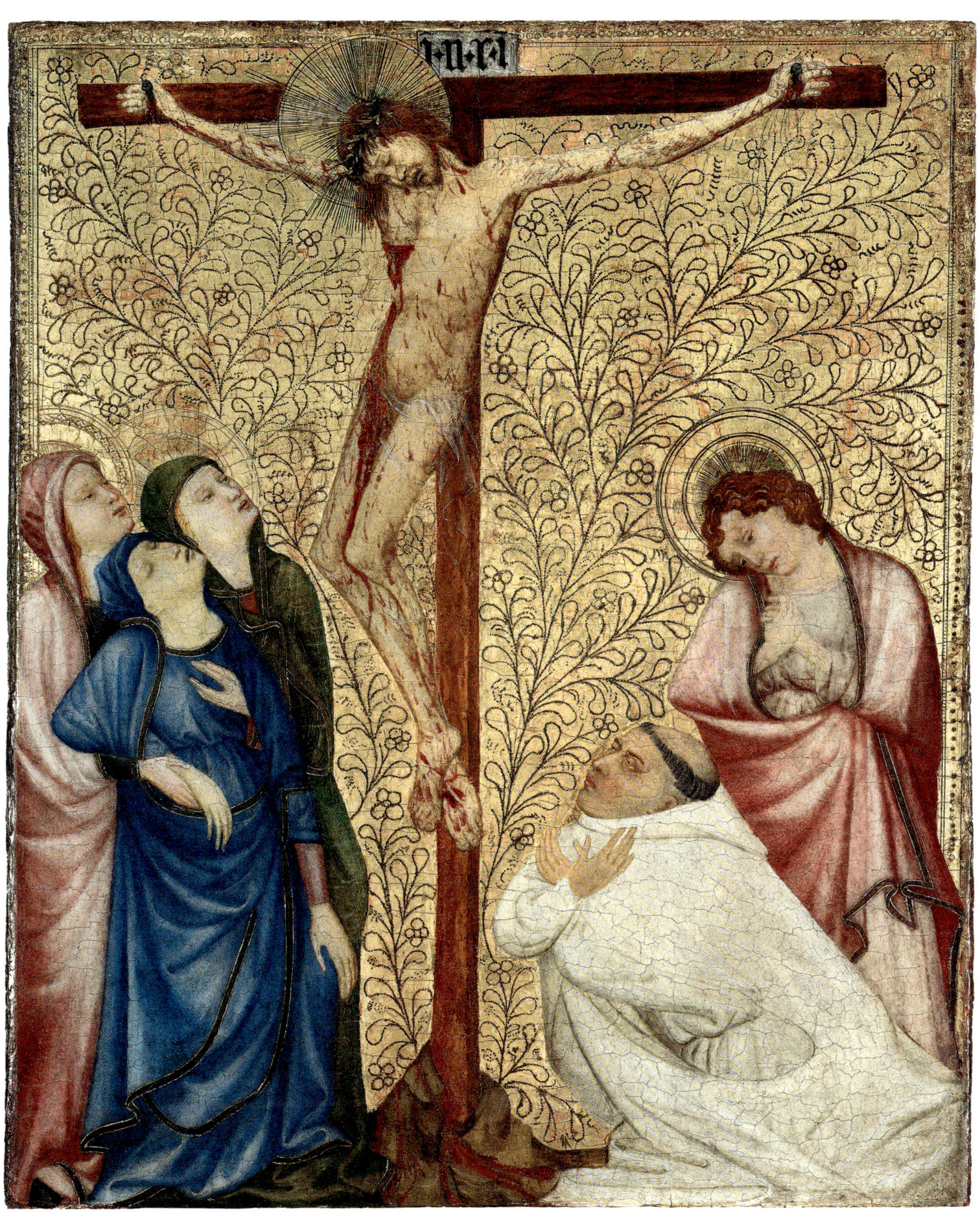

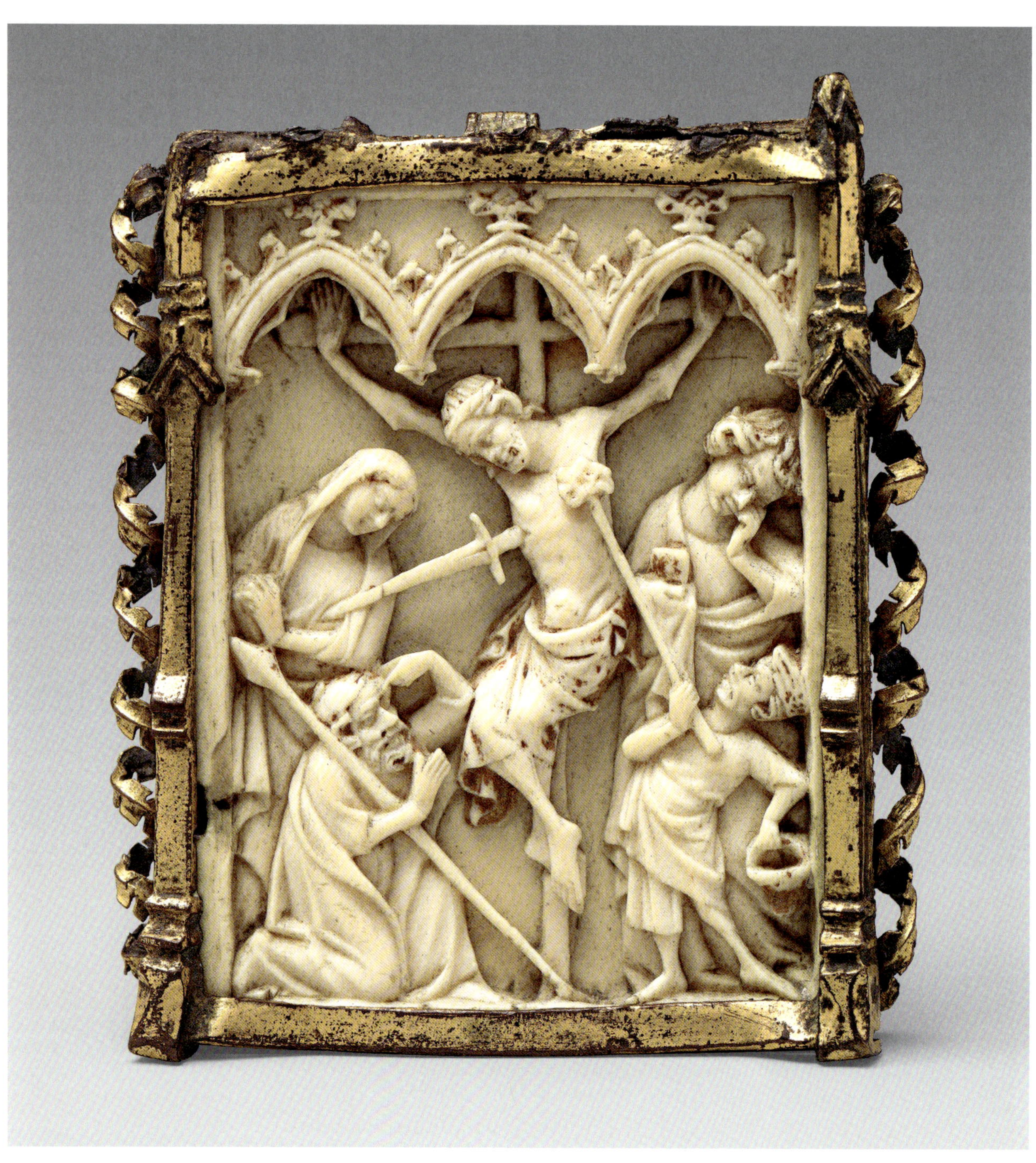

5. **Pax with a Crucifixion, showing a sword emerging from the wound of Christ and piercing the heart of the Virgin. South German, ca. 1360–70 (ivory); 15th century (frame). Elephant ivory and gilded copper**

Christ's side and piercing the Virgin's chest.[24] As in the Champmol painting, the Virgin Mary provided an ideal model for ardent believers who sought to take on the physical suffering of Christ. Empathetic suffering is here represented and encouraged through the language of son-to-mother penetration, a deliberate wounding that serves as a powerful sign of their bond. Originally part of a small devotional diptych, the ivory was transformed into a pax in the fifteenth century with the addition of a gilded copper frame and handle. During the Christian liturgy, the priest would invite the congregation to kiss it, wiping its surface in between each kiss. As the lips of believers touched the carved bodies of Christ and Mary on the ivory, they publicly engaged in an act of sympathetic devotion. Much about this ivory might seem startling, even excessive, in the way that it reimagines relationships and facilitates physical communion across time; its meaning and power cannot be contained by medieval categories or our own. But it is precisely this quality—this queerness—that makes the ivory such an effective devotional tool.

✧ ✧ ✧

This catalogue and the exhibition it accompanies are an exploration of the visual language of desire in its many forms. The essays build upon decades of work by scholars who have pioneered and refined the study of gender and sexuality in medieval Europe. Their contributions include numerous groundbreaking studies written in the 1980s and 1990s that drew from and developed women's history, feminism, and gay and lesbian studies alongside more recent work by those who overtly reference queer and transgender theories and methods.[25] Although the term *queer* has historically been used as a homophobic slur, activists and theorists at the height of the AIDS epidemic reclaimed the word as a marker of identity as well as a body of thought.[26] Early practitioners of queer theory understood queer as a position against the normative; it questioned and contested what was considered legitimate, especially with regard to gender and sexuality.[27] And while the Middle Ages does not need queer theory, we as its students benefit from its use, for it allows us to account for the complexity of medieval desires in ways that our own conventional conceptions of love, eroticism, and relationships can prevent us from seeing.

Spectrum of Desire takes inspiration from the call of queer theory to open up interpretive possibilities to allow a broader understanding of kinship, friendship, emotions, and love. While the exhibition and book do not focus on the sexuality of artists, they do consider how medieval audiences may have responded to images of same-gender desire or gender-fluid people. By and large, however, we are not invested in "outing" the past by stating that someone was lesbian or gay, for instance. Instead, we lean into the indeterminacy of our objects and the feelings, relationships, and desires they might express. We might ponder the nature of the relationship between two men on a leather box, for instance, who reach out for one another across its lock (FIG. 4).[28] Many works of art seem to deliberately represent subjects and interactions in ways that defy a single reading. We witness the collapsing of multiple binaries, whether secular/sacred, male/female, friend/lover, or marital/mystical. Queering as a method allows for all these possibilities and makes way for an understanding of objects that is not foreclosed by the limits of our own contemporary classifications or reductive presumptions about the past.

Although modern queer theorists have sometimes contrasted queer to that which is normative, we want to be careful about distinguishing between medieval norms—if we can indeed call them that—and our own. Scholars like Karma Lochrie have made a strong case that there was no "normal" in the Middle Ages and that many aspects of this period's history are inherently queer, meaning that they buck our norms today but were often an integral part of power structures in the past, most notably the Christian Church.[29] Roland Betancourt has made a similar argument about gender variance in the lives of saints, for instance; more than thirty Christian saints were born female and lived as male, and their stories circulated widely in text and image throughout the medieval and Byzantine world.[30] These saints are queer in the way

Fig. 4. **Front of PL. 15 showing two men reaching for one another**

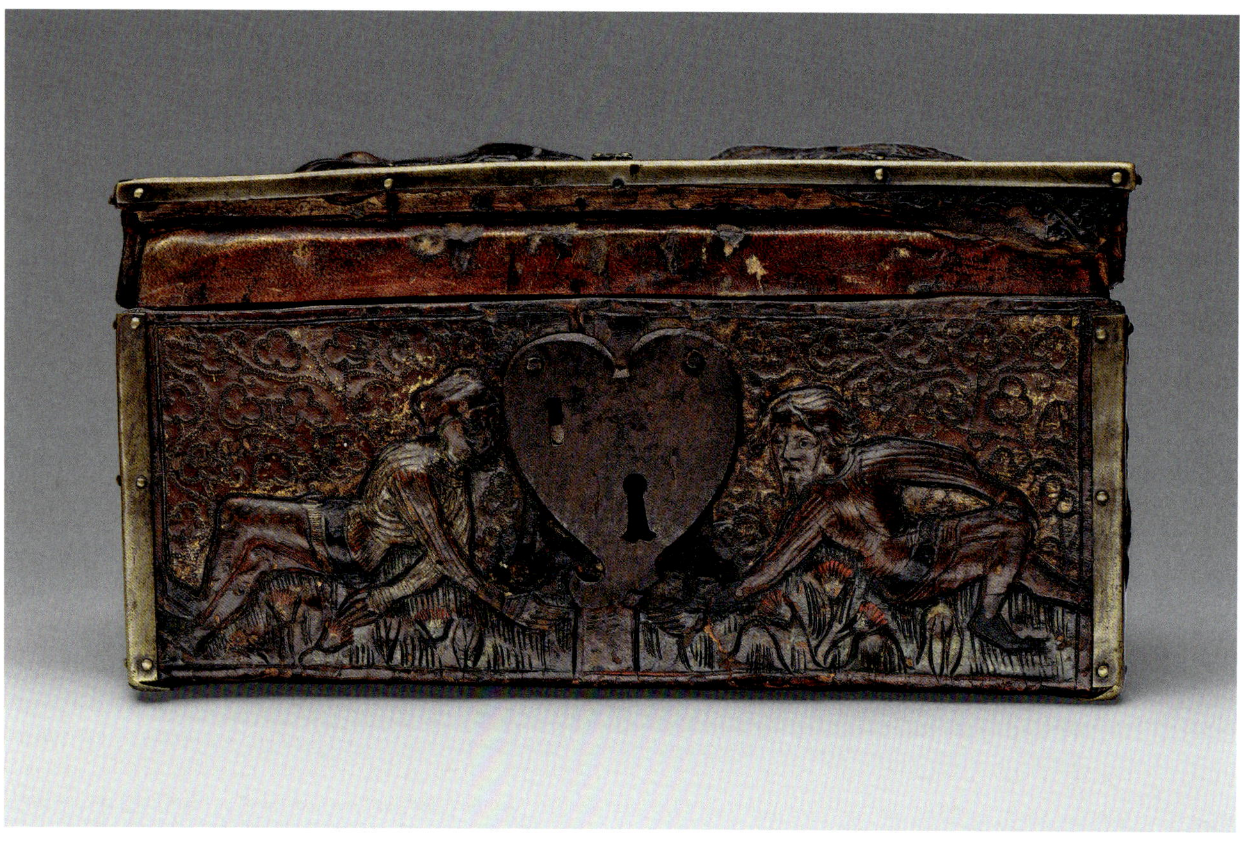

that they disrupt a modern gender binary and the false, yet rampant, presumption that this binary has always existed, but they were hardly marginal figures in the Middle Ages. Indeed, these gender-variant saints were highly esteemed and venerated, and their narratives can resonate with the lives of transgender people today.

Spectrum of Desire foregrounds works of art, presenting them as crucial sites of experimentation, performance, and even play. All of the artworks, even those sometimes deemed secular, were informed by a Christian world view, itself structured by scripture, exegesis, and canon law. Although Christianity was certainly not the only religion practiced in medieval Europe, it was the predominant one. Focusing on Christianity, then, is a way to attend to the specificity of how this hegemonic religion profoundly shaped notions of love, sex, and gender in the medieval past.[31]

Our first essay, "Bodies in Flux," considers how desire affected the representation of bodies and their capacity to change. It also serves as a primer on how to read medieval bodies in all their diversity. The second essay, "Medieval Erotica," turns to objects that unleashed the erotic imagination through their interaction with the body. The third essay, "Marital and Mystical Unions," considers the intertwined iconography of marriage, sexual penetration, and spiritual transcendence. The book concludes with a series of short essays by scholars who each focus on a single object and variously queer it by attending to aspects that have been overlooked or understudied.

To examine how people expressed desire more than five hundred years ago is to remind ourselves of a common humanity that reaches across time. There is much in how medieval people thought about their bodies and about love that we will recognize. They spent a significant amount of time defining and enforcing gender differences, even as they found freedom and poetry in blurring or disregarding those distinctions. Our own notion of romantic love draws a direct line to medieval ideals of love, where suffering was often used as a measure of its intensity.

At the same time, this catalogue and exhibition alert us to the historical specificities of the medieval moment and in turn our own. Medieval people talked about sex—described it, mocked it, legislated it, and in some ways feared it—just as we do. But unlike us, they also saw the vocabulary and physical sensations of sex as one of the most fitting ways to convey their deep desire for God. Some of the greatest Christian thinkers of the medieval period elaborated on the lingering, deep kisses they sought with the Lord. Devout believers prayed that they might climb into bed with Jesus. Secular and sacred commingle in the art discussed here, precisely because they were never distinct notions in the Middle Ages.

Today, this pairing of religion and the erotic might seem strange, even unsettling. Yet while the language of Christian devotion at present is ostensibly less eroticized than it was during the medieval period, sex and the Church continue to be intertwined, especially in the ways that religious leaders have privileged certain models of family, love, and sexual relations above others.[32] This rigidity in thinking also extends to the realm of gender; the male-female binary has been treated as natural and timeless. In medieval Christianity, however, the lines between male and female were frequently blurred, especially in the case of major religious figures, including saints, angels, and Christ. In other words, religion has never been distinct from questions of gender and sex, and the objects in *Spectrum of Desire* will, we hope, invite closer scrutiny of the varied relationships between them across time.

In their explorations of the body, gender, sexuality, and desire, medieval objects reveal the rich imagination of artists and viewers. At times, we can perceive a through line from past to present, especially when showing how certain stigmas and rhetorical tropes—like the idea of same-sex desire as something "against nature"—came into formation during this period and continue to haunt us today. But, we also see that ideas about how to live or whom to love were much less rigid in the past than we might have thought. The categories that medieval people used to make sense of desire are often not our own, yet they nonetheless reverberate with our present and invite us to reflect on the ways that desire—in all its forms—structures our own lives, identities, and relationships.[32] These works of art can open us up to other modes of living, loving, and being in the world; they are powerful reminders that things need not remain fixed.

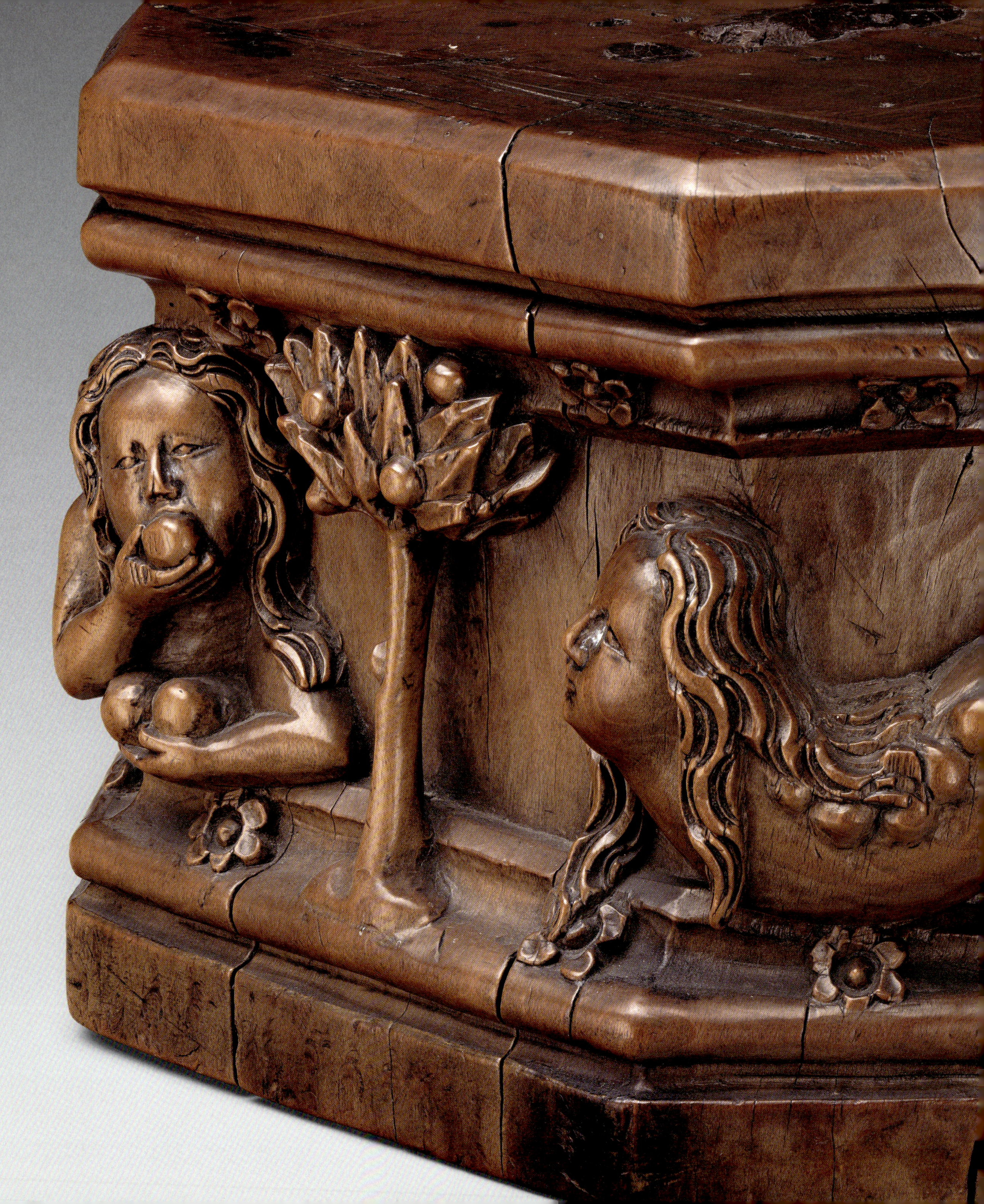

NANCY THEBAUT

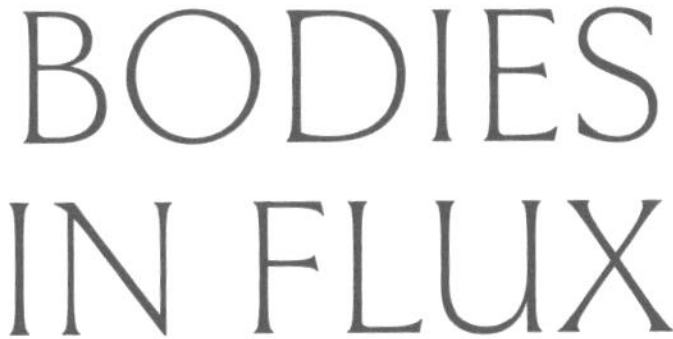

BODIES IN FLUX

A fifteenth-century Rhenish tapestry treats the study and discernment of bodies as a riddle to be solved. King Solomon sits upon a throne and faces the Queen of Sheba, who holds two flowers in her right hand and points to two seemingly identical children with her left.[1] The artist has imagined and elaborated on a passage in the Hebrew Bible, in which Sheba tested the famed wisdom of Solomon by asking him a series of difficult questions (PL. 6). The queen's riddle and the king's reply are inscribed on two interlocking banderols. Sheba states: "Tell me, King, whether the flowers and children are of the same or different kind," and Solomon responds, "The bee does not pass up a good flower; kneeling shows the female style."[2] In her desire to challenge the king, the queen has created a scenario in which the identification of difference—presumably boy/girl and real/artificial—is difficult, if not impossible. Solomon's solution to this quandary is to observe the actions of the children and the bee: one child kneels in the tapestry, thus revealing her "female style," and the bee will ultimately land on the living flower.

Set within a lush garden, the narrative seems to suggest the power of Nature, which medieval people understood as both the natural world and a set of norms or preexisting ideals that were inviolate. Despite the queen's best efforts to make the flowers and children appear identical, the true nature of each will ultimately reveal itself upon closer inspection. Late medieval viewers delighted in thinking about the relationship between nature and artifice, to which countless texts and this tapestry attest. For while Solomon's reply suggests nature's triumph, the image is far less conclusive: woven by human hands with the very materials of the natural world—wool, linen, precious metals, and plant-based dyes—the tapestry's artists have refashioned nature to their own liking.

Close observation further reveals that images of the natural world within the tapestry are marked by human intervention. The plants and trees are hardly wild, but part of a manicured garden within an otherwise arid landscape; Sheba's dress lies heavily atop the flowers, causing their stems to sharply bend toward the ground; and Solomon's massive, canopied throne is also markedly out of place. Nature succumbs to the will of the artist and to the humans figured within the scene. In other words, although Solomon's

6. **Two riddles of the Queen of Sheba.**
Upper Rhenish, ca. 1490–1500. Linen warp; wool, linen and metallic wefts

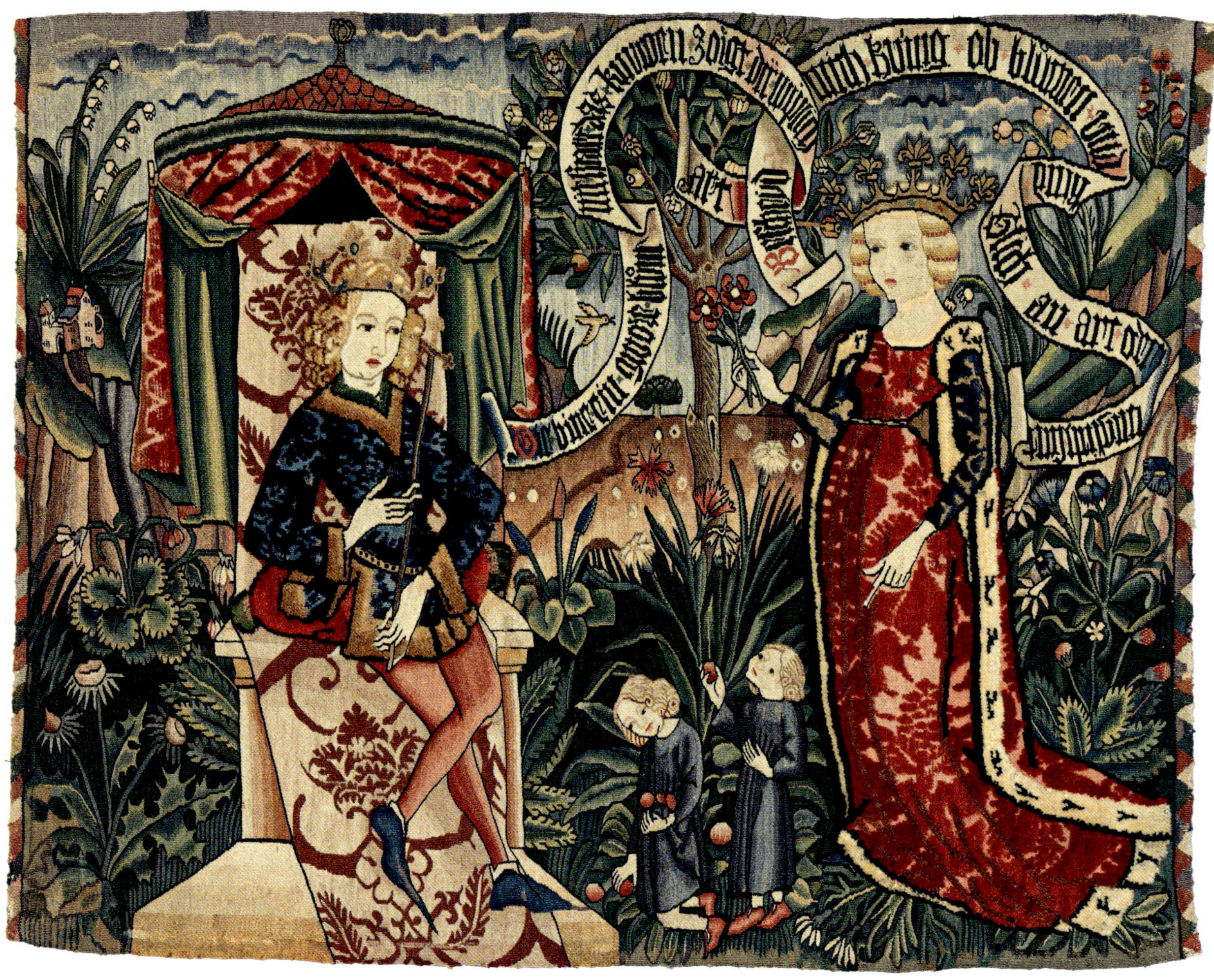

reply insists on Nature's truths and infallibility, the artist's stance is more ambivalent: bodies, like the natural world itself, can be reshaped according to one's desires.

Sheba's question provides a generative starting point for a discussion of how to read medieval bodies in all their diversity.[3] It takes a different tack than Solomon, however, in its response. Focusing on works of art made between the fourteenth and sixteenth centuries in northern Europe, when the policing of bodies and acts deemed "unnatural" was on the rise, we examine the ways that artists represented bodies and their capacity to change.

The mutability of bodies might at first seem resolutely modern. After all, it is a central tenet of queer theory and activism, from notions of gender performativity to the defense of bodily autonomy.[4] But change was also an important point of intellectual inquiry and belief in the Middle Ages.[5] The Christian doctrine of bodily resurrection proved an especially fecund ground for thinking about bodily transformations and continuity as it related to identity.[6] Caroline Walker Bynum recounts the range of ways that medieval theologians theorized the Resurrection, which included the "flowering of a dry tree after winter, the donning of new clothes...the hatching of an egg...the reforging of a statue that has been melted down, the growth of the fetus from a drop of semen...[and] the reassembling of broken potsherds."[7] Change was linked to creation, biological and artistic. It should be no surprise, then, that images were a particularly evocative means for exploring this key component of Christian thought.

Bodily transformations were understood to be the result of a variety of causes, both internal and external, and chief among them was desire. From concupiscence to courtly love, the longings and fantasies of medieval subjects reshaped their very appearance for better or worse. As cultural theorist Lauren Berlant explains, the "attachments that desire engenders constantly reorganize the body in...state(s) of 'becoming'[,] which in turn radically reshape the body as an erotic zone, a zone of meaning, value, and power."[8] This framework is useful when thinking about the body as a locus of desire in medieval art: its surface is a topography that renders visible the ways that desire constructs but also disrupts the subject.[9]

Representations of bodies are never neutral. The objects discussed here were made during an era when there was increased suspicion, control, and punishment of particular people, acts, and relationships.[10] At times, these works of art appear to reinforce the bigotry of their moment, but at others, they offer important sites of experimentation, even exploration, of how one could live or whom one could love.[11] Moreover, while much of European medieval art, like the tapestry of Sheba and Solomon, tends to foreground hegemonic subjects, a queer approach can make way for the study of sexual, gender, and racial minorities. It can simultaneously pull back the curtain on the construction of value systems that we continue to grapple with today, yet also—at times to our surprise—reveal that apparent subversions of these systems, like the gender binary, were an integral part of medieval Christianity and its images.

FIRST BODIES: CREATION AND CARE

Medical and spiritual understandings of the body coincide in a fifteenth-century manuscript illumination of Adam and Eve (PL. 7).[12] God stands at the center of a circular earth within a starry sky and with arms outstretched, as if pausing to admire the totality of his creation, from the fish in the river below to the sun and moon overhead. Surrounded by angels, God is entirely golden; his facial features against this gilded ground are barely visible, perhaps evidence of a reader's efforts to touch his face. His divine will is the driving desire that prompts the making of these multiple bodies.[13] In the Book of Genesis, God first makes Adam "of the slime of the earth" (Genesis 2:7) and then forms Eve from one of Adam's ribs while he is fast asleep (Genesis 2:21–22). The artist has chosen to depict the creation of Eve as if suspended in time: she emerges from Adam's side and joins her hands in prayer. Devotion to God precedes bodily integrity.

The painting is the frontispiece to a household medical compendium known as *Le Régime du corps* (*The Regimen of the Body*), a text written in 1256 by Italian physician Aldobrandino da Siena (d. 1296/1299) at the request of Beatrice de Savoie (d. 1267), countess of Provence and mother to four royal daughters. The first of its kind in a vernacular language, the *Régime* circulated widely and was likely used by wealthy women in the care of themselves and their families.[14] Aldobrandino is painted below the Creation and given pride of place within the letter *D* of *Dieu* (God). Dressed like a medical doctor and standing in a pulpit as if delivering a lecture, he points to the adjacent text, the prologue to the *Régime*. Here, we learn that the body is made of the four humors (blood, yellow bile, black bile, and phlegm) that derive their qualities from the four elements (earth, water, air, and fire) and is in a constant stage of change; it can become "corrupt, gets young, gets old, changes, and cannot remain in one state."[15] The science of *phisike* (physiognomy), Aldobrandino triumphantly declares, can help humans care "for the health [God] gave" them.[16] Readers learn the art of this science in the pages that

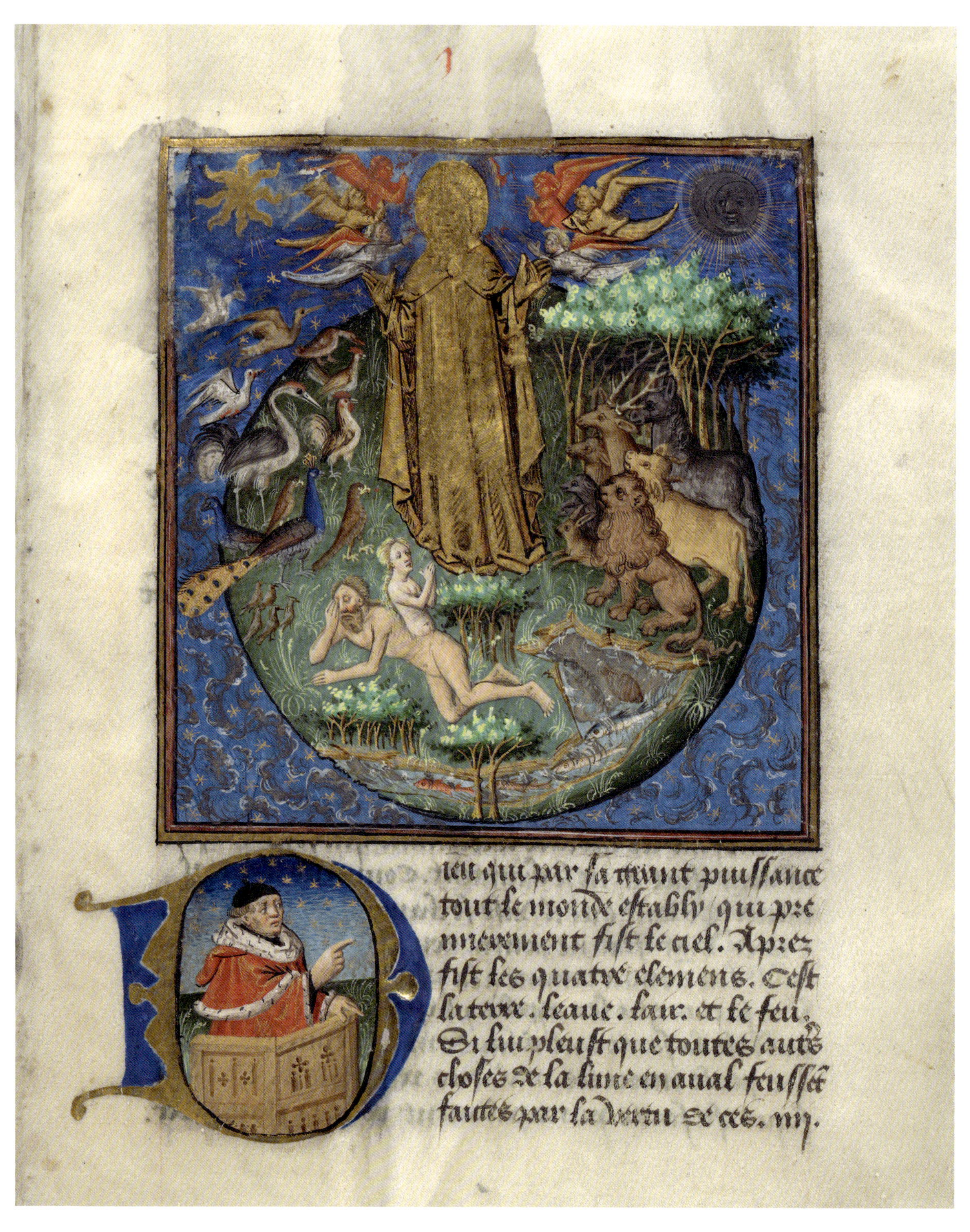

7. **Creation with Adam and Eve as the primal androgyne from *Le Régime du corps* (*The Regimen of the Body*). French, ca. 1440–50. Opaque watercolor, gold, silver and iron gall ink on parchment**

follow, including "how one can, by nature, know man and woman from the outside."[17]

This lesson in reading bodies "from the outside" is ultimately one in reading images, too, and the Creation painting invites the viewer to put this skill into practice. Adam and Eve's bodies offer an important case study in human anatomy and physiognomy, namely sexual (in)differentiation and the medieval theory of *complexio*, or complexion and temperament, which roughly correspond to the careful study of form and color.[18] Adam and Eve are joined at the waist; depicted thus, they encourage the viewer to anticipate their separation and momentarily pause on their bi-sexed body. While their genitalia are sexually indistinct, their upper halves are marked as male and female: Adam has a beard, and Eve has breasts. Theologians spilled significant ink over how to characterize this single, unified body. Considered by some to be a "primal androgyne" and by others as a perfect *hermaphroditus*, or a body with both male and female characteristics, Adam and Eve's shared form was an object of analysis to various ends, including the condemnation of actual intersex people.[19] The angels that hover next to God also subvert a sex binary. Theologians like Thomas Aquinas understood angels as neither male nor female: they do not assume bodies and thus bypass gender categories altogether.[20]

Beyond form, color is central to the discernment of the first human bodies. Eve's skin is pale pink, whereas Adam's is dark beige. In the medical context, skin was subject to scrutiny by doctors and natural philosophers, who widely agreed that the color of one's flesh was determined in part by the balance of the four elements and fluids (humors) within the body.[21] The proportions of these fluids informed one's temperament (sanguine, choleric, melancholic, phlegmatic) and the quality of one's body (hot, cold, dry, and/or moist), which were in turn linked to gender, skin color, and geographical origin. According to this logic, European women were cold and moist, as manifested externally by their white skin, and European men were hot and dry, and thus slightly darker in complexion. The "wrong" color was a sign of poor health; *Le Régime du corps* declares that (for presumably a European man) a complexion that is "green, pale, black, or dark purple" can be a sign of "bad habits, a lack of sense, and a bad nature."[22]

Black skin in other contexts, however, took on entirely different meaning. Medieval medical students encountered a range of sources claiming that people with black skin—regardless of sex—were thought to have more inner heat, caused in part by the hotter climate in which they lived.[23] As in much of the history of medicine, these theories could be tools of racist thought: the inner heat of Black women in Africa, for instance, was thought to make them far more sexually active than white women, as Peter Biller has shown in his study of thirteenth-century university texts.[24]

The frontispiece and opening lines of *Le Régime du corps* participate in the construction of religious and medical knowledge. On the precipice of change, Adam and Eve's shared body offers a starting point for the creation and care of all human bodies, albeit from a specifically white, European, and Christian perspective. All the while, there are aspects of this image that are remarkably queer and tender. The first humans are figured as an intersex body, in all its beauty, and Eve with her alert, devotional pose doubles as an image of the possibly female reader or the text's female patron, Beatrice de Savoie. She took on the role of Aldobrandino, even God himself, in her own efforts to care for the bodies of the people she loved.

FALLING BODIES: ILLICIT ACTS AND SUGGESTIONS OF *SODOMIA*

Desire was also a disruptive force that could irrevocably change bodies. Following the creation of Adam and Eve, things quickly go awry: a serpent tempts Eve to eat the forbidden fruit from the Tree of Knowledge, which she then shares with Adam (Genesis 3:1–6).[25] This act of original sin marks the Fall, when Adam and Eve transition from a state of innocence to one of carnal knowledge. They suddenly experienced concupiscence, lust, and libido.[26] For Christian theologians, Adam and Eve's sexual awakening had grave implications, namely that their descendants would also experience the same wayward desires and possess a weakened will to resist them.[27] Eve and a female-headed serpent face off in a small boxwood carving made in the late fifteenth century, now at The Cloisters, that figures the Fall as the moment when the human body is physically altered by desire (PL. 8).[28] Lying on her belly, Eve bites into an apple, her lips curling around its upper edges, and she suggestively holds another two apples at her chest.[29] At center is the fruit tree, and at right is a female-headed serpent whose wavy locks and serpentine body make her a mirror image of Eve. This hybrid creature was possibly understood as Lilith, Adam's first (and demonic) wife, according to Jewish commentaries on the Hebrew Bible that were adopted by Christian authors.[30]

The sculpture was never intended to be viewed on its own, however: a statue of the Virgin Mary was likely once placed atop the boxwood base. Prostrate below Mary's feet, Eve and the serpent were physically and metaphorically abased. Their bodies and behavior were negative precursors of the Virgin Mary, through whom Christ would redeem humanity for Eve

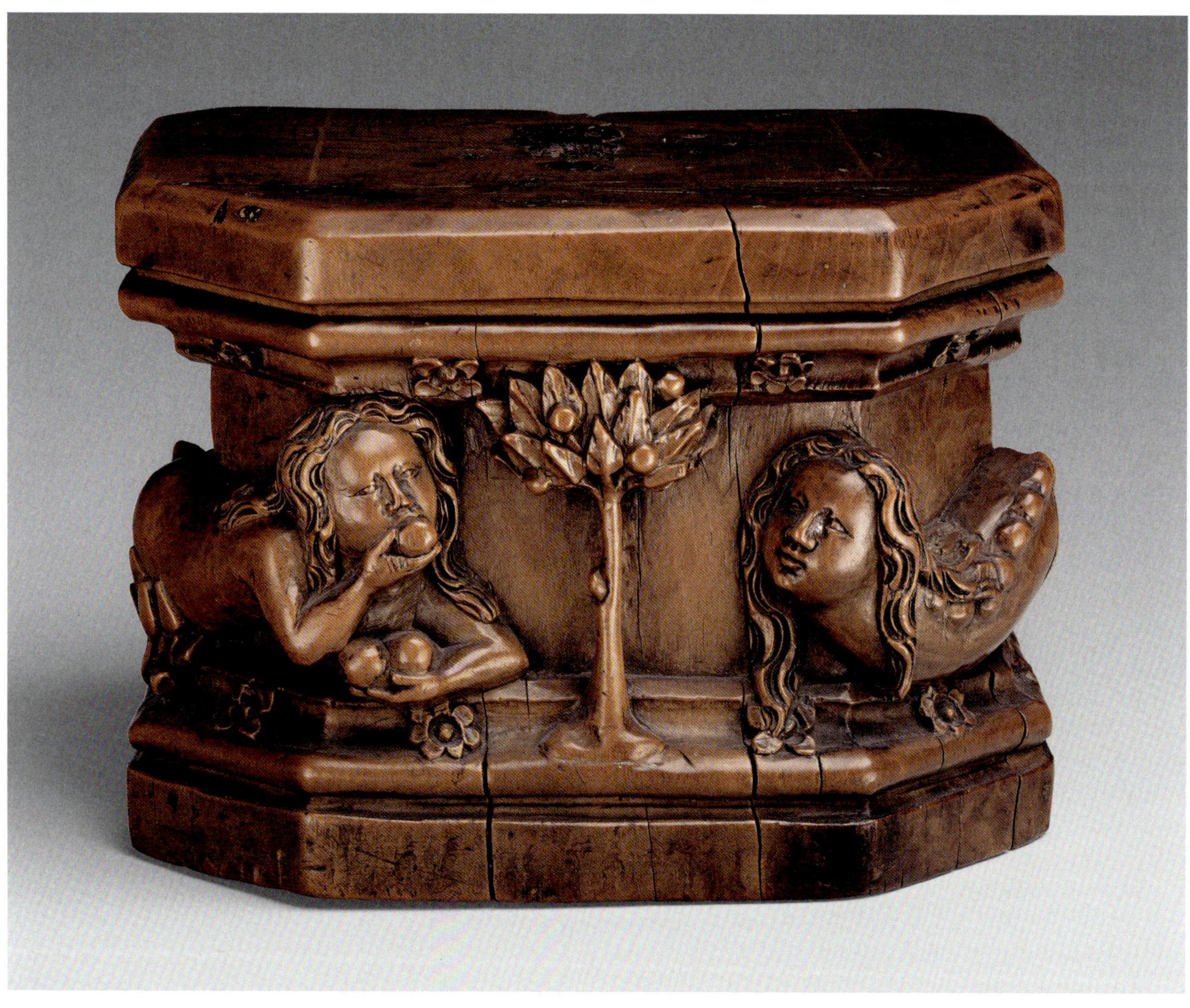

8. **Base for a statuette with Eve and a female-headed serpent. Netherlandish, 1470–80. Boxwood**

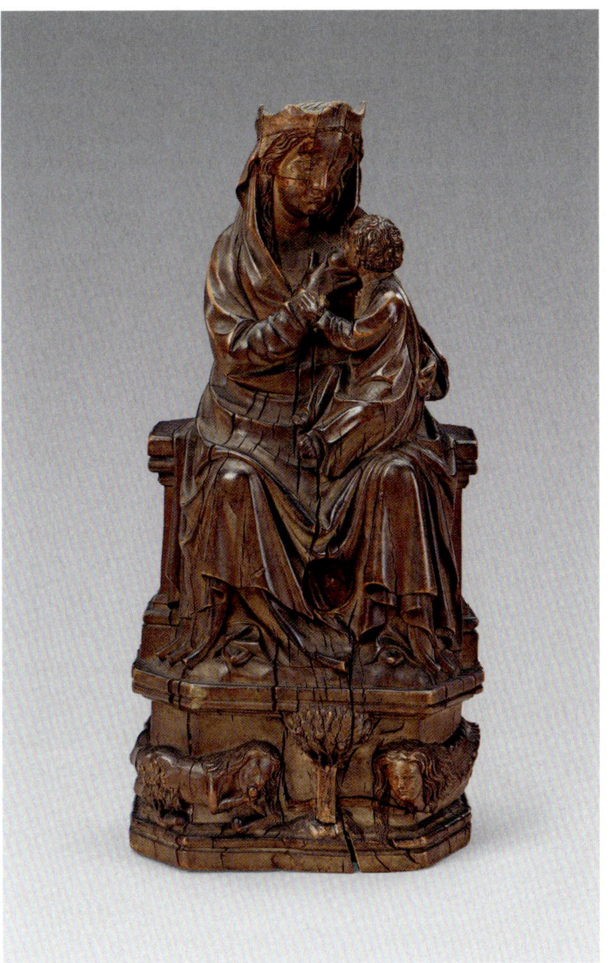

Fig. 5. **Virgin and Child with Eve and female-headed serpent. Netherlandish(?), possibly 16th century. Possibly boxwood, 15⅛ × 6⅝ in. (38.5 × 16.8 cm). Victoria and Albert Museum, London (4440-1857)**

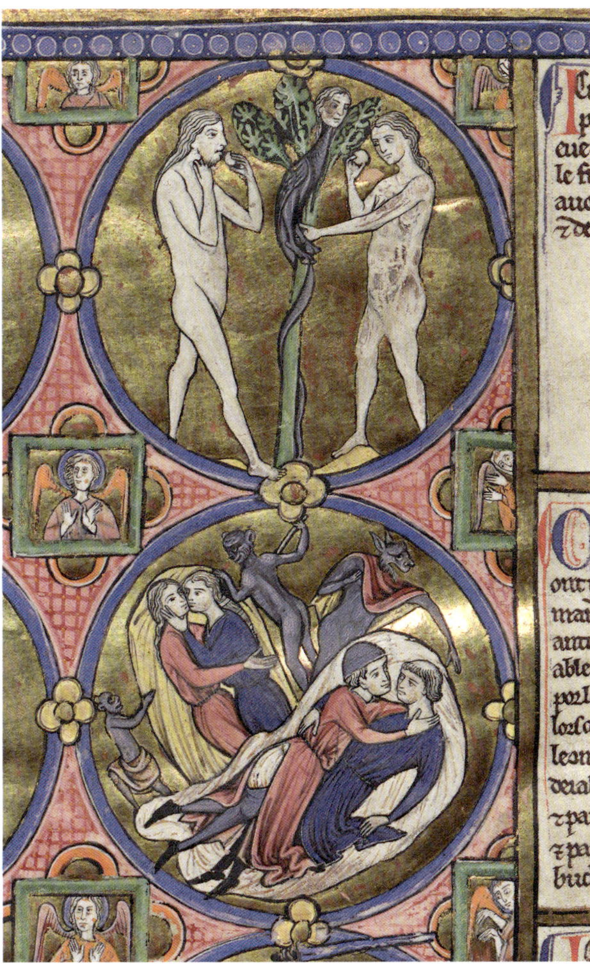

Fig. 6. **Adam, Eve, and female-headed serpent; same-sex couples embracing. From a moralized Bible. Paris, ca. 1220–30. Opaque watercolor, gold leaf, and iron gall ink on parchment, 13½ × 10¼ in. (34 × 26 cm). Austrian National Library, Vienna (MS Cod. 2554, fol. 2r)**

and Adam's sin. A sixteenth-century sculpture in the Victoria and Albert Museum, London, provides a sense of the original appearance of The Cloisters sculpture (FIG. 5).[31] Here, the Virgin feeds Christ from her breast, a source of spiritual nourishment. In the image of Eve below, breasts become the forbidden fruit. Eve transforms into the very objects of her temptation, namely apples and the female snake. In the case of The Cloisters base, the fine grain of the boxwood carving allows for exquisite detail that enhances the subject's sensuousness.

The formal similarity between Eve and the serpent is in keeping with medieval thinkers' misogynistic reading of the biblical narrative. It also condemns a particular kind of lust associated with the Fall by artists and theologians alike: inappropriate desire for oneself and same-sex desire.[32] The Cloisters base is hardly the first to represent the Fall in this way. One of the most explicit examples appears in the opening folios of a moralized Bible made around 1220 for Blanche of Castile, Queen of France (d. 1252). Two same-sex couples are in the throes of an unambiguous embrace; two women kiss and two men of different faiths (Jewish and Christian) wrap their arms around each other (FIG. 6).[33] The lower painting serves as a commentary on the Fall, depicted above, in which the female-headed serpent tempts Eve to eat the fruit. This trope persisted for several centuries.[34] In a sixteenth-century print by Lucas Cranach the Elder, Eve and the snake are in suggestively close proximity: their faces touch as the creature whispers into Eve's ear, and its phallic tail grazes her inner thigh (FIG. 7).

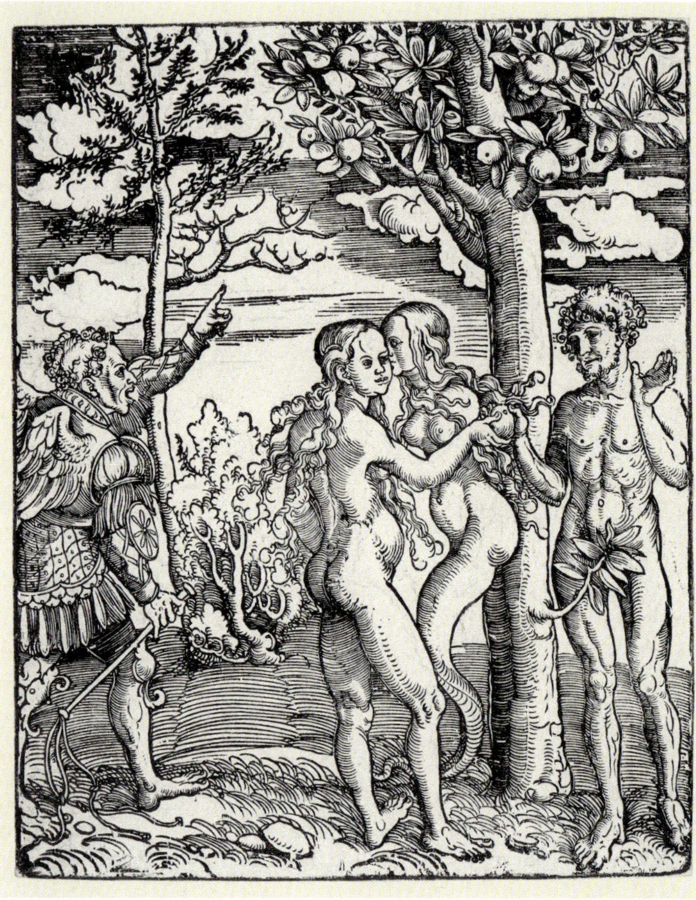

Fig. 7. **The Fall of Man, showing Eve with the female-headed serpent whispering in her ear, 1500–15. Lucas Cranach the Elder (German, 1472–1553). Black printing ink on paper, 11 × 8¾ in. (28.1 × 22.2 cm). British Museum, London (0518.12)**

The allusion to same-sex desire and its perilous consequences would not have been lost on the medieval viewer. It was part of a capacious category of sins known as *sodomia*, whose English translation, "sodomy," is misleading in its limited meaning.[35] In one of the first significant treatises on the topic, the twelfth-century monk Peter Damian listed some of the sexual acts *sodomia* entailed, including masturbation, "penetration in the rear," sex "between the thighs," and mutual rubbing of "manly parts."[36] He also proposed its root cause as the Fall, specifically Eve's "perverse" female desire.[37] Subsequent theologians expanded the definition to include crimes relating to gender presentation and heresy. Although this categorization of sex, gender, and belief might seem at a distant remove from today, it had lasting power. Historians agree that it was during the Middle Ages that "a peculiarly Western sexual ethos gradually took shape," and that the Church, specifically canon law, "played a crucial role in its formation."[38]

While canon law oversaw the policing and punishment of *sodomia* through the early fourteenth century, lay authorities began to exercise increasing scrutiny over the sexual conduct of its citizens thereafter. Cities adopted local statutes and ordinances to condemn various forms of nonmarital sex, including those associated with *sodomia*.[39] Punishments became deadly: the annals of the city of Basel, Switzerland, record the first known death of someone accused of committing sodomy, a man named Lord Haspisperch, who was killed in 1277.[40] In the case of late-medieval Bruges, ninety people were killed for the crime of *sodomia* between 1385 and 1515. Court records indicate that eighty-three were men, and seven were women.[41]

We know little about these individuals and the relationships they risked at great cost. Occasionally archives can offer a partial view of their lives, as in the case of Katherina Hetzeldorfer. Originally from Nuremberg, she was accused in the city of Speyer of having sex with women and presenting as male.[42] Hetzeldorfer's trial records reveal the court's preoccupation with her appropriation of male behavior, dress, and anatomy (specifically a red leather dildo), on which the court especially fixated.[43] Much goes unmentioned, however, including how Hetzeldorfer understood her own relationship to gender, as well as the precise crime of which she was accused.[44] Was it her presentation as male or sexual acts with women that were most offensive to those in power?[45] For crimes unnamed, Hetzeldorfer was tragically drowned in 1477.

Francesca Sautman and Pamela Sheingorn have proposed that images can help us "catch glimpses" of the acts, relationships, and people who remain unnamed.[46] The Cloisters carving can paradoxically prompt us to seek out and recover people like Hetzeldorfer precisely because of its overt condemnation of same-sex desire. In so doing, it also serves as a powerful reminder of the ways that objects could be complicit in the marginalization of and physical violence toward sexual and gender minorities.

FLUID BODIES AFTER THE FALL: SAINTS WILGEFORTIS & MARINOS

Visual narrative could also offer a world in which the transgression of a gender binary was not subject to persecution. More than thirty saints changed their social, sexed, and gender presentation over the course of their lifetimes, and artists embraced their representation.[47] This is particularly the case for those born with female-sexed bodies and presented as male, whom we would today describe as transmasculine. Their transition from female to male was understood as one of ascent, from the "material, passive, corporeal" female to the "active, rational, incorporeal" male.[48] In the context of this hierarchical understanding of gender, it is not surprising that stories of transfeminine saints are far less frequent; for a male-sexed person to adopt female attributes was considered a form of bodily debasement.[49]

God himself could enable such transformations. Such is the case of Saint Ontcommer, also known as Wilgefortis, an early Christian martyr who asked God to make her less attractive to deter a pagan suitor.[50] In response to her prayers, God gives her a beard. In a private prayer book made in the late fifteenth century in Antwerp, a tiny painting depicts the crucifixion of Wilgefortis, ordered by her father on account of her refusal to marry (PL. 9). Like many female saints, she preferred instead to be the spiritual bride of Christ. Wilgefortis has a faintly painted beard and wears a turquoise dress that outlines her breasts and waist. The painting of the saint and the adjacent prayer work in tandem to suggest not only that she is Christ's bride, but also that her body has merged with his. Outstretched on the cross, Wilgefortis' gender-variant body makes explicit her physical union with Christ as well as the power of bodily change to attain one's desires. (Christ's body, too, was understood by artists and theologians to possess both male and female attributes, as Bryan Keene explores in this catalogue).

The saint's physical transformation was not always a result of divine intervention, however, but of their own will and desire. A Belgian fifteenth-century copy of *The Golden Legend*, the most popular compendium of stories of saints' lives in the Middle Ages, depicts two episodes from the life of Saint Marin(e), commonly known as Marinos, to whom the narrator refers with both male and female pronouns (as we will here) (PL. 10).[51] Born with a female-sexed body, Marin(e) joins a monastery with her father following the death of her mother. The saint must accordingly present as male: he cuts his hair in the style of the monastic tonsure and wears the black Benedictine habit. For the remainder of his life, Marin(e) passes as male; it is only after his death, specifically during the preparation of his body for burial, that fellow monks see his female-sexed body.[52]

Whereas the text's narrator switches between male and female pronouns when recounting Marin(e)'s story, the artist only depicts Marin(e) with the visual vocabulary of a male, monastic body. At left, Marin(e), identified by the golden halo, kneels before a group of monks, one of whom holds a crozier. This scene likely depicts the moment when Marin(e) is falsely accused and then judged to be guilty of raping and impregnating a local woman. Marin(e) does not deny the charge and is thus banished from the monastery, to which the open archway at left might allude. At right, Marin(e) lays on his deathbed; he has returned to the monastery, and the monks care for him.[53] Absent from the painting is the discovery of the saint's female-sexed body, an otherwise typical inclusion in the representation of the saint's life.[54] Remarkably, the artist has depicted Marin(e) in accordance with the way that the saint—at least from the narrator's perspective—wished to live and be seen by others.[55]

Desire is again the impetus for bodily change, but of a different order than those examined thus far. Although initially framed as a response or even solution to narrative circumstance, Marin(e)'s desire to live as male ultimately comes from within.[56] Marin(e)'s male presentation certainly allows him to join his father in a monastery, but he resolutely holds onto his male identity and is reluctant to "out" himself, even when he could prove his innocence by doing so. The saint's silence, then, suggests evidence of a sincere attachment to his gender.[57] In depicting Marin(e) as a monk, the artist privileges the saint's desire to be seen as male and so affirms Marin(e)'s transmasculine identity, even at the risk of visual confusion. Although we will likely never know how medieval viewers whose own relationship with gender was fraught may have responded to this image, we can say with certainty that Marin(e)'s story, textual and visual, is part of transgender history.[58] As such, this painting invites the creation of community across time with those who identify as transgender and/or nonbinary today.

SIMEON BACHOS, "AETHIOPS," AND THE FOUNTAIN OF YOUTH

Although Marin(e)'s female-sexed body is unknown to his fellow monks until after his death, other gender- and sex-variant subjects were more open about their bodily changes, including so-called eunuchs, or castrated men.[59] The surgical removal of their testicles made them, to medieval viewers, neither male nor female, but something in between, akin to what we would today term nonbinary.[60] Specifically, the removal of a person's testicles was thought to make them lose heat and thus become less male: a eunuch (to whom we will refer with third-person pronouns) no longer grew facial hair and had whiter skin, a higher voice, a stronger sexual appetite, and uncontrollable emotions.[61] Many of these characteristics were also associated with women. Although this type of body modification did take place in Western Europe (with or without the person's consent), as narrative constructs, they were often non-European and specifically members of the Byzantine court.

Sex, race, and religion intersect in the representation of Simeon Bachos, who is today often referred to as

9. **A bearded Saint Wilgefortis on the Cross, from a Book of Hours. Netherlandish, ca. 1500. Opaque watercolor, gold, silver and ink on parchment**

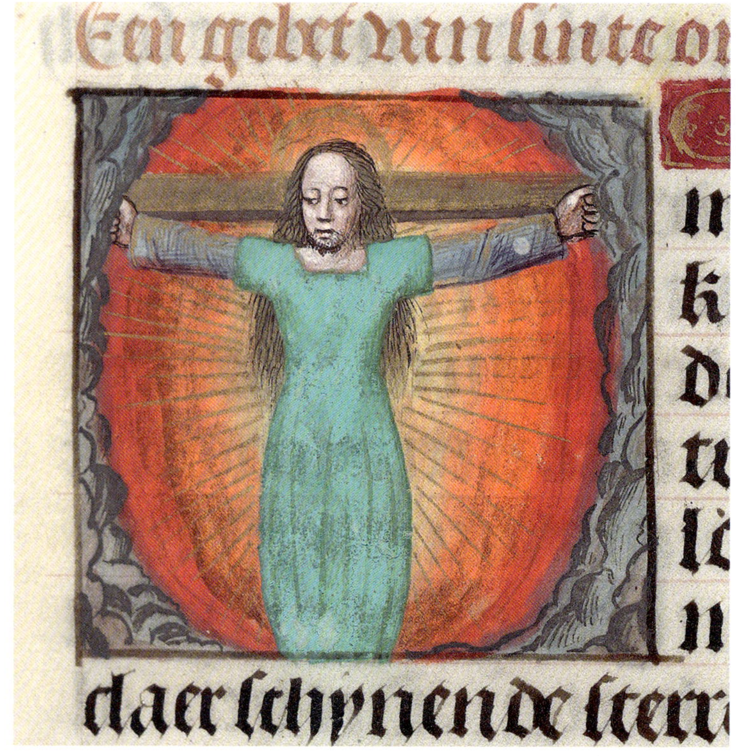

10. **Judgment of Saint Marinos; Death of Saint Marinos from *The Golden Legend*. Belgian, 1445–65. Opaque watercolor, gold leaf, silver and ink on parchment**

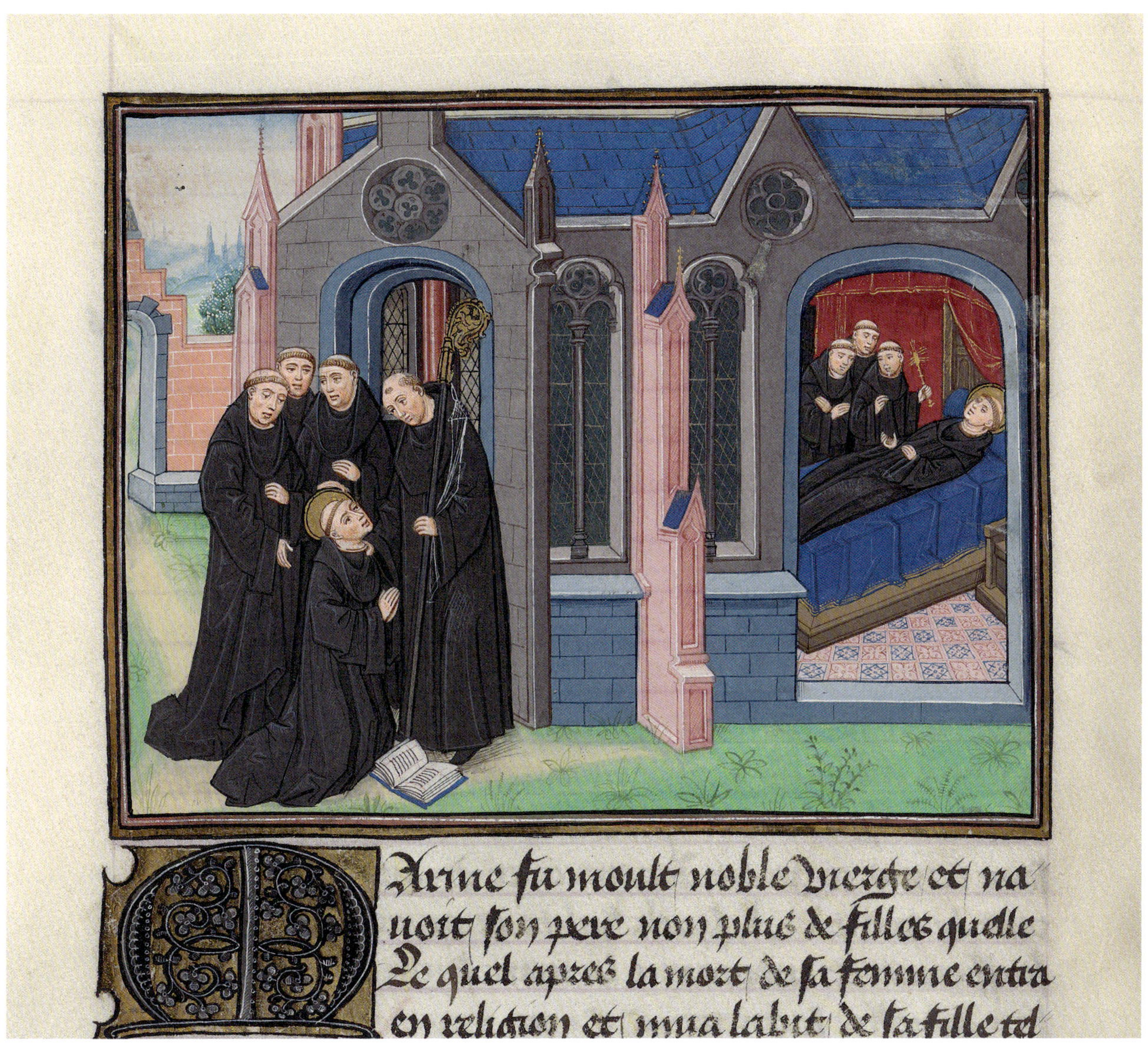

the "Ethiopian eunuch" (PL. 11).[62] A sixteenth-century Book of Hours made for Emperor Charles V (d. 1558) depicts the baptism of Simeon above a prayer to the Holy Spirit. The Acts of the Apostles (8:26–39) recounts that while Philip the Deacon was on his way from Jerusalem to Gaza, he encounters Simeon, who is described as "aethiops'"—the word is Greek for "burnt skin"—and as reading from the Book of Isaiah.[63] Philip explains the meaning of the text to Simeon, who then asks to be baptized. Their initial meeting is depicted at a distance on the left, and the baptism fills the foreground. With the sprinkling of water upon his head, Simeon's body will be transformed.

At this moment of conversion, the multiple differences between Philip and Simeon are visually conveyed through their bodies. Philip stands tall as he pours water over Simeon, who in turn bends his knees and hunches over. A quick comparison to the baptism

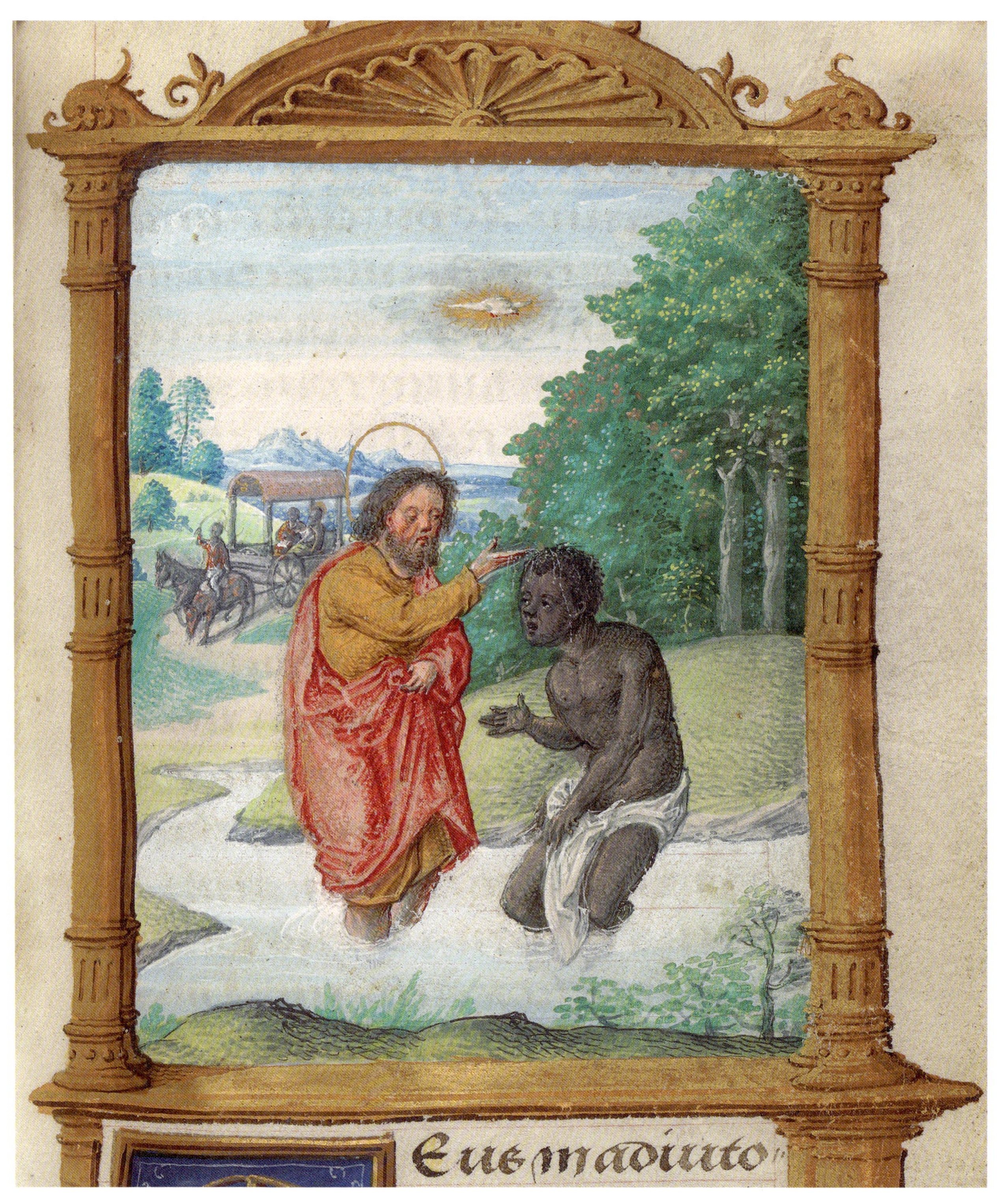

11. Philip the Deacon baptizes Simeon Bachos (the "Ethiopian Eunuch") from a Book of Hours. Master of Charles V. Opaque watercolor, gold leaf, silver and ink on parchment

Fig. 8. **African Magus, one of the Three Kings from an Adoration group. German, before 1489. Maple, paint, and gilding, 61½ × 17 × 13¼ in. (156.2 × 43.2 × 33.7 cm). The Metropolitan Museum of Art, New York, The Cloisters Collection, 1952 (52.83.2)**

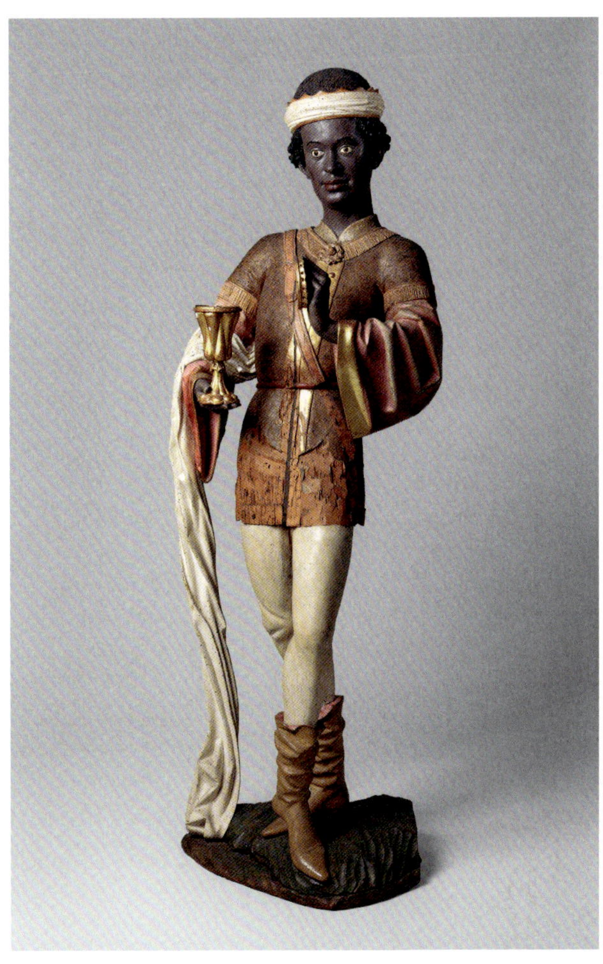

of Christ (fol. 126r) in the same manuscript reveals that their distinct poses are not simply the visual language of baptism. Rather, there is an expressed imbalance of power: Philip has spiritual authority that Simeon does not possess. Simeon also wears less clothing than Philip, inviting closer scrutiny of their bare skin. Simeon's left hand holds a white cloth in place, calling attention to their genital area, which gives them the social and sexual status of a eunuch. While Simeon's partial nudity is functional, it also contrasts their black skin with Philip's pink skin.

Skin color, as we have seen, can convey multiple meanings about a person in European medieval art. As scholars like Geraldine Heng have shown, black skin could suggest a physical reality (epidermal race) or a quality about that a person, including their geographic origins and religion and—in a deeply racist way—the infernal.[64] In this instance, Simeon's black skin emphasizes that they are non-European. Their precise origins, however, were nebulous: for medieval Europeans, the moniker "Ethiopia" (hereafter used without quotation marks) could refer to any place in which Black Africans lived, all of sub-Saharan Africa, and/or India.[65] This geographical confusion predated the Middle Ages. Greek historian Herodotus (d. 425 BCE) believed that Ethiopia constituted all inhabited land south of Egypt. In medieval art and narrative, Ethiopia was strongly associated with figures like the Queen of Sheba; Prester John, the mythical king of the Ethiopians (and keeper of the Fountain of Youth); Simeon; and Balthazar, one of the three kings who visited Christ after his birth.[66] The visual vocabularies for these figures varied greatly: whereas Sheba was often shown as white, Balthazar was regularly shown with black skin beginning in the fifteenth century and in the aristocratic dress of a European noble, as seen in a statue from Swabia, Germany (FIG. 8).[67]

Clothing also played an important role in a person being designated as Ethiopian. In the widely circulated pilgrimage guide *Peregrinatio in Terram Sanctam* (*Pilgrimage to the Holy Land*), Bernhard von Breydenbach (1440?–1497) presents a textual and visual inventory of diverse peoples that the European traveler might encounter in Jerusalem. Among them are two "Abyssians or Indians" (also understood as Ethiopians), specifically a priest and a layperson (PL. 12).[68] The priest wears a cloth wrapped around his head and no shoes, which the text below indicates is characteristic of Ethiopian men and women; there is no mention of the other outfit, which is likely an artistic invention. Skin color, however, contradicts the adjoining text that reads, "Indians [or Ethiopians] are all black like the Moors." Yellow and pink, not black or brown, partially cover the figures' faces and lips in a marked departure from the representation of Balthazar and Simeon.

At the time that Breydenbach was traveling to the Holy Land, Ethiopian pilgrims were regularly in Rome. A five-member embassy of Ethiopian Christians arrived

12. **Ethiopians of Jerusalem from *Peregrinatio in Terram Sanctam* (*Pilgrimage to the Holy Land*), 1486. Erhard Reuwich (artist). Black printing ink with watercolor on paper**

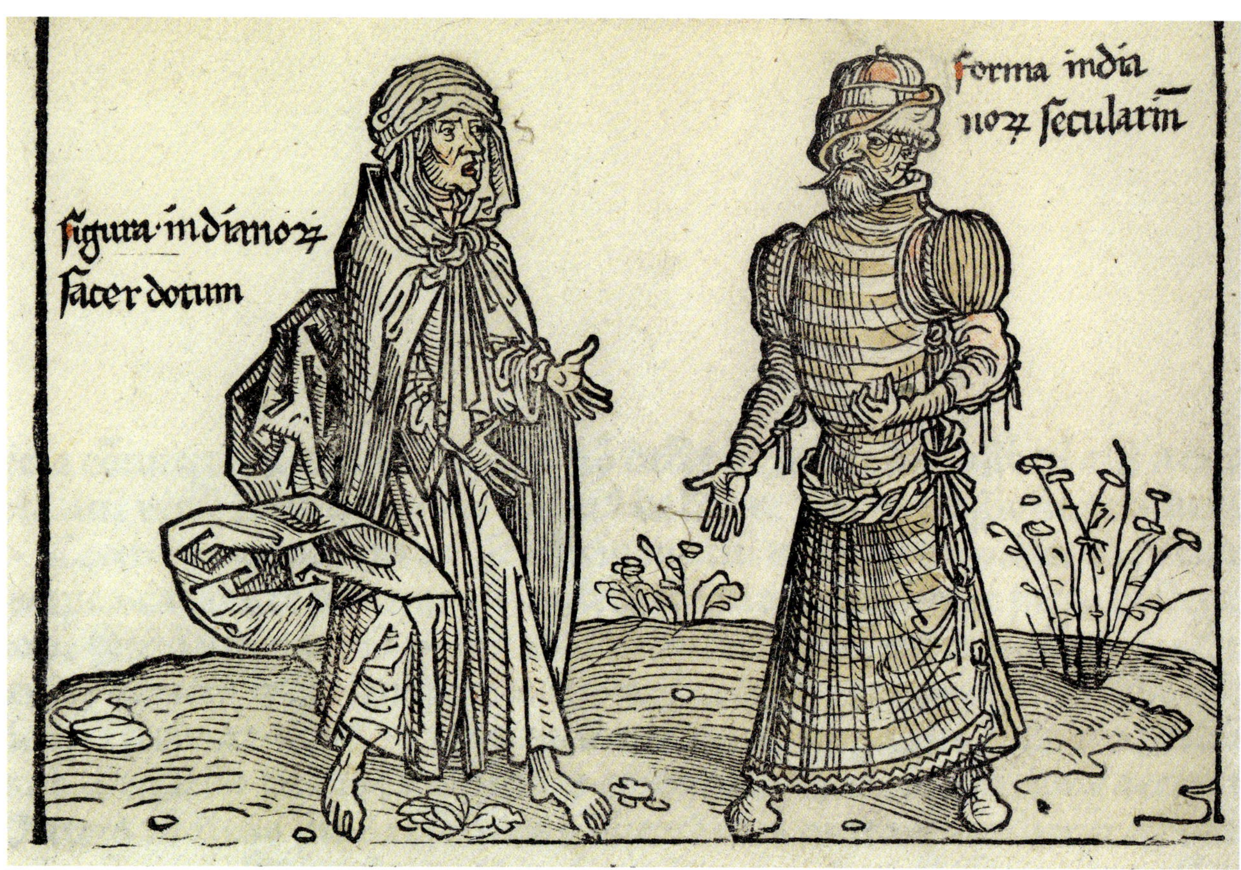

in 1404, and dozens more continued to travel there in the decades that followed. By the mid-sixteenth century, they held an institutional presence in Rome: under Pope Paul III (d. 1549), Santo Stefano became a home for Ethiopian pilgrims who needed a place to stay, study, or pray.[69] Beyond Rome, an increased number of Black Africans came to the European continent, many as servants or enslaved laborers.[70] The highly constructed image of Simeon was perhaps shaped by nebulous concepts of Ethiopians as well as by actual Black Africans whom the artist may have encountered in Europe. Painted within a manuscript for the Holy Roman Emperor, Charles V, Simeon's hunched-over body was almost certainly also viewed in relation to the rise of rampant colonization and enslavement of dark-skinned people both in Europe and overseas, and in which Charles was complicit.

While it is possible that Simeon resembles a Black person with whom the artist was familiar, the representation more likely uses the Black body as a rhetorical tool. Crouched over and nearly naked, Simeon's Black, castrated, not-quite-yet Christian, and non-European body participates in the construction of Philip's own body and identity as male, Christian, and European (although he was, in actuality, from the Middle East). In the context of this image of baptism, which was understood as a literal rebirth, Simeon's spiritual and corporeal change is framed as consensual but also as a kind of ascent aided by Philip, who represents by contrast the ideal of the white, male, Christian body.

Water also facilitates the transformation of bodies in an ivory relief carving of the legendary Fountain of Youth (PL. 13). The figures are foremost young, white, and aristocratic, and they too are connected to Ethiopia.[71] In his *Histories* of the Greco-Persian war, Herodotus recounts that the "long-lived Ethiopians . . . lived to be a hundred and twenty years old, while some even went beyond that age." The king of Ethiopia reveals that their longevity is made possible by a "fountain, wherein when they had washed, they found their flesh all glossy and sleek, as if they had bathed in oil."[72] The fountain is also mentioned in the *Alexander Romance* (it makes Alexander's servant immortal) and *Travels of Sir John Mandeville*, which places it in India. The miraculous properties of the fountain are also associated with the Pool of Bethesda, which healed a disabled man (John 5:2), as well as, more generally, with the salvific and transformational waters of baptism, which offered Christians a kind of spiritual rebirth, as depicted in the painting of Simeon.

Any reference to the fountain's non-European context is lost, however, in this ivory plaque that probably once covered a set of writing tablets. In the top section, a bearded man steps into the water and supports himself with a walking stick; he is elderly and disabled. At right, we see the water's miraculous effects: four youthful bodies engage in amorous exchange and courtship. The visual vocabulary of youth herein trumps that of gender: entirely nude, the figures' only distinguishing markers are the crowns or veils worn on the heads of the women. Below, three couples (or perhaps one couple three times over) are nearly identically dressed and perform an elaborate choreography of courtly love. At left, a crowned woman turns her head away, as if disinterested; at center, the man holds her hand; and at right, he flirtatiously touches her chin, and she in turn wraps her arm around his body, as if to acquiesce.

The ivory makes claims about the kinds of people who can participate in courtship and love. Distinct from the bearded man who carefully steps into the water, the couples are all resolutely young, noble, and able-bodied. Andreas Capellanus's *De Amore* (its title often translated as *The Art of Courtly Love*) of the twelfth century stipulates who can and cannot fall in love, and age, class, and ability are all important determinants. Capellanus notes that when it comes to love, "age is a bar, because after the sixtieth year in a man and the fiftieth in a woman . . . one may have intercourse [but] . . . passion cannot develop into love."[73] Young children are excluded from love, specifically "a girl under the age of twelve and a boy before the fourteenth year do not serve in love's army" (in theory at least, yet not always in practice, as arranged marriages confirm).[74] The text is also heavily concerned with class: eight dialogues between couples of varying classes suggest that a different social status could be a serious impediment to courtship. The Fountain of Youth ivory has made its subjects not only the perfect age for love, but also of the same class; their identical bodies assure their noble viewer that the ideal conditions of love and courtship have been met.

In their current state, the figures are also determinedly white. Small traces of pigment, like the green on the foliage that surrounds the couples, indicate that parts of the plaque were likely painted at some time in its history. Viewers associated the material and color of elephant ivory with European conceptions of female beauty. From the *Roman de la Rose* (*Romance of the Rose*) to personalized love letters, whiteness is central to descriptions of women's bodies. They have an "ivory breast" (*pectus eburnum*), white faces, and even "white gloves to keep . . . [their] white hands from turning brown."[75] White was also the color of both men and women in love: the fifteenth rule of love, according to Capellanus, specified that "every lover regularly turns pale in the presence of his beloved."[76]

The legend of the Fountain of Youth, once associated with Ethiopia and its mythical king, Prester John, is stripped of any evident connection to Black or non-European subjects. Instead, the focus is squarely on a fantasy of becoming young again, which results in the ability to participate in the rites of courtly love. The miraculous waters create near-identical bodies: noble, courtly, and barely differentiated by sex.[77] Below, the attainment of courtly love is hard-earned: it is a multistep process, moving from initial resistance to acquiescence. As James Schultz explains, the cause of courtly love was considered to be external to the body: it acts on its passive subject. We might understand, then, the woman's eventual embrace of her lover not as a result of her own internal desire, rather as owing to the fact that the sight of her partner has finally entered her eyes and heart. But even if medieval viewers conceived of the courtly lover to be passive, the ivory carving itself is active in the way that it suggests which bodies matter—and which do not—in the elitist art of love.

THE RIDDLE OF THE BODY

We now return to Sheba's riddle with which this essay began (SEE PL. 6). Recall that she tests Solomon's wisdom by asking him whether the flowers and the children are the same or different. By observing the bee's and children's actions, Solomon allows his wisdom to prevail: he can identify the flower that is living, and he can discern a difference in the children's style that is gendered. Despite Sheba's best attempts to create the illusion of sameness, Solomon can see difference.

Although the inscriptions on the tapestry suggest that all is resolved, the riddle continues for viewers, who attempt to make sense of Sheba's puzzle and Solomon's curtailed response. While the two children's poses are distinct, the two flowers remain identical. The birdlike bee is depicted at a crucial distance, and we do not yet know on which flower it will land. The viewer is left in a state of suspense: which flower is real, and which is artificial? The riddle remains open-ended and prompts the viewer to wonder whether there are other illusions of sameness in the tapestry that await their discernment.

Consider, for instance, Sheba and Solomon: while their clothing explicitly marks them as female and male according to late-medieval conventions, their appearance is otherwise quite similar. They are blond and pale-skinned; they wear crowns; and their poses are courtly. This visual illusion of sameness belies their geographic difference, however. Sheba, according to the Gospels of Luke and Matthew, was from the "uttermost parts of the Earth," which were understood by medieval exegetes as Africa, Ethiopia, or Saba.[78] But unlike other images of "aethiops" we have discussed, like Simeon, Balthazar, or the priest and layman in Breydenbach's *Peregrinatio*, Sheba is white and dressed like a European queen. Moreover, in the Song of Solomon, also known as the Song of Songs, a woman historically associated with the Queen of Sheba is described as "Black but beautiful…as the tents of Cedar, as the curtains of Solomon" (Song of Solomon 1:4). The conjunction "but" suggests that beauty and Black skin are mutually exclusive.[79] The artist, then, has chosen to privilege Sheba's beauty—associated from a European perspective with white skin—over her origins, elsewhere visually correlated with Black skin or exoticized clothing. Nature, or in this case, a naturalistic depiction of epidermal race, is eschewed by the artist; whiteness trumps the representation of geographic origin.

The tension between the natural and artistic lies at the heart of the tapestry's meaning. Recall that Solomon's reply suggests that Nature is all powerful; her creations cannot be distorted, and her laws cannot be broken. She is like the female personification of Nature in the *Roman de la Rose*, who makes "individual creatures to continue the species" and is in frequent conflict with Death, Corruption, and Art, who attempt to subvert or poorly emulate her creations.[80] In the realm of images, however, Nature's dominance can be questioned; the artist (or patron) has the final say.[81] By making it impossible for the viewer to identify the natural versus artificial flower, the artists slyly subvert Solomon's confident reply and assert the power of Art itself.[82]

By depicting bodies that were betwixt and between, changed or actively changing, late-medieval artists shaped a society-wide fascination with all that bodies could become.[83] They worked in Nature's image but were not beholden to her creation. Instead, they represented bodies to their own liking and repeatedly insisted on their mutability. In so doing, they made claims about the kinds of desires and bodies that mattered (to use Judith Butler's profound phrase) and were considered legitimate.[84] Made at a time when lay and ecclesiastical authorities persecuted people accused of so-called crimes against nature, medieval images could affirm or subvert these bigoted laws and logics, powerfully rendering visible the desires, longings, and fantasies of their subjects.[85]

13. **Plaque with the Fountain of Youth. French, ca. 1320–40. Elephant ivory**

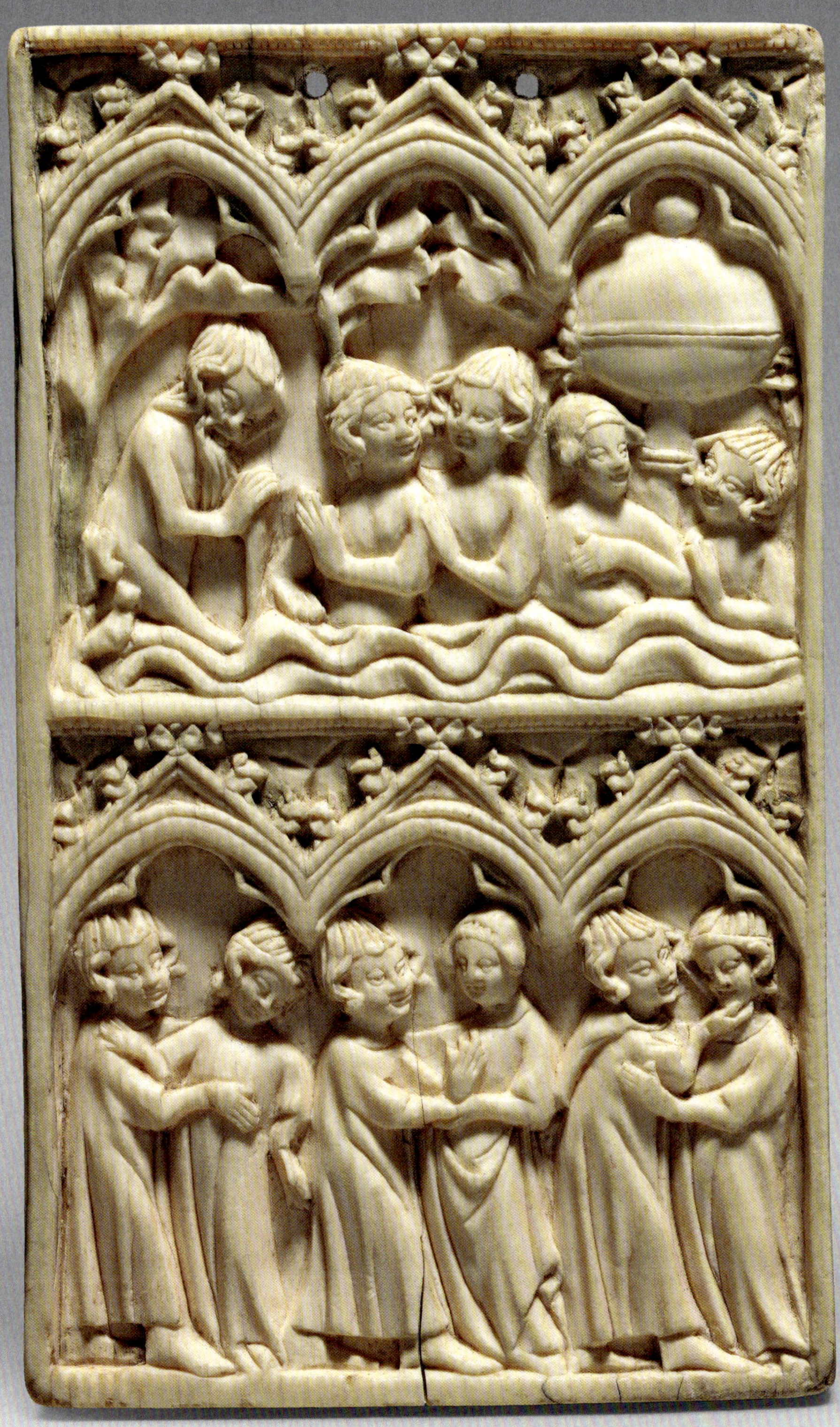

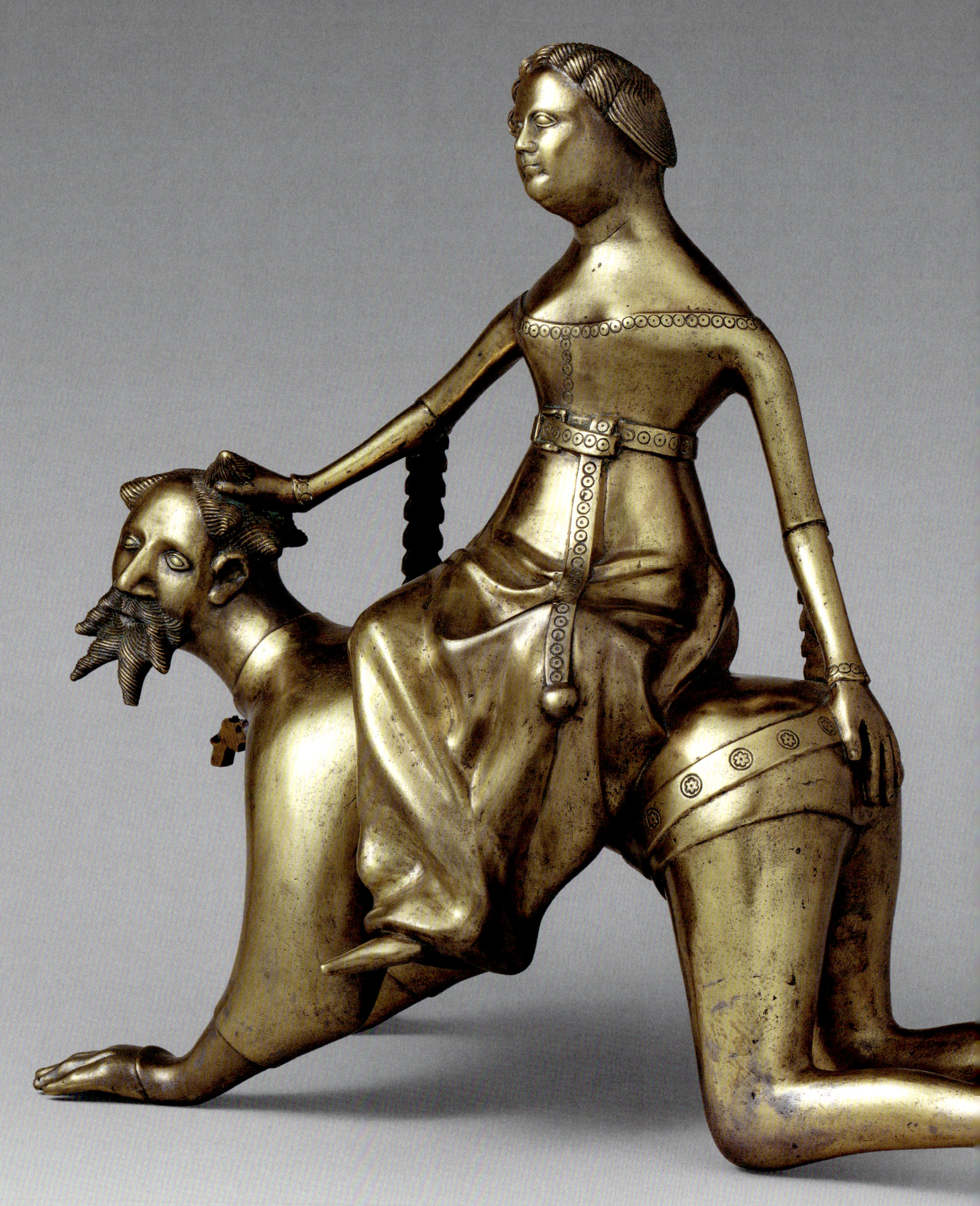

MELANIE HOLCOMB

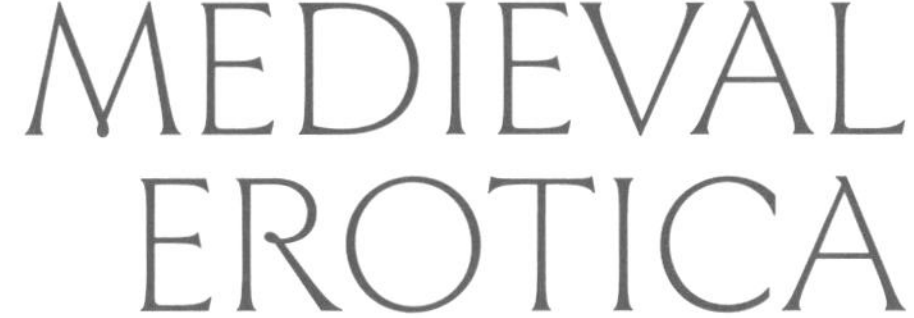

MEDIEVAL EROTICA

We only know the initials—B. and C.—of the two medieval women who, respectively, wrote and received a love letter now preserved in a manuscript in Munich. Composed in Latin rhyme likely sometime in the twelfth century, B.'s letter moves quickly from passionate endearment to heartfelt distress:

> To C., sweeter than honey or honeycomb, B. sends all the love there is to her love... why do you make delay so long, so far away? Why do you want your only one to die, [she] who sighs for you at every hour, at every moment, like a hungry little bird... as the turtledove, having lost its mate, perches forever on its little dried-up branch, so I lament endlessly till I shall enjoy your trust again.[1]

For the women, separation imposes an intolerable burden of time. The temporal sensation of delay swells into an affliction of space-time. Death hovers. Hours collapse into immeasurable moments, and yearning stretches into an eternity. "Desire," as Carolyn Dinshaw has astutely noted, "can—and sometimes must—create its own time."[2]

A fourteenth-century ivory box allows us to see how medieval objects, especially those that expressly take on the theme of desire, posit their own sense of time (PL. 14). The box presents a version of the well-known parable of the Prodigal Son. This moving tale follows a young man from his descent into profligate living to his subsequent redemption through paternal forgiveness. At first glance, the narrative on the box appears to unfold in a linear manner. The front panel launches the story, with the parents bestowing the early inheritance that the son has demanded. The action proceeds clockwise around the side as the son journeys away from home accompanied by his entourage. He turns another corner, and the orderly cadence of men on horseback gives way to a raucous display of debauched living. Showcasing an excess of food, drink, women, and erotic play, the back panel depicts a tavern interior, replete with a bountiful spread and a lifted curtain that offers a peek of bedroom activities. The final short side shows the son stripped to his underwear, playing a risqué game of chess before submitting to a washboard beating as punishment for not paying his bills (FIGS. 9, 10). Without clothing and money, the son

14. **Box with the parable of the Prodigal Son and scenes of lovers. French, 14th century. Elephant ivory**

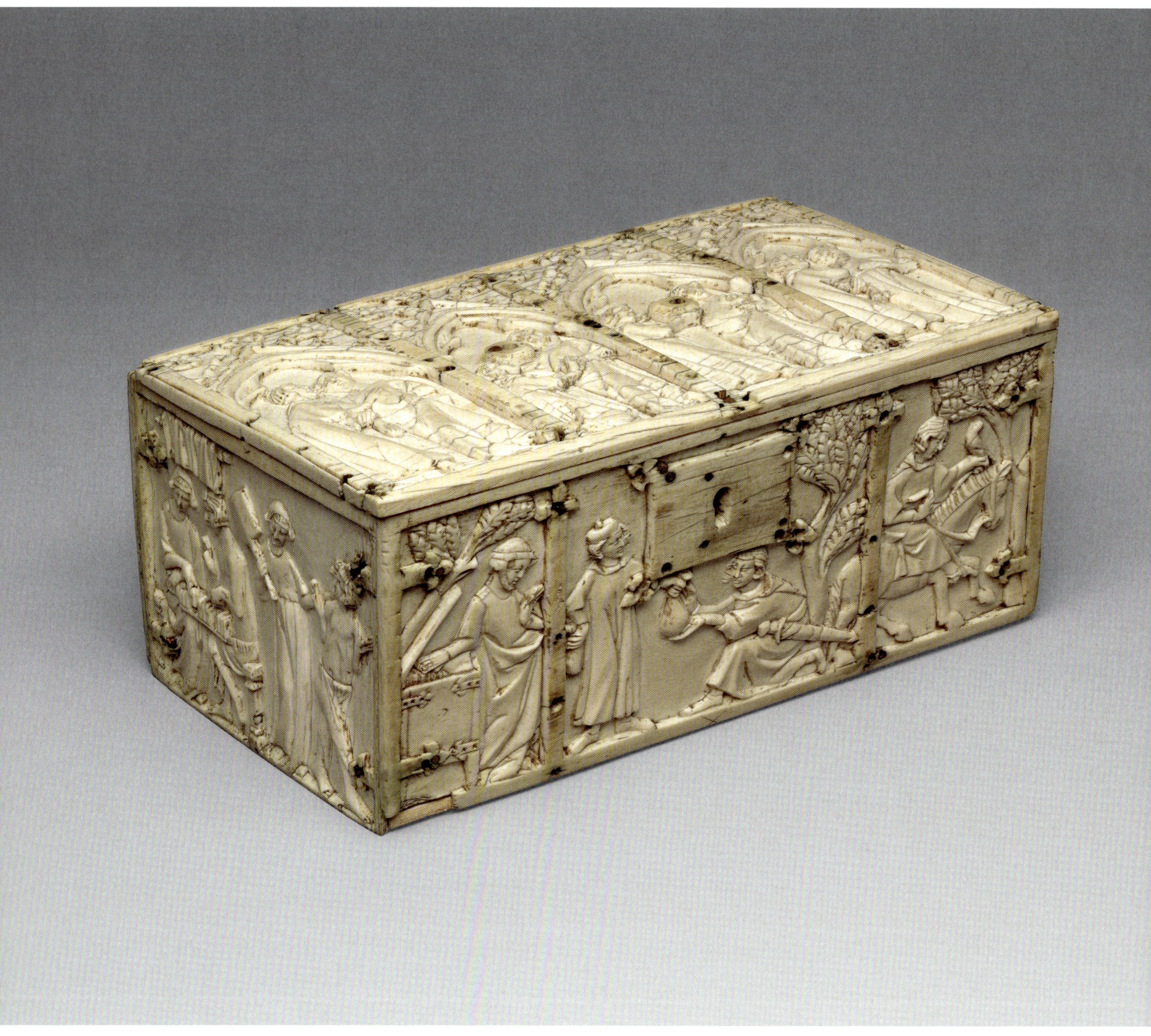

reaches his lowest moment, and we now await his return home to the arms of his merciful father. But the ivory carver provided no such conclusion. A moral never surfaces. Judgment is suspended. Time simply stops.

Few tales make a better argument for domestic rectitude as an antidote to carnal pursuits than that of the Prodigal Son. The parable exemplifies and extols what Jack Halberstam and other queer theorists call "straight time," a temporal trajectory driven by "reproduction and family, longevity, risk/safety, and inheritance."[3] In its many variations over the centuries, the story has been elaborated to commend the rightness of paternal lineage and the safety and inevitability of home while condemning the corrupting powers of gambling, drink, and excessive sexual indulgence. This box, however, seems to revel in the vices that the parable so famously renounces, rejecting the temporal and moral logic that undergirds the narrative.

Another artist might have utilized the lid to bring the young man—and the story's message—home, but this one chose to present a pleasing suite of couples under an arcade, engaged in the titillating to-and-fro of courtship (SEE FIG. 24).[4] We must accept, as Jean Campbell has suggested, the artist's or owner's

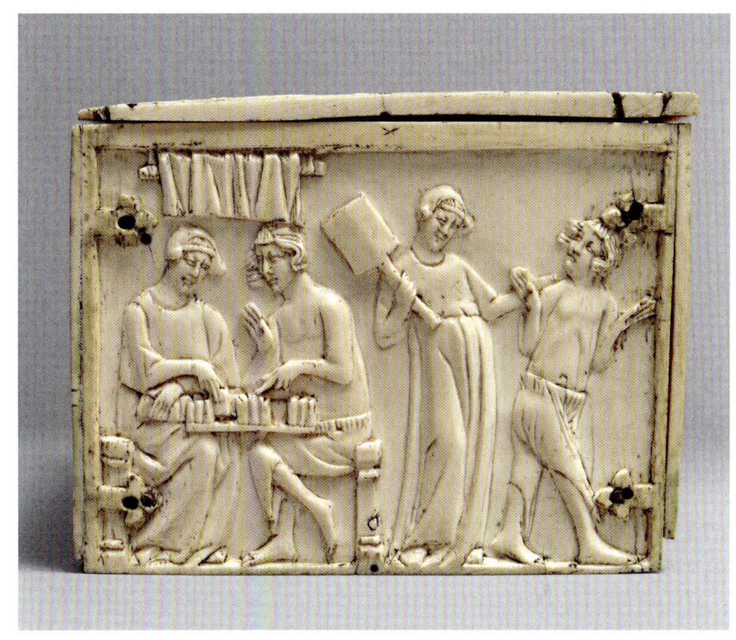

Fig. 9. **Left side of PL. 14 showing the Prodigal Son playing chess and being beaten on his backside**

Fig. 10. **Back of PL. 14 showing the Prodigal Son in a tavern and performing a sex act with a naked lover in bed**

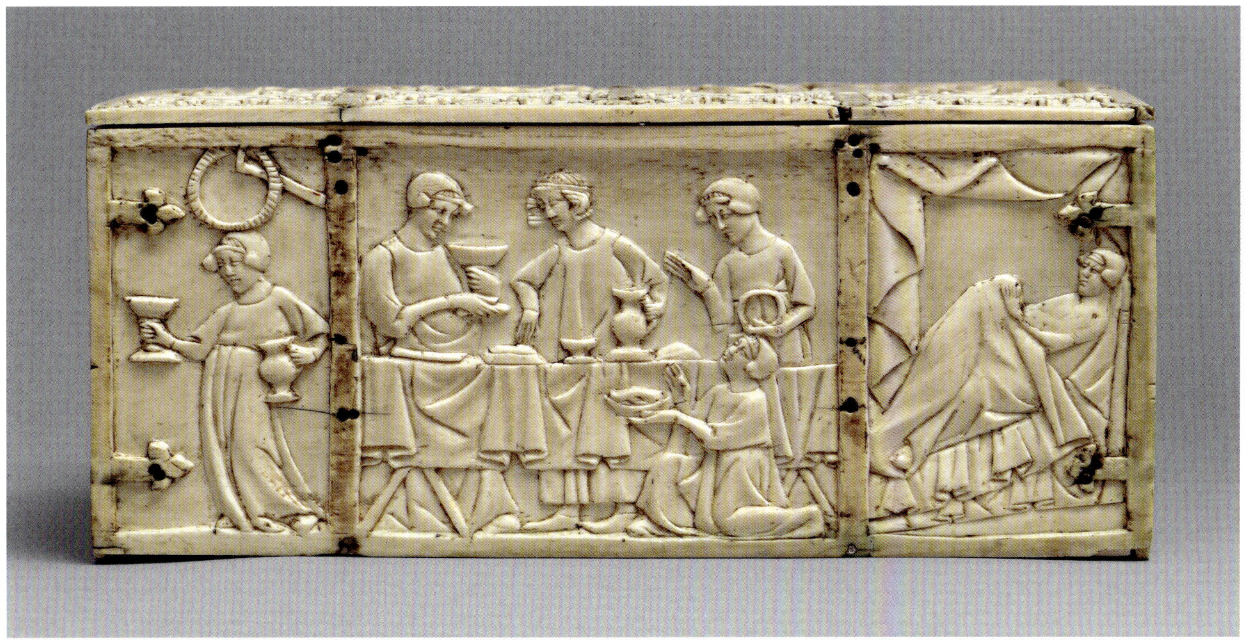

indifference to the narrative stakes of the biblical story.[5] The lid places the entire box in a state of suspended animation, so that the son's randy ways read less like a rake's progress than a primer of amorous activities. Desire does not always require consequences or serve as a means to an end. The scenes on the box unapologetically luxuriate in what might be called libidinal time, in which erotic pleasure takes many forms and never draws to a close.

The Prodigal Son box is an example of medieval erotica. Though the term erotica is notoriously difficult to define, in describing the box thus we need not get caught up in modern efforts to distinguish between erotica and pornography. (One clever reader of *The Guardian* characterized it as simply the height of the shelf it sat on![6]) Rather, we can take advantage of the word's inherent flexibility to embrace the sorts of works that are often secondary in discussions of medieval eroticism.[7] Our focus in this essay is objects rather than pictures: that is, works that participate in the erotic more than show it—though, as we see on the ivory box, they might do both. Unlike fetishes that displace the body as the site of desire, these objects fully incorporate, may even draw attention to, the body in the rituals they invite. They earn the designation of erotica on account of the imaginative possibilities they set in motion. Traveling among an array of such objects—belts, combs, writing tablets, and decorated small boxes—the present discussion explores how medieval erotica fostered haptic and relational practices that were key to their enjoyment.[8]

We know that medieval people understood three-dimensional objects as potent stimulants. One fourteenth-century text warns of the "carnal lusts" that arise from "comfortable beddings...delicious and soft shirts and smocks...pleasurable robes of scarlet and other comforts of the body."[9] In the early 1500s, reformer Ulrich Zwingli expanded on the long-standing trope that sculptures in the Church were a distraction by denouncing the practice of depicting saints in seductive contemporary costume. "There stands [statues of] Sebastian, a Maurice and the gentle John the Evangelist, so cavalier, soldier-like and pimpish that the women have had to make confession about them."[10] When the twelfth-century writer Andreas Capellanus in his Latin treatise *The Art of Courtly Love* writes that "love is an inborn suffering which results from the sight of, and uncontrolled thinking about, the beauty of the other sex," he links desire—"uncontrolled thinking"—specifically to vision. These other texts make clear though that objects promoted erotic feeling though the activation of multiple senses.[11]

If erotica has a broad range of meanings, desire and love have even more. The language of passionate love was applied far more expansively in the Middle Ages than today. A contemporary of Richard the Lionheart and Philip II Augustus wrote that Philip loved Richard "as his own soul," recounting how they "ate at the same table and from the same dish" and shared a bed in order to convey the extent of their devotion to one another.[12] We will never know what the two did in that bed, and it seems the wrong point of focus. Their relationship—royal, public, political, and expressly tied up with medieval ideas of power and virtue—existed within a category of intimacy we moderns no longer possess. Erotic, yes. Sexual, who knows?[13] Medieval treatises on friendship excluded women entirely, yet the love letter between B. and C. makes clear that medieval women experienced passionate friendship, collaboration, and love that was no less intense for its cultural elusiveness.[14] As we will see, erotica may be brought into conversation with the range of medieval relationships in which *eros* figured.

Desire certainly prompted the creation of many medieval works of art. What interests us here is the role that such works played in the creation of desire. How did they shape, fuel, and interact with this powerful sensation in order to enhance and extend it? Time thus serves as a useful framework in our exploration, as medieval objects like the Prodigal Son box were often exquisitely attuned to the temporal dimensions of desire. They participated in the peculiar, tension-filled span of time that constitutes yearning. Whether we call it courtship, romance, pursuit, or foreplay, it strains toward a type of union. As such, they promoted an erotics of time characterized by surprising openness, indeterminacy, and possibility.

15. **Box with scenes of lovers. Flemish, 14th century. Embossed leather, walnut, gold, paint, copper alloy and iron fittings**

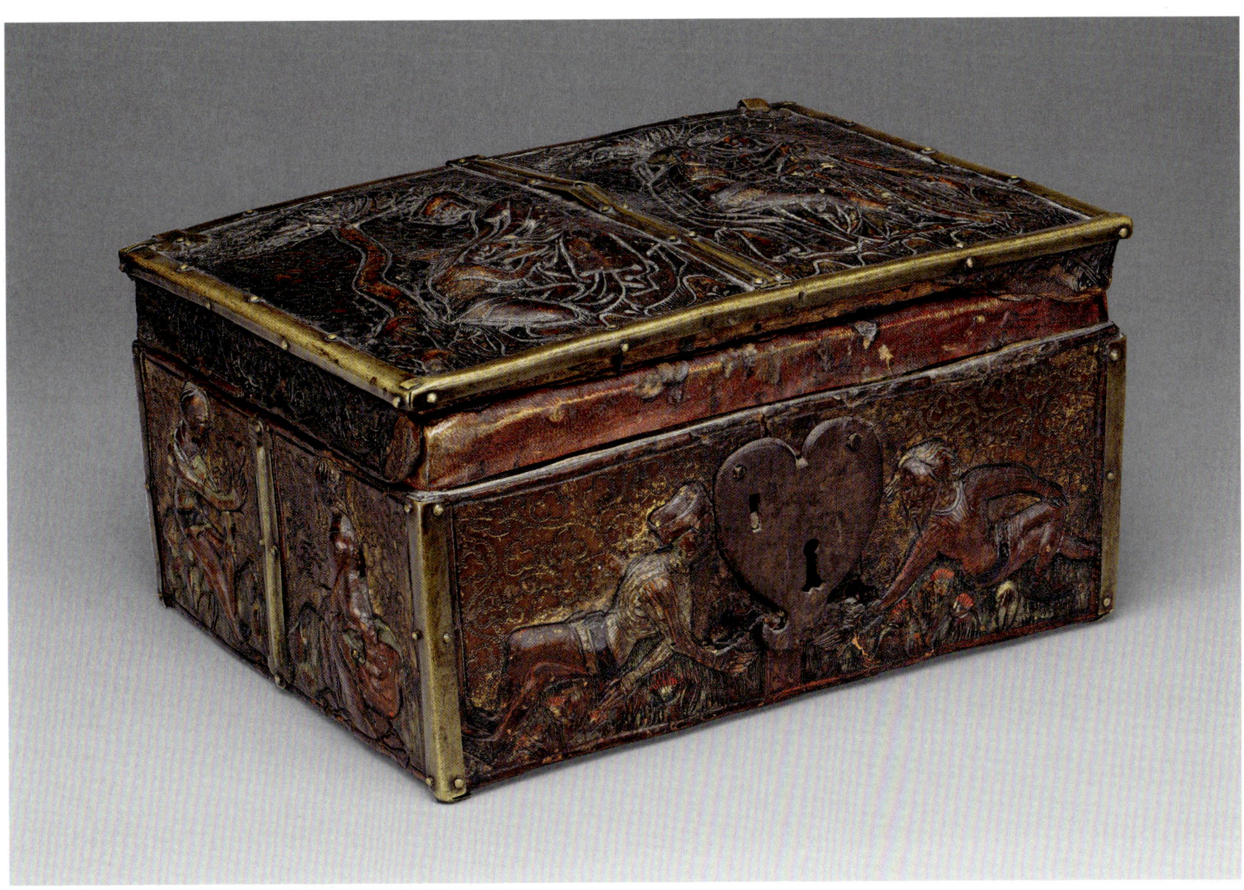

EMBODIED TIME

A fourteenth-century box covered in gilded and painted leather does not appear to recount a specific narrative, but rather places the bodies of lovers at center stage (PL. 15). The various couples promote consensual exchange, whether by reaching expectantly toward one another across a spatial divide or engaging in a passionate embrace. On one side, a man offers his heart for a floral wreath. On another, a woman trades her heart for an upright, overtly phallus-shaped plant. Allusions to the very kinds of objects we might imagine the box containing, these tokens of desire are carefully incised into the leather, their furrows a suggestive counterpoint to the smooth and supple volumes of the lovers' bodies.

A particularly evocative exchange on the back panel depicts a reclining woman offering a belt, akin to some surviving examples, to a bearded man lying opposite her (FIG. 11, PL. 16). Threaded between her fingers, its buckle dangling invitingly before her, the belt lures the man toward her. It is also an extension of his reach, as if an invisible current flows from his fingertips to hers, along the gentle curve of the belt's length, directly, inexorably, to her lap. The man wears his own belt, dark and hefty in contrast to the slender contours of hers. While several medieval stories associate women's belts with fertility, seductiveness, or fidelity, men's belts seem to play an outsize role in mediating relationships with other men, particularly at court.[15] King Henry III, for instance, gifted elaborate belts to the Archbishop of Cologne and his brother in gratitude for their help in negotiating his sister Isabella's marriage to Emperor Frederick II.[16] When sending her off to her betrothed, Henry ordered twenty-four belts for her to distribute to foreign dignitaries on his behalf.[17] Henry himself was the recipient of a silk and gold embroidered belt with a silver buckle from his chief minister Hubert de Burgh, who presented it in an effort to heal a long-standing rift between them.[18] At the Burgundian court, Philip the Bold gave relatively simple belts of silver to servants and lavished his brothers, cousins, and other aristocrats with weighty gold belts laden with jewels and enamels, particularly at the great gift-giving holiday of New Year's Day.[19] Belts were also assets of high enough value that they could serve as collateral for loans from peers and moneylenders.[20]

As tokens of love, loyalty, rank, and rivalry, such gifts operated within the bounds of male friendships, passionate and otherwise, that were cultivated with-

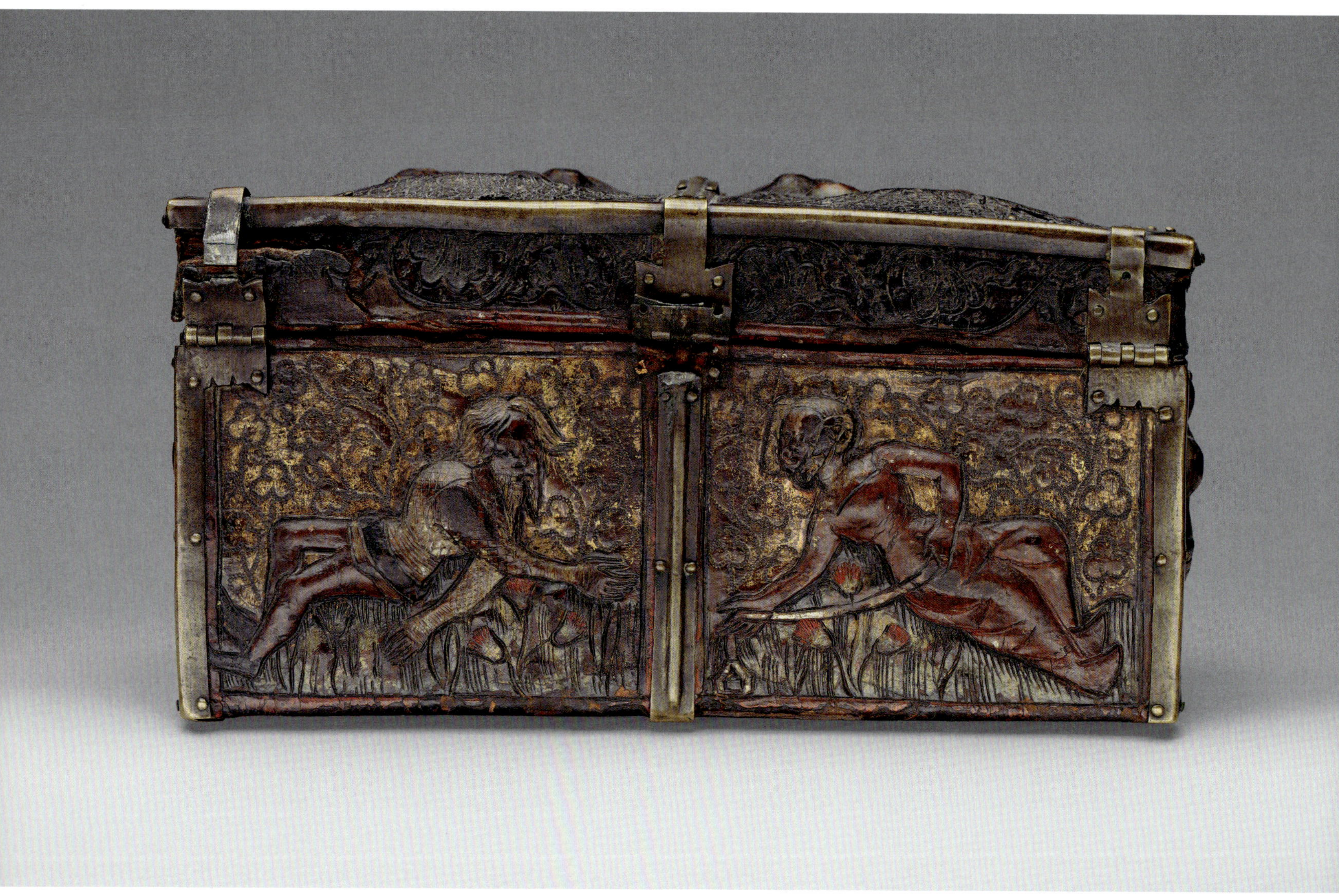

FIG. 11. **Back of PL. 15 showing a woman offering a man her belt**

16. **Belt. North Italian, ca. 1330–50. Silver, with traces of gilding and enamel; modern textile support**

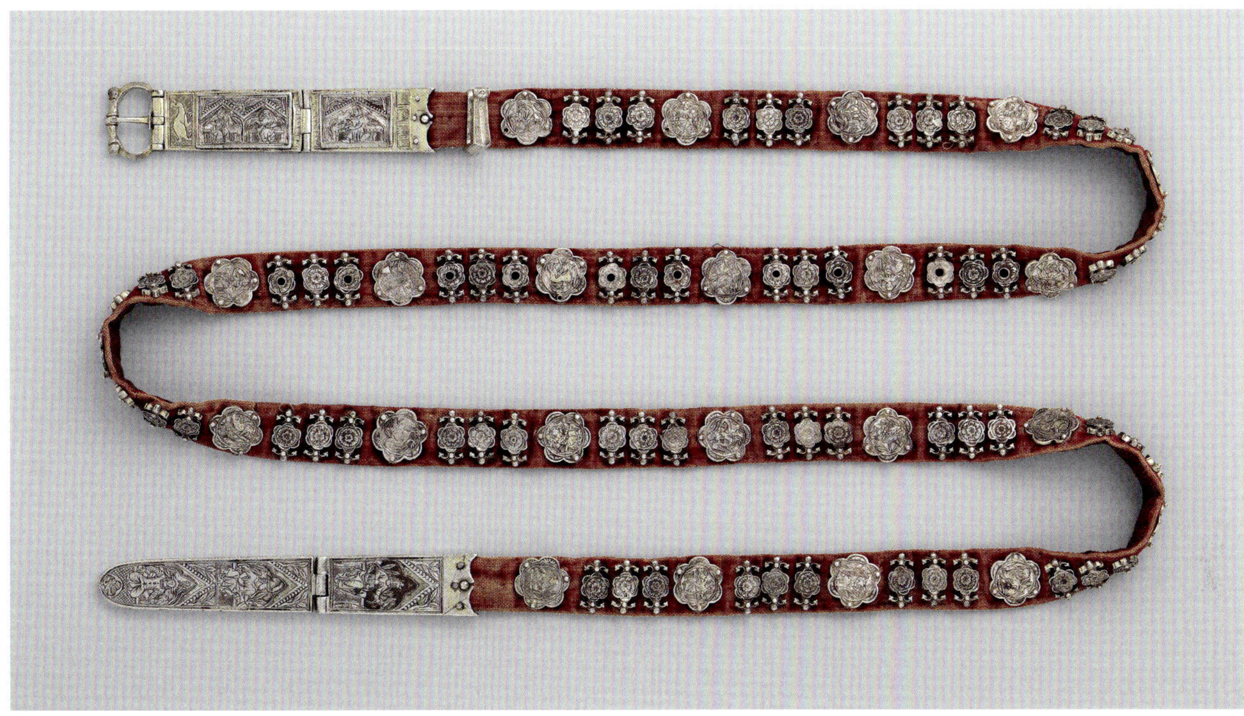

in the homosocial spheres of royal and ducal courts.[21] The simultaneously competitive and homoerotic undercurrents of belt display are made manifest in *The Belt*, a thirteenth-century German story by Dietrich von der Glezze, in which a magic belt guarantees the wearer honor, happiness, and victory over any opponent.[22] Decorated with some fifty precious stones from faraway Morocco, India, and Greece, it outshines any of the dazzling textiles that a "shining knight" might wear with it. It inspires an invitation to court, induces the infidelity of a chaste wife, and ultimately persuades the knight Konrad to "lie down" with Henry of Swabia, the belt's wearer, and "do all the wonderful things that [Henry] can imagine and think of, and especially what any man usually does with his wife."[23] The comic and stabilizing twist of this complicated story is that Henry of Swabia is in fact Konrad's wife in disguise. Nonetheless, its plotline assumes charismatic love between men at court, fueled by a display of masculine virtues that includes a splendid appearance and prowess at chivalric pursuits.

Combs, like belts, could implicate a body in the thrall of desire.[24] *The Art of Courtly Love* by Andreas Capellanus counts combs as suitable gifts of courtship from a lover to his lady along with jewelry, belts, gloves, mirrors, and small dishes and trays. These objects, we are told, were useful to the "cultivation of appearance" and readily called to mind the giver.[25] Combs are especially evocative in this context because they insert a man's presence into women's private spaces, where women were permitted to take off their hair-coverings. The very shape of a comb alludes to the fingers of a hand, allowing a suitor, at a remove, to stroke his loved one's hair. One Arthurian tale recounts how Lancelot kissed and touched (100,000 times) the strands of hair he loosened from a comb belonging to Guinevere.[26]

The erotic nature of hair combing derived in part from the protracted intimacy it implied and from its sensuous languor. Patience is a necessity in taming unruly hair. As tangles and knots give way, painful tugs on the scalp settle into rhythmic caresses. The scene on the lid of the leather box shows a man sitting comfortably crossed-legged at a woman's feet, his head resting on her lap and his locks spilling across her skirt (FIG. 12). Precise tooling makes visible silky strands passing through the comb's rigid teeth. Clearly, fantasies of shared grooming were not limited to men combing the hair of women. Fourteenth-century trial records of the mountain village of Montaillou in southern France imply that delousing could also carry an erotic charge, at least in settings outside of large cities and aristocratic courts. During a two-year affair, local noblewoman Béatrice de Planissoles would delouse her lover, Pierre Clergue, a priest and one of the village's leading citizens, "in bed, by the fire or by the window" as they talked and made love.[27]

If the containment of hair conveyed respectability and self-restraint, its loosening suggested unleashed sexuality. Certain accoutrements like a comb or handheld mirror could be read as a sign of demure beauty or dangerous seductiveness.[28] Men were held to a different standard, but they too were expected to conform to prescribed social codes. Beards and a full head of hair signaled virility, but excessive and unruly hair was the mark of foreigners, barbarians, and the sexually unbridled.[29] The mythical wild man was entirely covered in fur (SEE FIG. 16).[30]

Hair rituals were integral to men's homosocial and homoaffective relations. As good health was associated with regular grooming, men consulted surgeons and

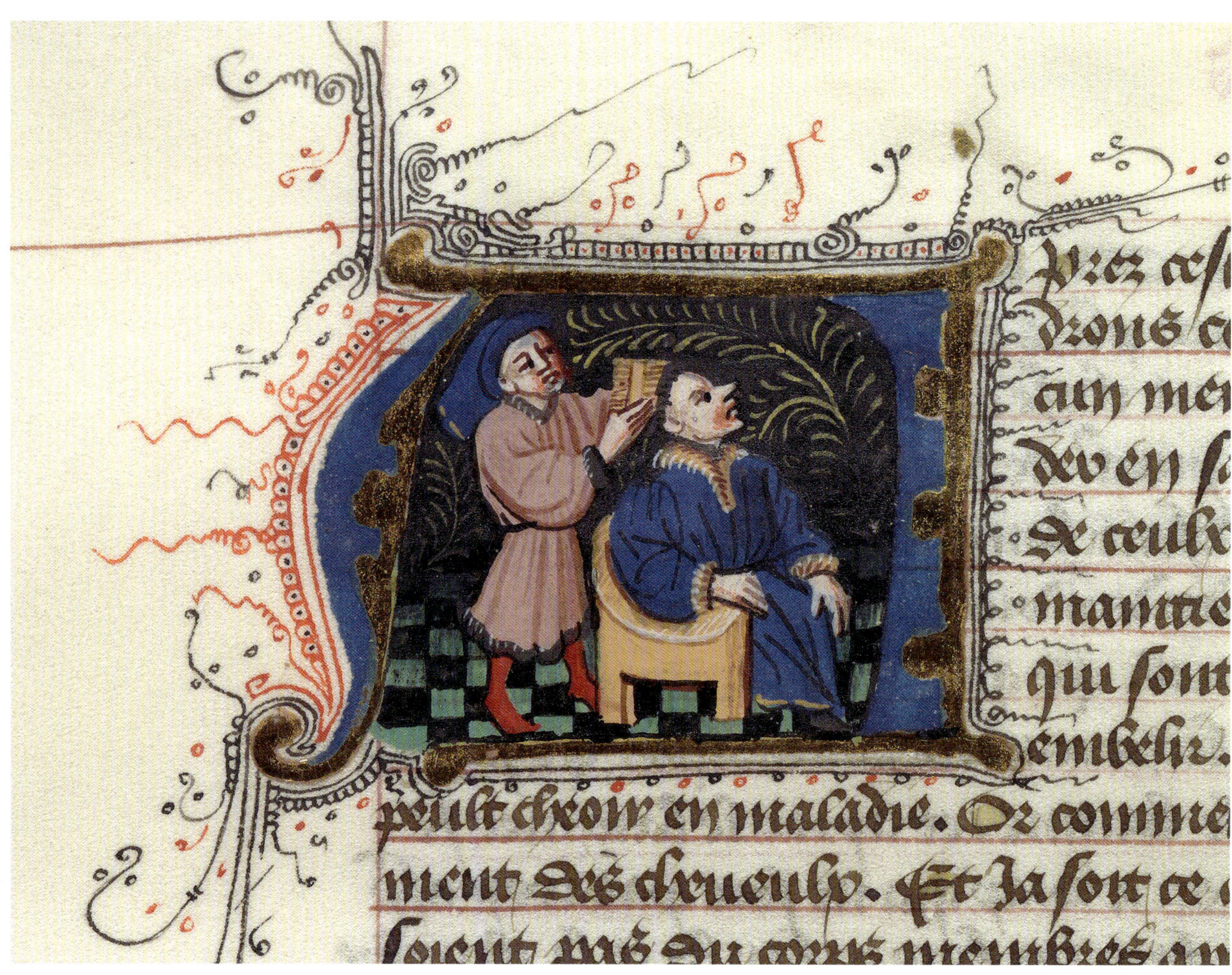

17. **Hair combing from *Le Régime du corps* (*The Regimen of the Body*). French, ca. 1440–50. Opaque watercolor, gold, silver and iron gall on parchment**

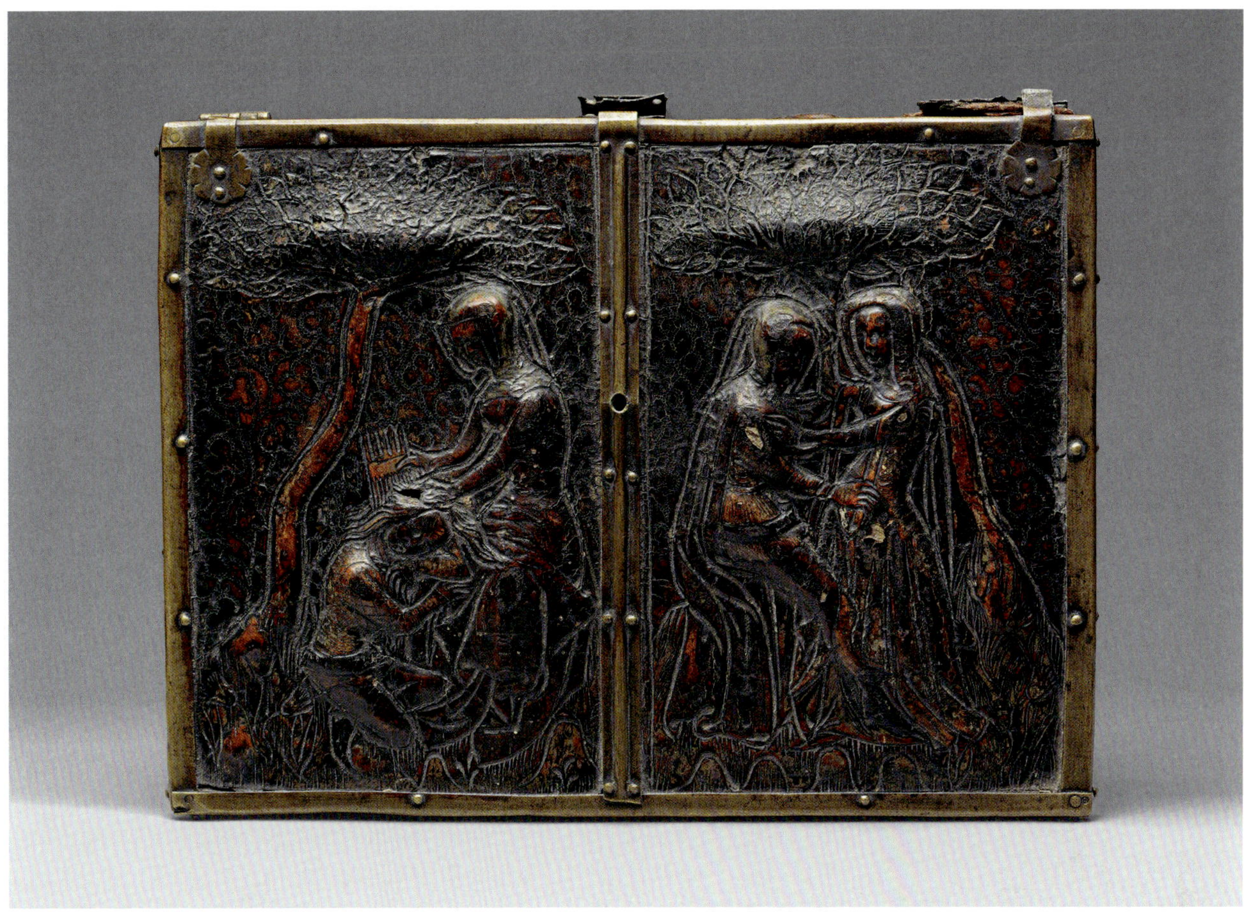

Fig. 12. **Lid of PL. 15 showing a woman combing the hair of a man kneeling before her and lovers embracing**

barbers to treat the scalp and hair. Surviving inventories imply that men may even have been the principal consumers of luxury combs and mirrors. Over generations the Desgrez family in Paris sold combs to dukes and kings, often in a set with mirrors, hair-parters, and brushes, all made of ivory. Philip the Bold was a loyal customer, at one point buying and replacing ivory combs for himself and family members, notably his son and nephew, every few months.[31] The duke's accounting records remind us that specially commissioned leather boxes and silk bags were de rigueur for the safekeeping of all these objects of masculine luxury, vanity, and health.

The medieval health guide known as *Le Régime du corps* speaks of the importance of hair for beautifying the body.[32] It also offered detailed advice on how to dye hair, remove it, and tackle lice. Though the text does not mention brushing or combing, an accompanying illustration showing the latter stands in for the myriad washings and applications of unguents and dyes that the text prescribes. A seated nobleman surrenders to the ivory comb in the hands of his youthful barber (PL. 17). The wispy feather that sweeps over him contributes to the dreamlike stupor suggested by his upturned head and distant gaze. Extending the language of philosopher Michel Foucault in his descrip-

18. **Comb with a scene of the hunt. French or Italian, 15th or 16th century. Elephant ivory, paint and gold**

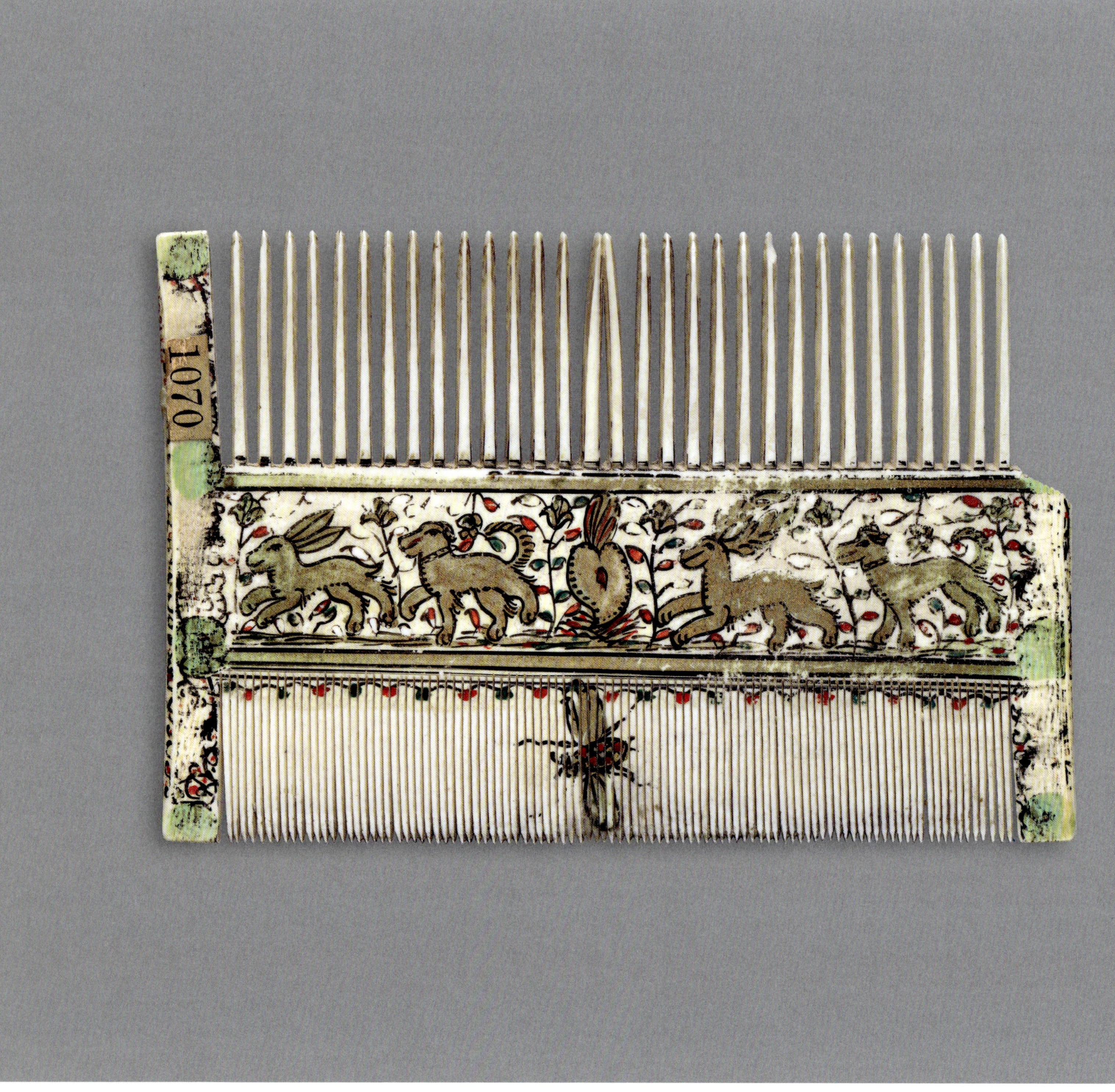

tion of sexuality, hair in this image serves as a "transfer point for relations of power" between old and young, nobleman and servant.[33] The potential for *sodomia* could lurk in the practices of hygiene, as is clear in a moralizing painting from a fifteenth-century manuscript that illustrates the vice of lust by showing a monk longingly gazing at a young man combing his hair.[34]

The facture and decoration of combs added to the satisfactions of grooming. Themes of love and its pursuit were expressed with hearts, scenes of the hunt, and displays of courting couples. Whether the smooth warmth of boxwood or the creamy softness of ivory, materials used for making the finest combs balanced tactile enjoyment and durability. Royal inventories occasionally mention combs made of the even more luxurious materials of silver, gold, and enamel.[35] "Take pleasure" commands an inscription on a boxwood example from the fifteenth century, which allowed its owner to open and shut doors to hidden compartments.[36] The playful embellishments on an ivory comb of the same date seem to make the same request (PL. 18). The artist has painted winged insects on the comb's narrow teeth, as if they have just landed. No lice these, the pretty little bugs make light of the task of grooming.[37] Hair-combing may have allowed lovers to extend times of intimacy, but some of its delights were only fleeting.

EPISTOLARY TIME

Other luxury objects that drew the body into amorous expression include ivory writing tablets (PLS. 2, 19, AND 24; FIG. 13). Diminutive in scale—most are four to five inches tall—they could be attached to the belt as a constant reminder of the words sent to or received from a lover. Their very form invited somatic engagement, requiring the user to first disengage them from a belt and then from a protective fabric sheath or leather box. If the tablet was a single plaque, a user would need to turn it over. Unbound multi-tablet sets required the user to shuffle plaques strung together by a linen or leather cord, whereas bound sets could be leafed through like books.[38]

More than pen and parchment, the writing tablet and stylus were fundamental to medieval literacy.[39] Made from thin pieces of wood, bone, ivory, or metal, a writing tablet provided a framed recess and hard surface for a thin layer of wax, into which one could inscribe letters, numbers, or sketches using a sharpened stylus. The "eraser" end of the stylus could take the form of a small triangle, which, when heated, could be employed to smooth the wax for reuse. The portability and erasability of the tablet provided the ideal technology for a merchant's tallies, a student's exercises, or a poet's drafts.

The many ivory tablets that survive undoubtedly owe their preservation to their sculpted decoration, which could draw from both secular and sacred motifs.[40] A cover need not prescribe content, but surely the selection of a scene of courting couples over, say, a crucifixion tells us something about the context of a tablet's purchase if not its ongoing use. Nothing would prevent medieval owners from using ivory tablets for their accounts, itineraries, and tables, as suggested by the small number of wooden tablets that retain wax and traces of their original writings. But might their erotic decoration, small size, and effaceable surface lend them to activities and identities marked by ephemerality, even secretness?

The concept of wax tablets harboring taboo thoughts surfaces in a story recounted by the monk Bernardus Noricus (d. 1326), who tells how a cleric was divinely punished with temporary blindness because he carried around wax tablets inappropriately inscribed with love poems.[41] The forbidden cross-religious romance of Floris (a Muslim) and Blanchefleur (a Christian), as told in a thirteenth-century version of their eponymous tale, began with flirtatious verses written on ivory tablets.[42] A secret affair, attested to by the so-called Letters of Two Lovers, now preserved in a library in Troyes, was in part conducted through wax tablets passed back and forth between the two lovers.[43] The lone example of an actual ivory booklet that survives with original wax and inscriptions is preserved in Namur. It presents a cohesive package, in which love is pronounced in every detail (FIGS. 14, 15).[44] Generic scenes of lovers carved on the front and back

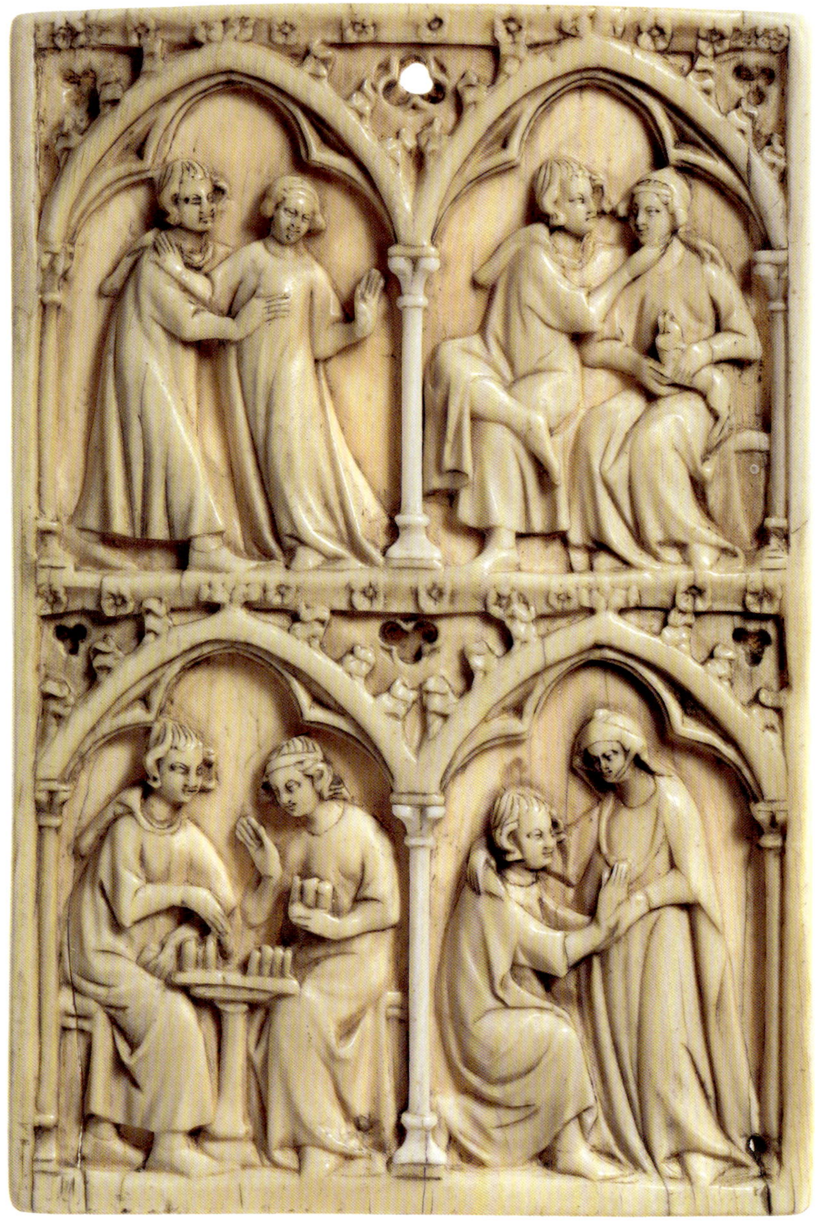

19. **Writing tablet with lovers engaged in activities of courtship. French, 14th century. Elephant ivory**

Fig. 13. **Back of PL. 2 showing flirtatious lovers**

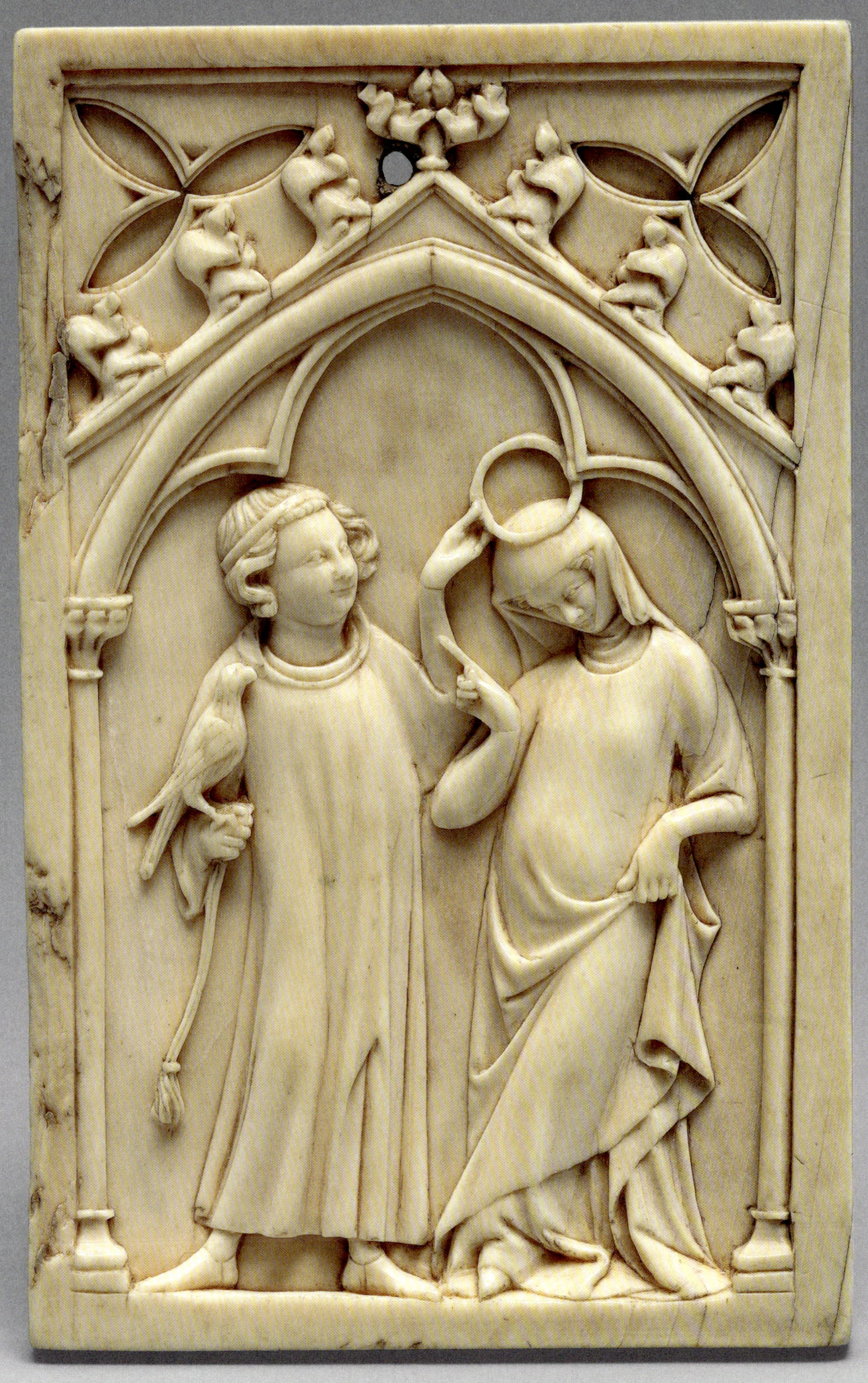

Fig. 14. **Detail of FIG. 15, showing leaves of an ivory tablet with red wax that originally contained private love lyrics**

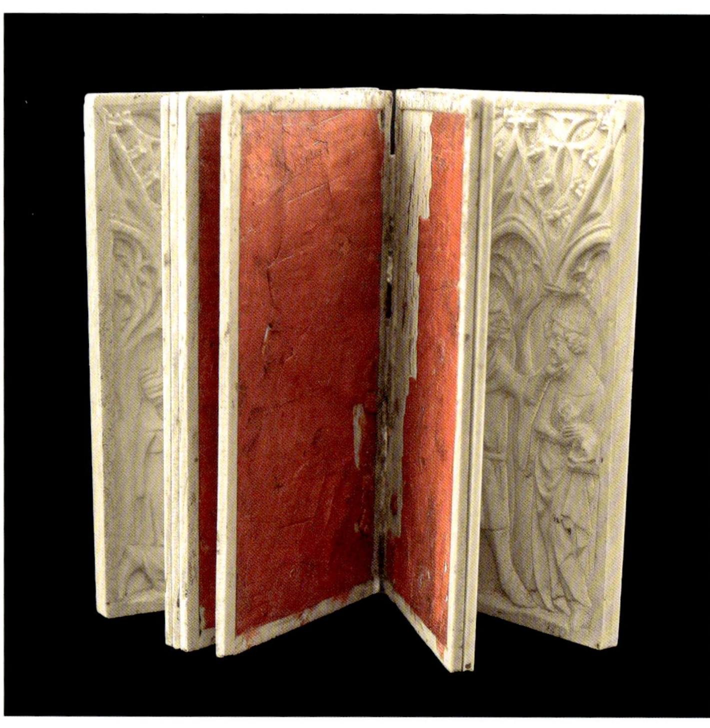

ivory covers encase love lyrics ("Amour me fait souvent... Desir") inscribed in fancy red wax, rather than workaday black. A leather box displaying scenes from the tragic love story *Tristan and Isolde* also survives. It protects the ensemble, which, remarkably, includes its original silver stylus. This thoroughgoing treatment of the theme of love makes a powerful claim for reading ivory tablets as touchstones within a history of emotion. Their prominent display in a museum today should not prevent us from also interpreting them within a history of privacy.[45]

The emotional life of medieval lovers is difficult to grasp precisely because our knowledge of it is heavily biased toward its public expression. A medieval letter was generally a political statement, and medieval poetry a rhetorical performance.[46] Love letters and love poetry—often one and the same—followed rigid rules of vocabulary, composition, and cadence. They were generally preserved through careful copying in medieval manuscripts, because they flattered the writer or exemplified the form.[47] The chance survival of less polished works, almost certainly intended for a single reader, is therefore nothing short of extraordinary.

Among such rare gems is a three-letter interchange between an unnamed woman and her male teacher, addressed only by the initial H, preserved in the Bavarian State Library, Munich. One of her letters underscores the central role of language, spoken and written, in the cultivation of romance:

> For from the day that I first saw you
> I began to love you.
> You penetrated my heart's inmost being
> forcefully,
> and, through the advance of your most
> joyous conversation,
> have, wondrous to tell, arranged your own
> seat there,
> and, lest any impulse should topple it,
> have fastened it most firmly by your
> letter writing,
> as if the seat were a stool, or rather,
> a throne.[48]

In the original Latin the letter showcases the rhythms and rhymes of an accomplished student of the language, but it does not follow a prescriptive literary model. Rather, as Peter Dronke has argued, we see someone testing her skills, exploring the themes of friendship and fidelity through an imaginative blending of classical, biblical, and vernacular language.[49]

Experimentation with language and feeling is even more fully on display in a curious cache of some fifty epigrams and verses written by a teacher and his convent pupils, also stored in the Munich library and known as the Regensburg Songs.[50] As the famous romance between Abelard and Heloise demonstrates, the teacher-student relationship was ripe for erotization, and the Latin school exercises from Regensburg regularly veer into a much broader emotional range than rote repetitions of "amo, amas, amat." They touch upon love's often conflicting condition: "I shall hate him if I can, if not, against my will I shall love him." They express jealousies banal—"I am very sad, because you prefer Bertha to me"—and poetic: "You deceive me, embracing me in words, other women in deed." They arrange nighttime trysts: "It is your lover who writes—do not betray him! I implore you to come to the old chapel at dawn. Then the bed will reveal to you all that my heart now keeps hidden." One of the songs even alludes to the gift of cord from which wax tablets are hung and flirtatiously reminds the teacher who received it to remember the student who gave it, as tablets swing at his side.

It is impossible to know if these texts presented real emotions or actions. We can claim with more certainty that they represented for their authors early forays into new terrain, both in Latin composition and romantic feeling. Little wonder that scholars have characterized the Regensburg Songs as a rare instance of direct preservation from wax tablets to parchment. Their tentativeness, clumsiness, and candor are the

Fig. 15. **Writing tablet, box, and stylus. Elephant ivory. French, 1341–60. Tablet 3¼ × 1⅞ in. (8.3 × 4.6 cm). Musée provincial des Arts anciens du Namurois-Trésor d'Oignies, Namur (Coll. Fondation Roi Baudouin. Dépôt à la Société archéologique de Namur, inv. 29)**

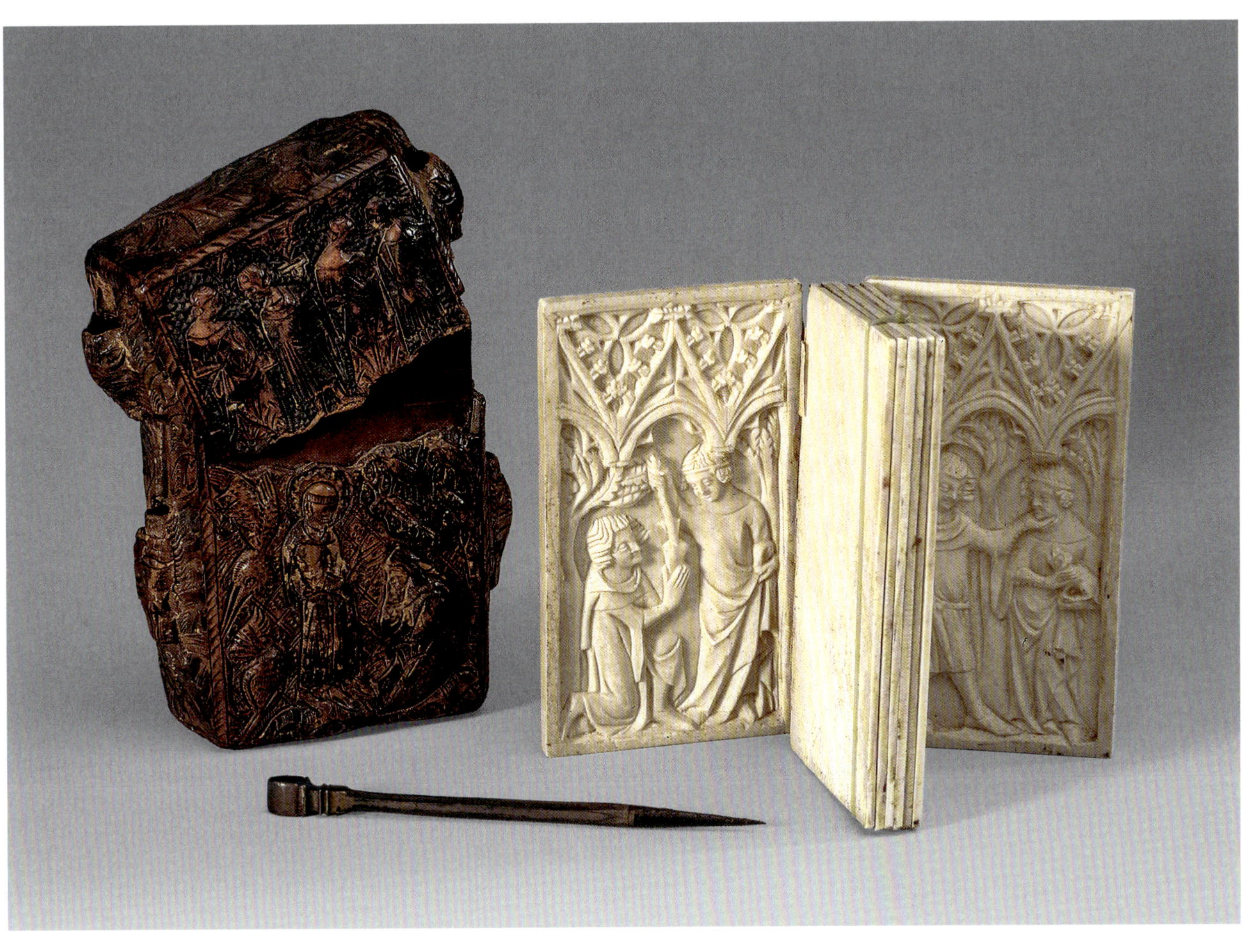

20. **Drawings of five half-figures including wildmen from a sketchbook, ca. 1400 (fol. 2r). Circle of Jacquemart de Hesdin. Metalpoint on prepared ground with dilute watercolor washes on boxwood**

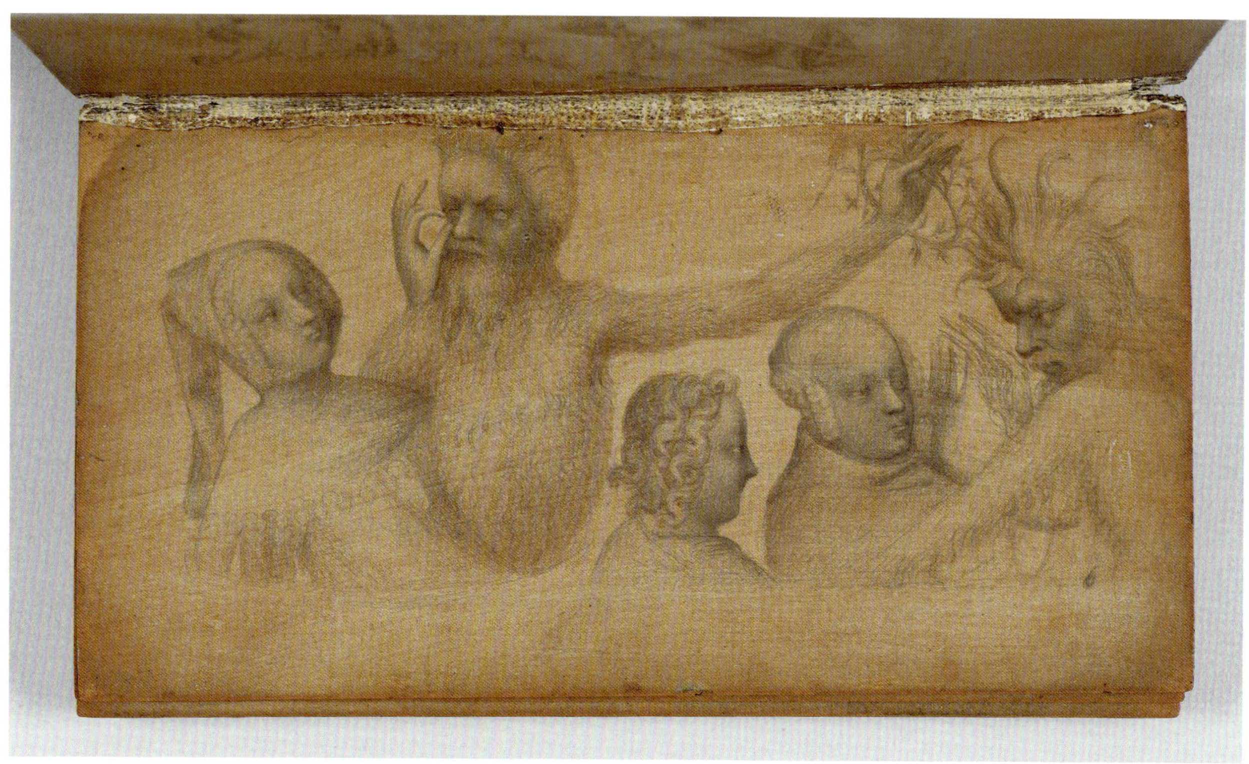

hallmarks of writers' drafts, perhaps filled with sentiments intended for erasure.

Reading ivory tablets around and through archival bias may provide access, however fleeting, to gendered and queer subjectivities that otherwise elude us. The trope of humility pervades the love letters, with women regretting that their words lack the elegance of distinguished male orators. Considering the context of many of the surviving letters, this language may be a function of the deference students paid to teachers, but a claim of inferiority also lowers the stakes, freeing the writer to step outside the bounds of normative literary form. Given that women had limited opportunities to learn and practice formal rhetoric, erasable wax tablets, of ivory or other materials, might have provided welcome, private spaces for women's writings.

Emma Le Pouésard has pointed to the ways in which the stories and iconography of medieval secular ivories often promoted feminine agency, drawing our attention to the "overlooked, hidden or ... potentially queer representations" that appear there.[51] The letter between B. and C., with which this essay began, underscores the appropriateness of that endeavor. Ivory tablets, like the homosocial spaces of convent and court, surely opened the possibilities of the permissible. Another medieval letter between two women does more than hint at the nuanced eroticisms that privacy afforded.

> To G—, her one-and-only rose, from A—the bond of precious love. What strength have I, that I may bear it, that I may have patience while you are gone? ... When I remember the kisses you gave, and with what words of joy you caressed my little breasts, I want to die as I am not allowed to see you.... Return, sweet love! ... know that I cannot bear your absence longer. Farewell, remember me.[52]

21. **Drawings of four figures, including a king from a sketchbook, ca. 1400 (fol. 3v). Circle of Jacquemart de Hesdin. Metalpoint on prepared ground with dilute watercolor washes on boxwood**

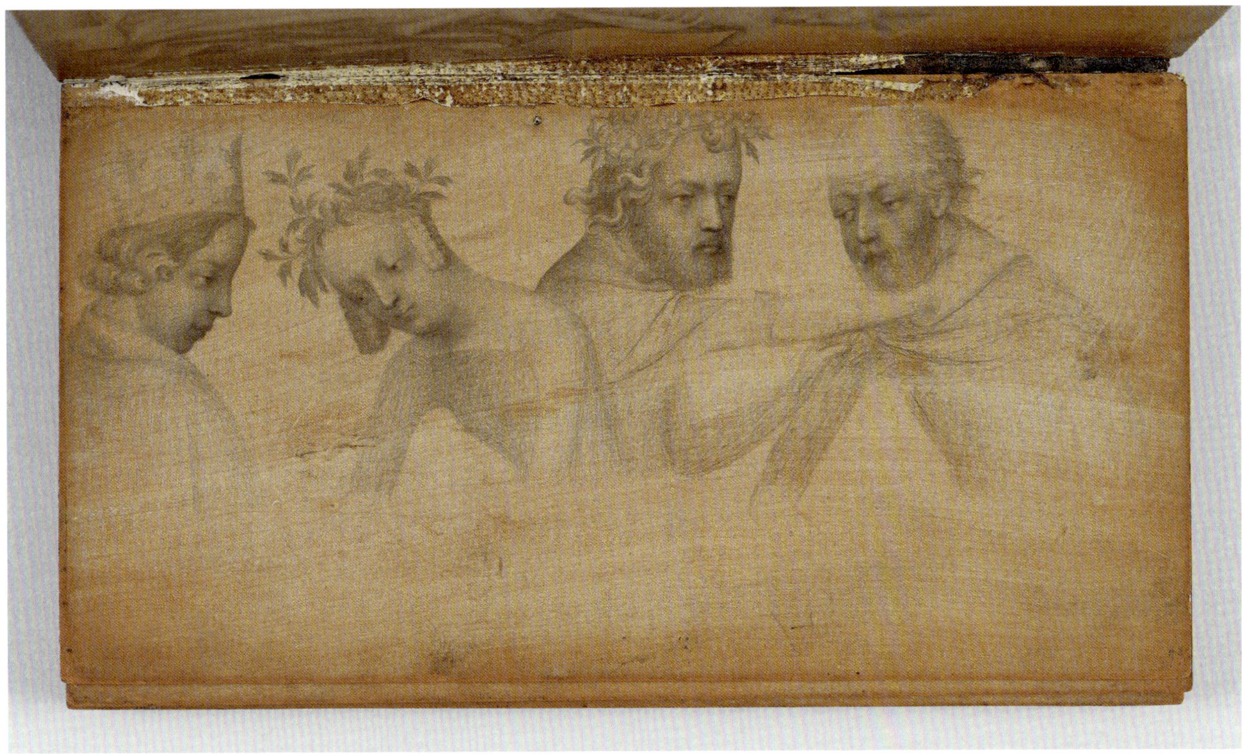

So paltry is first-person evidence of female-to-female relationships in the Middle Ages that it is difficult to know how to interpret A.'s letter to G. It uses the language of heroic pain, more often spoken by a man in the guise of an ideal courtly lover, to describe the pangs of separation. Its reference to kisses and caresses may refer to the deeply felt sensations of affection or to actual past acts. Whether A. and G. are friends or lovers, or more likely occupy an historic category we have yet to define, the letter unequivocally attests to a strong social bond between two women. It affirms forms of "female fellowship, community and even love," which necessarily played out in private spheres during the Middle Ages and which scholars are only beginning to uncover.[53] A friendship, a romance fueled by letter-writing, depends upon the contraction and dilation of time. The wait between the sending and receiving of messages is as crucial in kindling desire as the composition and content of the messages themselves. Ivory writing tablets are monuments to epistolary time. They remain the public and permanent trace of the private and the evanescent.

If wax tablets lent themselves to the expression of intimacies between two people, they may well have also provided a private space for an individual to record quick sketches, nascent ideas, and unspoken thoughts. A sketchbook in The Morgan Library & Museum, New York, may have provided such a repository (PLS. 20, 21). Though made of boxwood and lacking recesses for wax, the sketchbook, owing to its small size and its structure as a notebook of six thin panels held together by strips of parchment, calls to mind ivory counterparts. Scattered over the panels are an array of images and image types, all rendered in delicate metalpoint, likely silver. They range from foliate, drapery, and figural studies, to religious subjects, to portrayals of different couples variously and evocatively engaged with one another. These include a man and woman coyly facing each other; two men, one grasping the shoulders and cloak of the other; and two pairings of women with a wild man, the symbol of savage sexuality (FIG. 20). The arms of one pair are entwined allowing the woman to close the wild man's eye while the other couple ambiguously faces off in a moment of attack. Or is it tenderness?[54]

Some forty artists' sketchbooks, most on parchment, survive from the Middle Ages, but few operate as the Morgan sketchbook does, with an air of tentativeness, with images in disparate stages of finish and ample evidence of erasure and reuse.[55] The relationships between the figures are difficult to explain. They are not rote copies from another source, nor do they come across as instructive motifs for a workshop. This is a sketchbook in the modern sense of the word, where ideas were tested, discarded, or advanced, maybe for a painting that never came to fruition or is now lost. Or perhaps they were created with no intended end use, but rather provided an outlet for an artist to trace an erotic line, explore a diversity of suggestive couplings, and open up possibilities of desire.

Fig. 16. **Right side of PL. 22 showing knight defeating a wild man and Gawain receiving keys to the Castle of the Maidens**

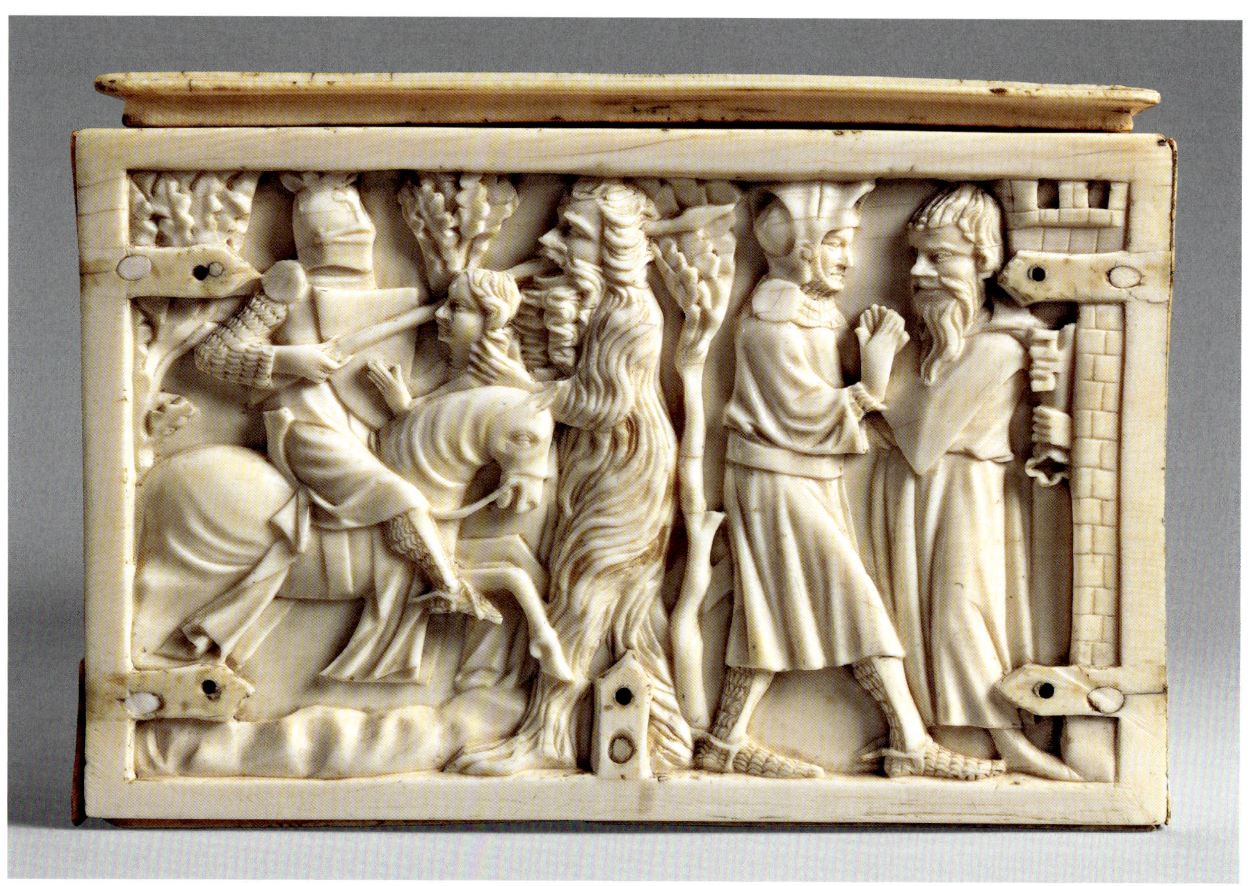

22. **Box with romance scenes. French, 14th century. Elephant ivory**

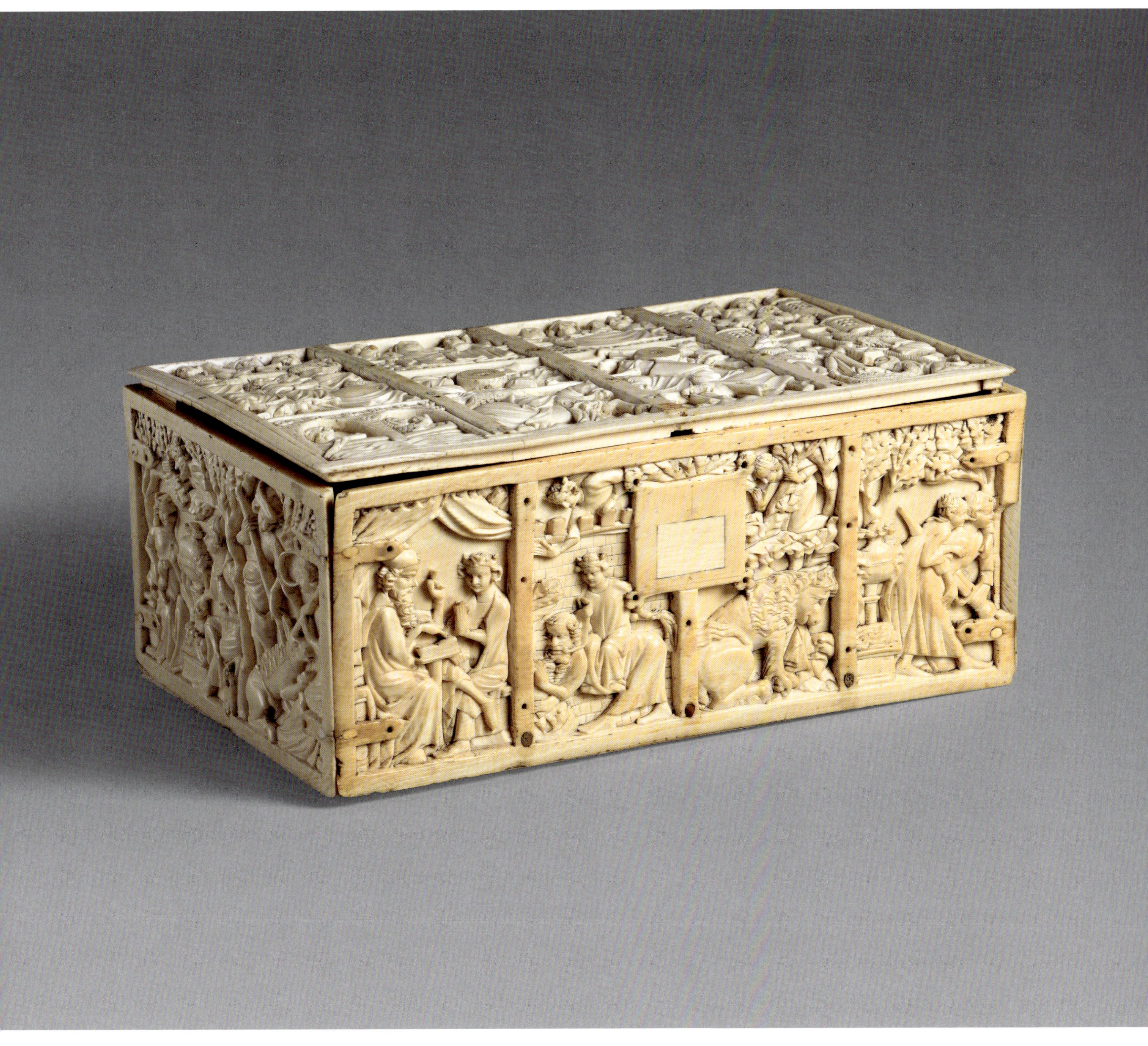

The late-medieval German poem *The Monastery of Love* is an imaginary travelogue to the everlasting domain of Lady Minne, the Goddess of Love. Although evoking the structure, hierarchy, and utopian ideals of a cloistered community, this subversive world amusingly houses lovers engaged in courtly pursuits such as dancing and jousting, rather than monks and nuns devoted to prayer and work. The narrator-traveler marvels at the beauty and harmony of the ersatz monastery, but, still dissatisfied, he tells his guide that he yearns to lay eyes on Lady Love herself. "Have you gone mad?" she chastises. "If you cannot see Minne here...you need ask no further." Minne can only be seen in the effect she has on people. The lesson for the narrator and the reader is that love is manifested and perpetuated not by the figure of Minne but by the activities and interactions of lovers.[56]

An early fourteenth-century French ivory box, dense with scenes from tales of courtly romance, operates on the same principle (PL. 22, FIG. 16). Most of the vignettes are drawn from popular written stories that circulated in France and beyond including *Lancelot, Perceval, Bestiaire d'amour, Pyramus and Thisbe*, the Tristan legend, and the Phyllis and Aristotle story.

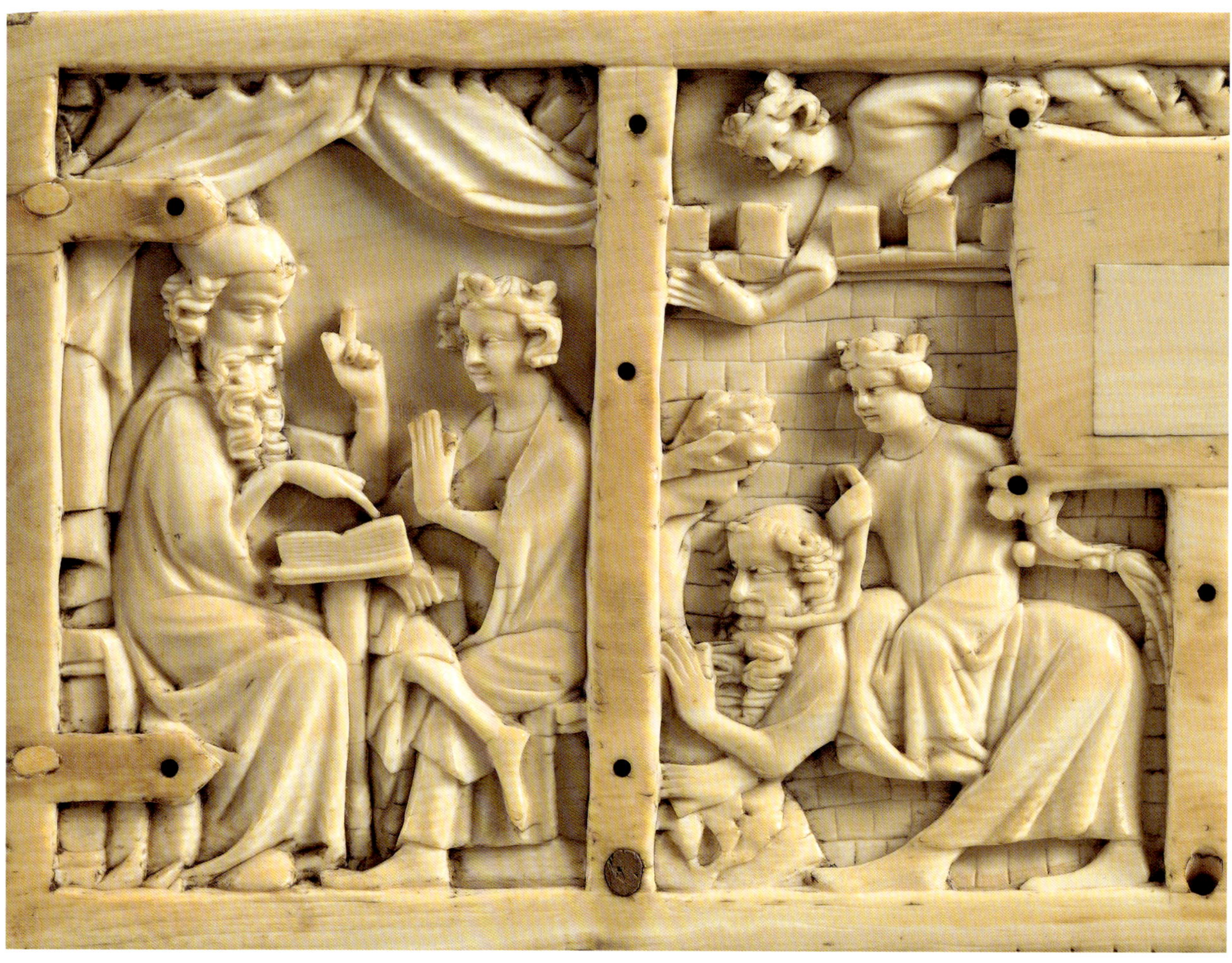

Fig. 17. **Detail of PL. 22 showing Aristotle teaching Alexander, and Phyllis humiliating Aristotle by riding him as a beast while Alexander watches**

23. **Aquamanile in the form of Aristotle and Phyllis. South Netherlandish, late 14th or early 15th century. Copper alloy**

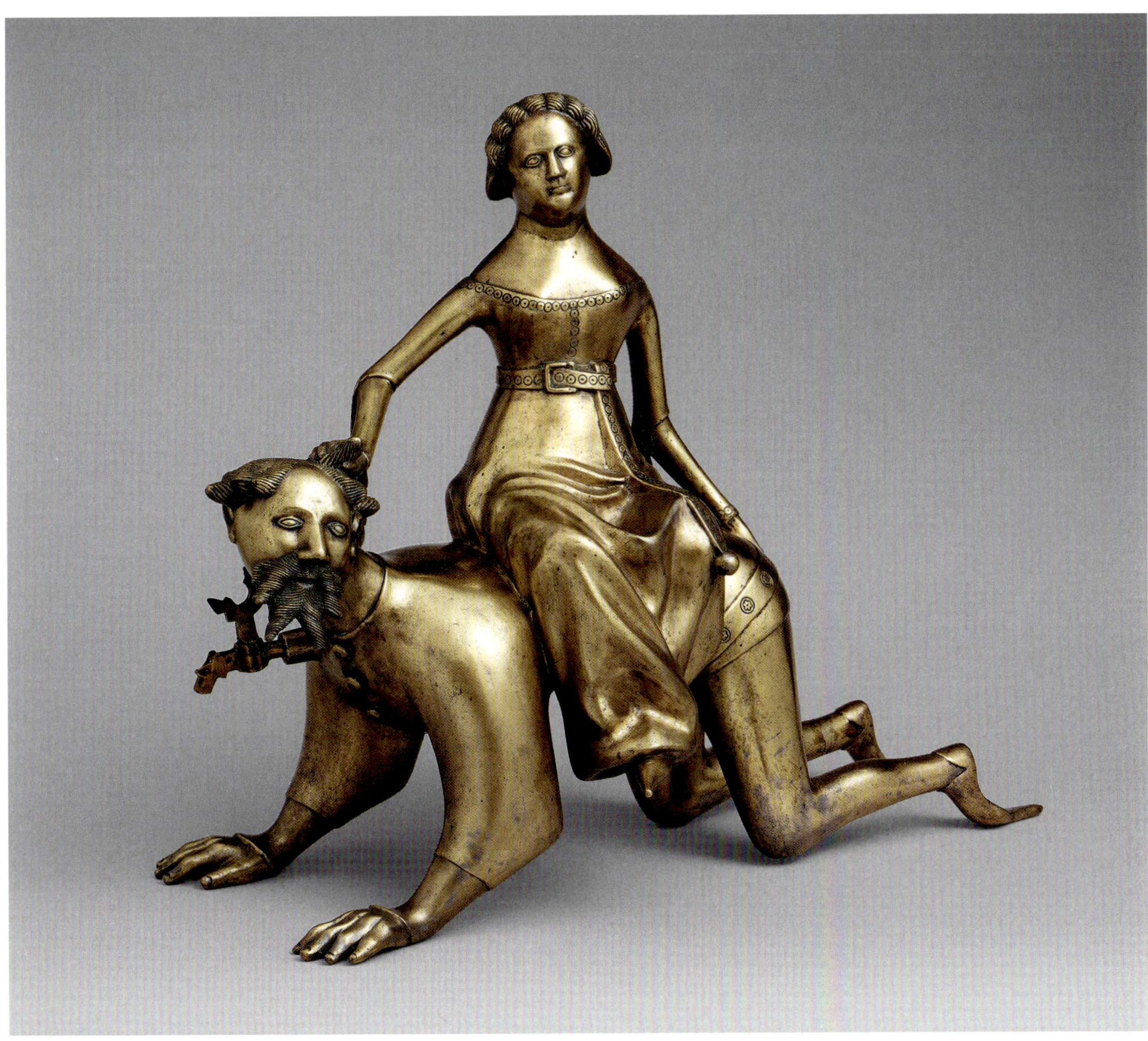

Paula Mae Carns has characterized this box and others like it as visual compilations akin to the story collections that appear in medieval manuscripts.[57] The owner of the chest, similar to the narrator in *The Monastery of Love*, is presented with a panorama of love's activities. These emblematic pictures, like their textual counterparts, are the means by which courtship and amorous performance are shaped, repeated, and reenacted, sustaining both the transmission of the tales and the models of romance they offer.

As varied as the scenes are, common themes emerge. Whether showing figures in treetops, on castle parapets, or just outside a castle wall, almost every panel of the small chest includes someone looking for or at love. Love, after all, as Capellanus wrote, results "from the sight of . . . the beauty of the other sex."[58] The decoration of the box explores the power, lure, and risks of vision, while at the same time placing desire itself under scrutiny. Desire invites humiliation in the story of Phyllis and Aristotle, danger in the stories of

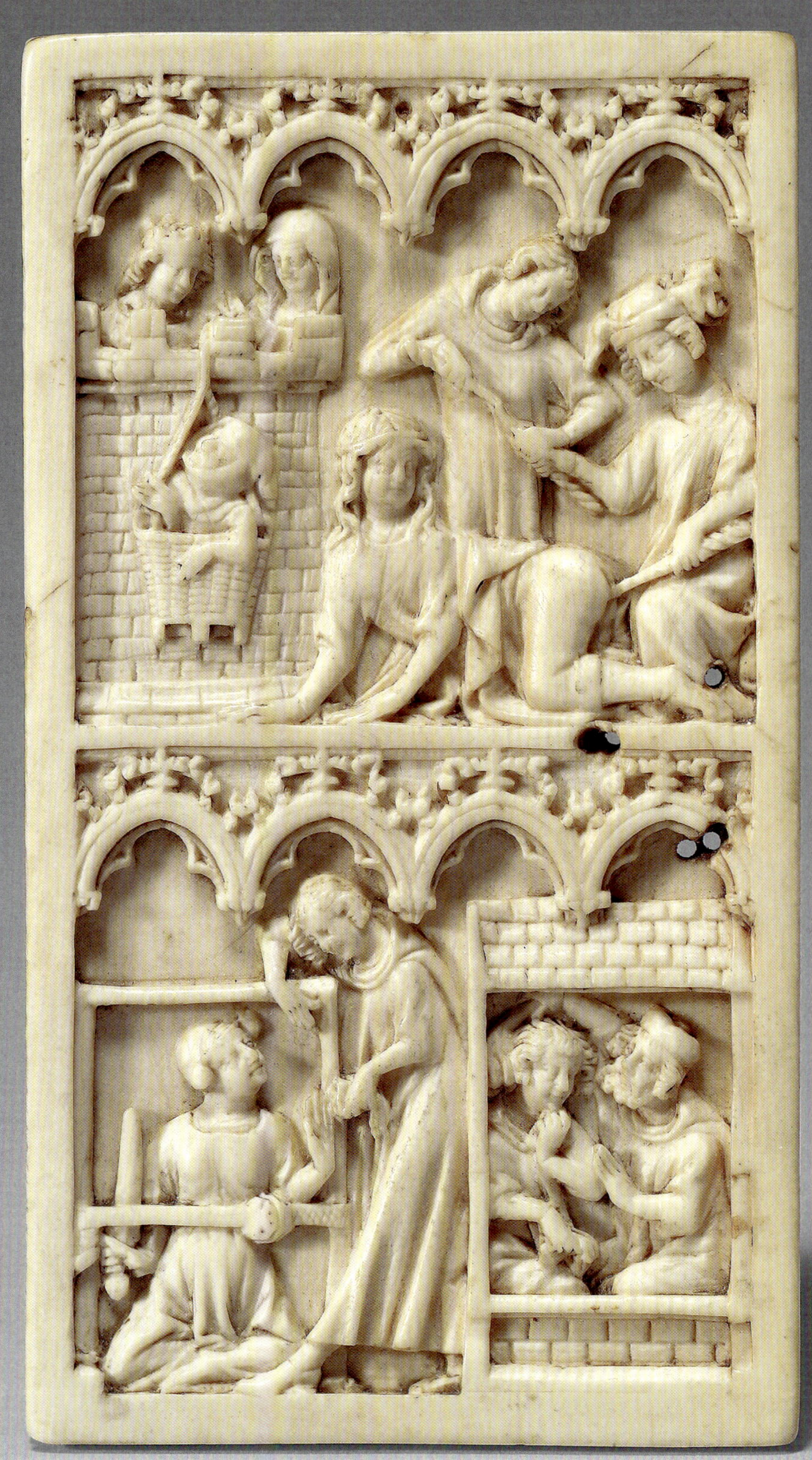

24. **Cover of a writing tablet with the story of Febilla and Virgil. French, 1340–60. Elephant ivory**

Gawain and Lancelot, and death in the tale of Pyramus and Thisbe. Rampant weaponry in the form of swords, spears, and javelins that appear on every face serves as a reminder of the pain, sometimes sweet, of piercing desire. The carvings also speak to an aggressive masculinity so exaggerated that it is difficult to know whether the instruments of a chivalrous male are being mocked or valorized.[59]

The scenes showing Phyllis and Aristotle stand somewhat apart within this extravagant phallophilic display (FIG. 17). The tale—a medieval invention—recounts how the philosopher Aristotle chastises his student Alexander the Great for spending too much time with a woman, sometimes called Phyllis, rather than attending to his duties as king and military leader. When Alexander tells Phyllis that he has been instructed to stay away from her, she takes matters into her own hands. She offers Aristotle sexual favors if he will agree to let her ride him like a horse, staging the activity so that Alexander can see it. Aristotle's authority undermined, Alexander resumes his romance with Phyllis.[60]

The story was a favorite of medieval artists, drawing laughs and, depending on context, demonstrating either the dangers or the triumph of love (PL. 23).[61] The latter seems very much at play on the ivory chest, reinforced by assumptions that proper courtly love was a young person's game. The scene extends hierarchical inversions of gender and age that were current in the Middle Ages into an exploration of their erotic potential. The sexual context is clear, and the whip in Phyllis's hand and the bridle in Aristotle's mouth give precision to its physical expression. Theatricality is built into the story and its depiction. Aristotle may not have agreed to the audience, but he consented to his degrading role. The story of Aristotle's masochistic humiliation was met with success in part because it both confirmed and undermined the binary opposition of dominance (coded male) and submission (coded female) that characterized general discourses on medieval sexuality.[62] As Ruth Karras has pointed out, the sexual act was understood less as a mutual endeavor and more as something done by someone to someone else.[63]

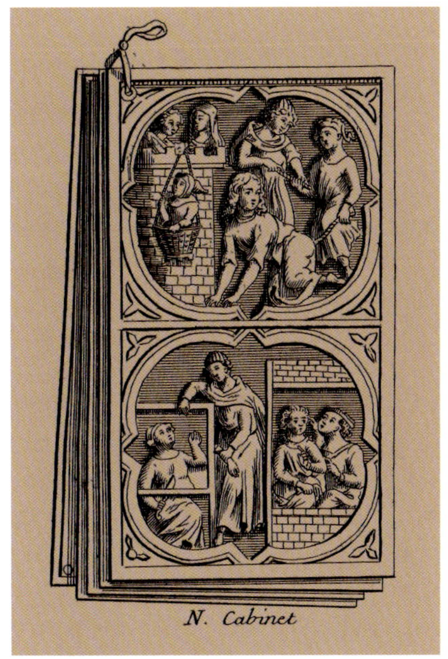

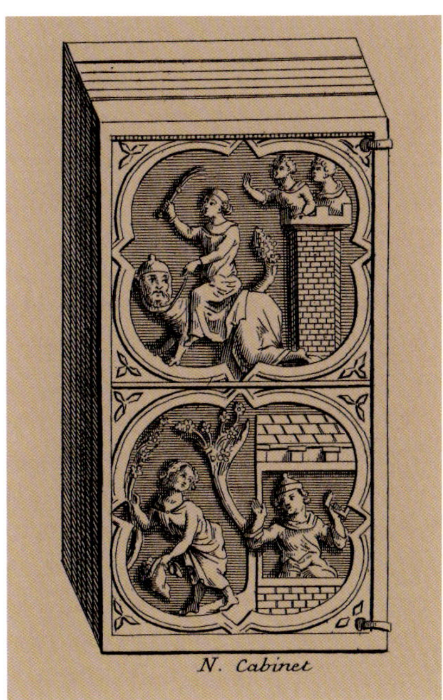

Fig. 18. **Detail of ivory writing tablets depicting Febilla and Virgil (top), Phyllis and Aristotle (below) in B. de Montfaucon, *L'Antiquité expliquée et représentée en figures* (Paris, 1722). Vol. III, pt. 2, p. 359, pl. CXCIV**

Evocations of cross-gender masochism must be set against legal and social structures that locked medieval women into nonconsensual submission.[64] As scholars have shown, poetic language or an expert brushstroke can mask the violence of rape.[65] But was there a script of "counter-conduct" for women, a performance, an opening that gave them agency as the submissive partner?[66] Sarah Salih presents several case studies of medieval women who willingly capitulated to a marital obligation of "unpleasant sex," if not for erotic gratification, then for the public satisfactions of social conformity or self-definition.[67] Martha Easton has argued that sexualized images of female martyrdom might have afforded an enjoyable experience for female viewers in that they portray a woman who has encouraged her own victimization and will reap the ultimate spiritual reward from it.[68] With care, scholars have teased out evidence of women's consent within an asymmetrical dynamic of sexual power.[69] Uncovering representations of women's physical pleasure in such contexts is far more elusive.[70]

A mid-fourteenth-century ivory writing tablet may attempt to provide such a script, though its success is a matter of debate (PL. 24). The carving of particularly fine quality depicts a woman on all fours engaged in an unusually explicit sex act.[71] Several late-medieval texts recount how the poet-sorcerer Virgil pursued a Roman princess, sometimes called Febilla, who played a trick on him. In response, she hoists him up in a basket so that he might visit her in a tower, yet she leaves him, humiliatingly, hanging in midair, an episode shown at the left on the ivory.[72] Virgil then enacts his retribution by extinguishing all the lights in the city and magically placing a hot piece of coal inside of Febilla's body. To illuminate the city, people must put their candles in Febilla's anus or vagina. The ivory depicts the rekindling as an almost mechanized assembly line, a perverse bucket brigade of candle-lighting. So forthright and disturbing is this depiction of anal penetration that museums holding such works of art understandably leave them in their storeroom.

An eighteenth-century engraving of a now-lost ivory writing booklet indicates that the Febilla panel was once paired with another one showing Phyllis seducing and riding Aristotle (FIG. 18). Though no writing tablets illustrating the Phyllis and Aristotle story survive, we can readily imagine it through a rearrangement of scenes on our ivory box. The stories of Febilla and Phyllis are similar in that they involve ancient writers and public embarrassment, and the booklet's ivory carver took pains to set them up as parallel, with towers on the outer edges and Febilla and Aristotle both on hands and knees. Febilla's calm demeanor, turned head, and hiked-up skirt intimate that she, like Aristotle, has consented to her situation, and the conspicuousness of her carefully modeled bottom encourages surprise, laughter, and titillation. Indeed, the images seem to tap into the wide range of "butt jokes," commonplace in medieval marginalia, fabliaux, and farces that found amusement in farts and in sex *par derrieres*, but the connection only goes so far.[73] The licentious women and sexually demanding wives who figure in French fables all notably belonged to the lower classes. Febilla, by contrast, was a princess. The Aristotle and Febilla stories thus sit squarely within the courtly romance genre, making them worthy subjects for ivory-carving. And their backsides mentioned therein are not relegated to the margins, but given pride of place. The depiction of the Febilla scene especially was a curious, seemingly indecorous choice.[74]

On its own, the ivory representation of Febilla exemplifies the misogynist stereotypes of feminine sexual voracity that pervaded medieval literary, artistic, theological, legalistic, and medical cultures. It grotesquely seems to justify, or satirize, rape. But directly juxtaposed with the Aristotle and Phyllis panel, as we see in the engraving, the Febilla panel undergoes a subtle shift in its meaning. In that pairing, Febilla's submission would have been explicitly set against Phyllis's dominance. The two ivories together would have drawn attention to the seductiveness of power, in all its crudeness, and argue for its instability. The writing booklet, with its complementary front and back covers, thus would have posed a comic and erotic question, one that could be posited by simply flipping the booklet over: who's on top? The cleverness lay in offering two versions of what we moderns would call sadomasochistic role-playing.[75] That was its punch line and its provocation.

The Aristotle and Febilla stories, of course, are not exactly parallel. Only when reduced to a visual shorthand could the philosopher's humiliation be equated with the princess's violation. Both stories, though, are fantasies in the guise of history. They use temporal and paradigmatic distance—Aristotle and Virgil predate the Christian era—from the viewer's present to explore the erotic limits of humiliation and cruelty. The written source-texts imply that Febilla is not a masochist but the victim of a sadist.[76] The ivory depiction rejects that logic by placing Febilla in the same position as Aristotle in the game of sexual domination. In so doing, it proposes that she consented to her own ritualized humiliation. Pleasure proceeds to the ivory's owner, where power resides in her or his hands, in the orchestration and manipulation of sexual fantasy.[77]

HAPPILY EVER AFTER?

Inventories, account records, court poetry, romance tales, and works of art confirm that the objects we have called erotica circulated among members of the courtly class as love tokens, cultural and literal currency, and playthings.[78] There are even occasional references to male and female buyers purchasing such pieces for personal pleasure.[79] One item in the accounts of Philip the Bold provides a bracing reminder of other uses for these works. On February 14, 1388, the Duke of Burgundy sent his wife, Margaret III of Flanders, a gold buckle encrusted with a ruby and pearls that depicted the God of Love.[80] Margaret was instructed to give the buckle to the duke's nephew Louis II of Anjou and his mother, Marie of Blois, a few weeks later.[81] During those early months of 1388, Philip and his brother the duc de Berry were helping negotiate the marriage of Louis to Yolande of Aragon to ensure a political alliance between two strategic regions.[82] Louis was ten years old when he received this auspicious gift. His intended fiancé was six.

With the gift to little Louis, we are far from the fairy tale world of ardent young adults that medieval texts and images conjure. We are reminded that amorous relationships were highly regulated beginning in childhood. Works that toyed with the idea of romantic love may have suggested imaginative possibilities—"a vision of choice"—but they could also exert social control, not simply offering fantasies of desire but imposing them.[83] The God of Love was invoked on the golden buckle to assert "straight time," in all its severity. The seemingly whimsical motif was a frank reminder to a young boy of the requirements of aristocratic masculinity and of his political, familial, and social obligations to wed an even younger girl he had never met. The path of Cupid's arrows could be directed by a ruthlessly powerful hand.

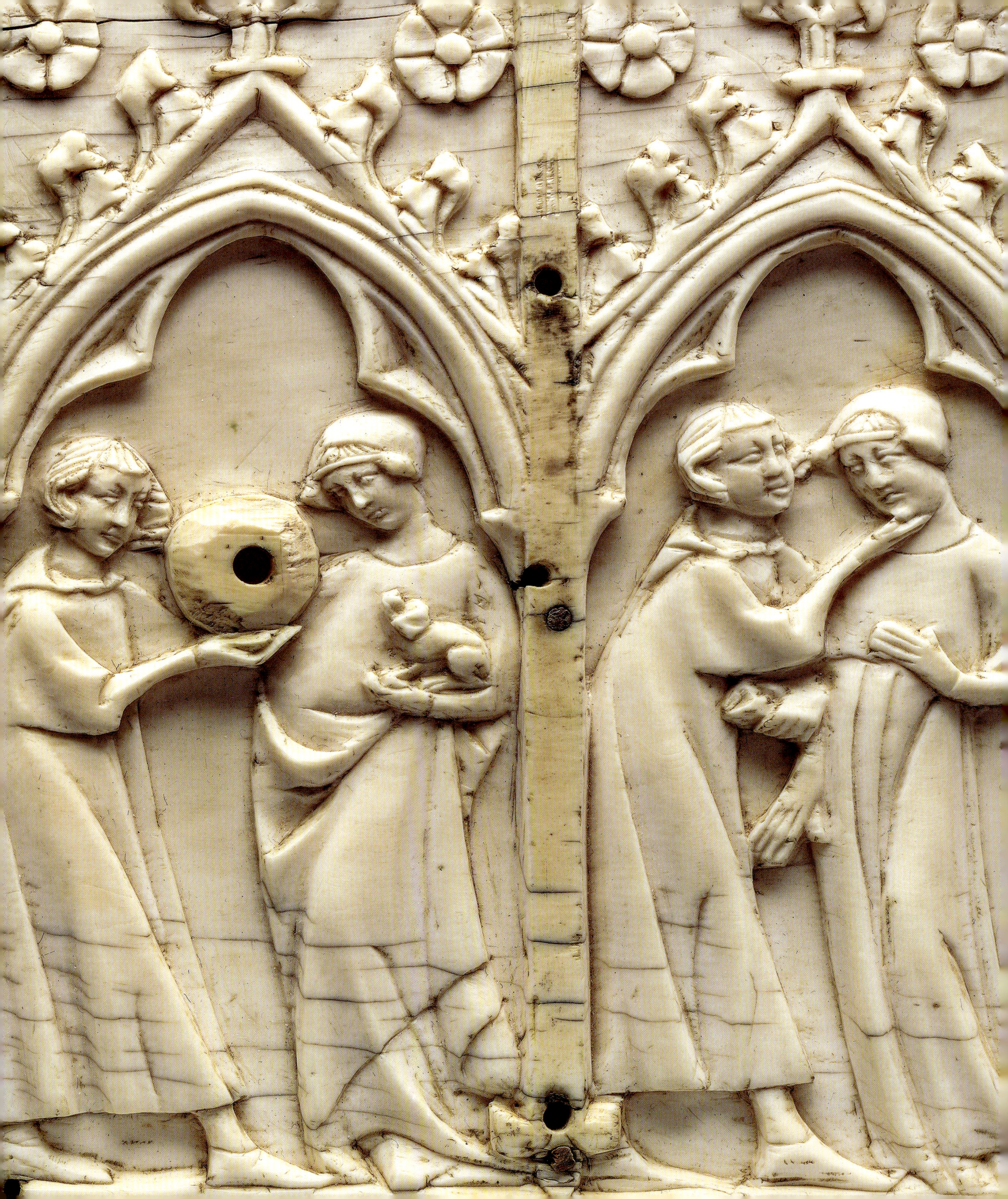

MELANIE HOLCOMB AND
NANCY THEBAUT

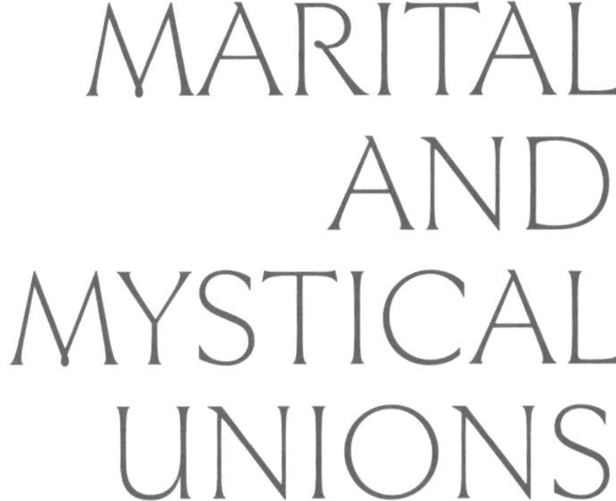

MARITAL AND MYSTICAL UNIONS

A blaze of brilliant color in a thicket of text, a small painting from an Italian legal manuscript conveys at a glance the sense and substance of the writings it embellishes. The single leaf is apparently all that survives from an early fourteenth-century copy of the *Decretals* of Gregory IX, a foundational collection of papal rulings issued in 1234 (PL. 25; FIG. 19).[1] The picture, showing a nuptial mass, serves as a signpost of sorts. Crowning two columns of text, it directs the reader to the beginning of the *Decretals*' fourth book, which is devoted to the vast juridical category of marriage.

Within a neatly ruled frame a young couple kneels in prayerful submission, flanked by family and witnesses separated by gender. A priest at center, a golden cross at his chest and book in hand, bridges the two halves of the picture. His authority is further conveyed by his frontal pose and conspicuous height. The pages that once followed addressed a host of legal complexities regarding licit and illicit unions. They were debated, clarified, and regulated through hundreds of papal and episcopal letters, a framing explanatory gloss, and numerous subsequent annotations. The image, with its distinct sections of color and orderly arrangement of figures, breaks up the dense verbiage to remind medieval viewers of the centrality of holy matrimony in delineating social roles, and of the duty of the Church in arbitrating it. Nothing sentimental about this wedding scene, just a straightforward statement of fundamental principles.

The staid illustration is an appropriate accompaniment to a text that drily explains conjugality in terms of "the impediment of public propriety," "present tense contracts," and "carnal intercourse."[2] Images outside legal contexts depict the wedded state in far more affecting ways, disclosing the sentiments and physical sensations it aroused.[3] The marital bond was a consuming medieval ideal, upheld by legislation, ritual, literature, and art. As a concept and metaphor, it could extend well beyond the bounds of the narrowly defined institution that canon law so meticulously regulated, embracing relationships and experiences that a *Decretals* codex would never picture.

While a conjugal union was the most readily available paradigm for expressing the culmination of many kinds of desire, both sacred and profane, it was not the only one. Medieval people described and depicted the consummation of desire as a "happy drunkenness" or a "great delectation," as a pregnancy or a feast, as a surrender or a wound.[4] Sexual and sexualized acts provided an especially varied and rich source of subject matter for artists. Late-medieval works of art encouraged, critiqued, and structured the exploration and experience of unions both within and beyond the realm of wedlock. This essay examines how, why, and for whom such images were used. We first consider the ways that visual representations shaped expectations of marriage. Works of art frequently offered lessons or warnings about how the roles of husband and wife should be performed. We then turn to the visual language of coitus before discussing works that represent and facilitate other kinds of union, namely the emotional, spiritual, and erotic connections between a person and the divine. Remarkably, it is precisely when sex and marriage are rejected that depictions of union intimate physical pleasure and open up a range of relational possibilities.[5]

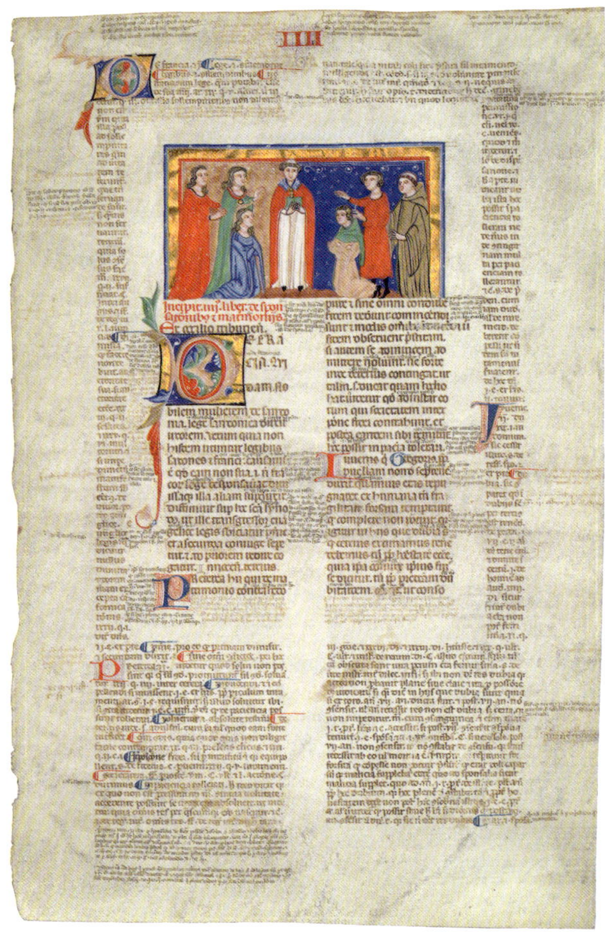

25. **Manuscript leaf with marriage scene from the *Decretals* of Gregory IX. Italian, ca. 1300. Opaque watercolor, gold leaf, and iron gall ink on parchment**

THE MODEL OF MARRIAGE

The mutual consent of spouses, voiced publicly, was the basis for legal matrimony in the Middle Ages.[6] Even as betrothals were frequently arranged by parents, at times when their children were very young, canon law made clear that the will of the nuptial pair—understood exclusively as a man and a woman—could override parental agreements. Works of art featuring husbands and wives reinforced the idea that marriage was an accord between only two parties. A painting from 1470 now in the Cleveland Museum of Art captures the enclosed world of a newlywed couple (SEE PL. 48). The groom's encircling embrace both establishes its boundaries and draws attention to the fundamental asymmetry of the relationship. Though husband and wife incurred a conjugal debt to one another, to use the medieval phrase for the expected mutuality of sexual obligation, men were nonetheless considered the superior partner.[7] His forward step, made more assertive by the eye-catching white of his tights, signals dominance. Her drawn skirt simulates a rounded

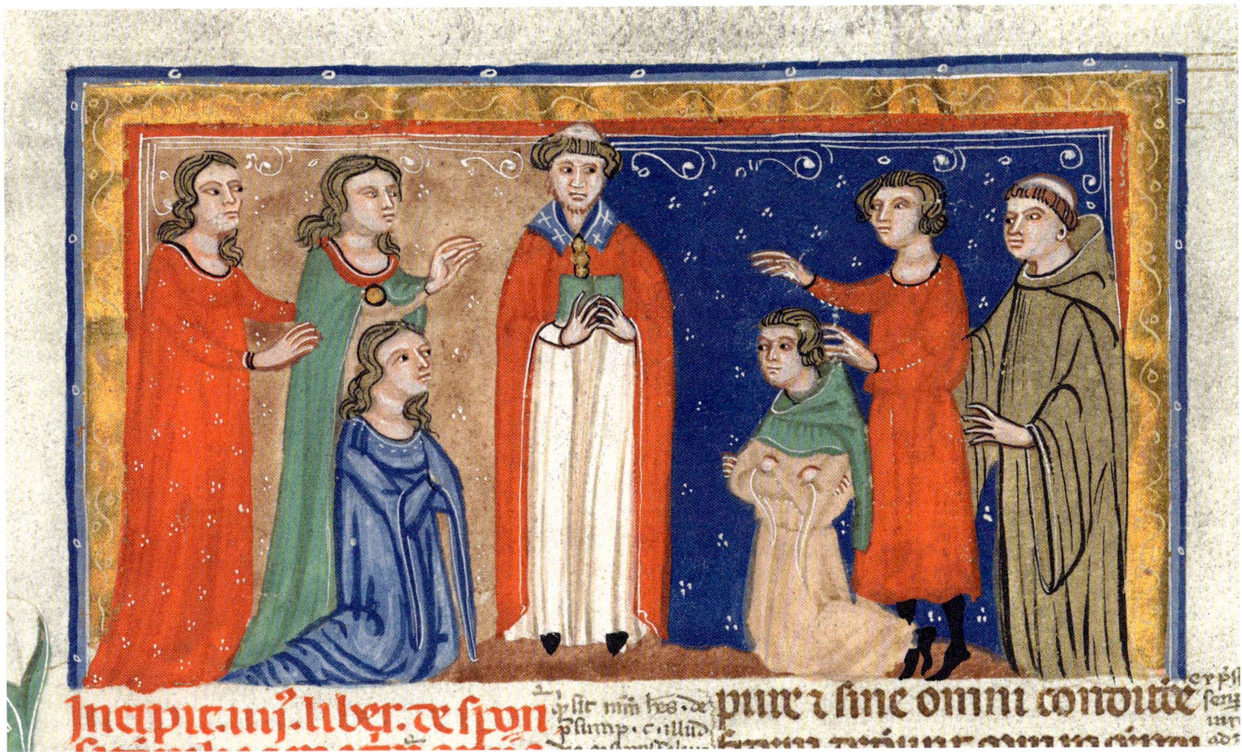

FIG. 19. **Detail of PL. 25 showing a nuptial mass**

belly on which her left hand rests in a gesture of anticipated fertility. Along with stabilizing gender roles, marriage properly channeled sexual desire, directing its dangerous energy toward procreation.

Depictions of couples made manifest the cultural work of wedlock, but they also modeled tenderness and reciprocity of feeling. The gentle interplay of the bride and groom's hands as he presents her with flowers evokes a quiet conversation between the two, while also showing off the rings that ceremonially mark their bond. (Medieval customs had not yet codified on which finger or hand a wedding ring could be worn.)[8] A painted sculpture of Joachim and Anne, parents of the Virgin Mary, strikes an even sweeter chord, in part because he so tenderly trains his gaze on her (PL. 26). The pair exemplified holy matrimony in the late Middle Ages, and Anne was considered a special intercessor for married women.[9] Like Abraham's wife Sarah from the Hebrew Scriptures, Anne miraculously became pregnant with her first child, the Virgin Mary, at an advanced age. Theologians who emphasized Mary's purity explained her conception in paradoxical terms, as a chaste impregnation.[10]

Almost certainly a fragment from an altarpiece, the sculpture shows what was understood to be the very moment of the Virgin's conception, when Anne and Joachim meet at the Golden Gate in Jerusalem. Though they are long married in this scene, the sculpture uses some of the same visual formulations as the marriage portrait. Joachim's leg lunges forward and his arm wraps around Anne's shoulders. The joining of their right hands, known as the *dextrarum iunctio*, a characteristic gesture of the wedding ceremony since antiquity, further emphasizes their wedded status.[11] Drapery enacts the sexual encounter that is not one. The dramatic sweep of Joachim's cloak both guards their intimacy and telegraphs its suggestive energy. Meanwhile, Anne's skirt, held up like a makeshift

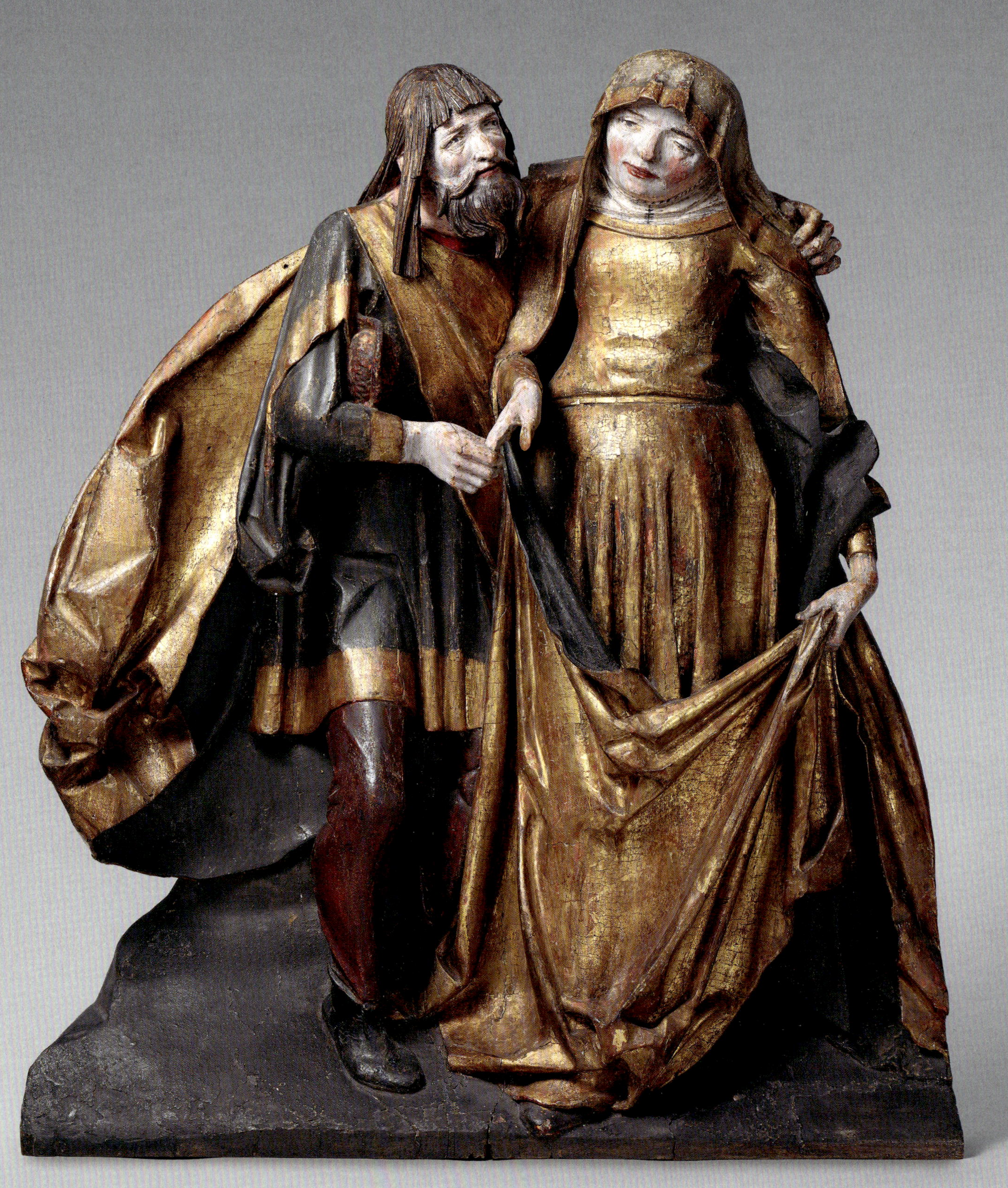

26. **Meeting of Saints Joachim and Anne at the Golden Gate, ca. 1515–20. Benedikt Dreyer. Oak with paint and gold**

basket for just-picked fruit, imparts her new physical state as sacred receptacle.

Wedding rites varied across late-medieval Europe, but they could begin with a ceremony of betrothal.[12] Once the families had agreed on the bride's dowry, they gathered to witness the couple's legal engagement. After the pair joined hands and exchanged vows, the groom gave a ring to the bride (and sometimes she gave him one, too). Jewelry thus served as a surety contract and public proof of a couple's mutual agreement.[13] But even before betrothal, rings were given to gain affection and were so powerfully associated with a conjugal commitment that women were warned to accept such gifts with caution. An unvirtuous man might use one to lure a woman into sexual relations, and a ring worn by an unmarried woman could imply promiscuity.[14] The diverse forms, inscriptions, and materials of rings drew from the widespread iconography of love and courtship. The shape and message of a fourteenth-century example convey the long-standing idea that love is kindled in the heart (PL. 27).[15] A gold repoussé band playfully connects courtship to a hunt, with monkeys as the hunters (PL. 28).[16] So-called fede rings provide the most obvious reference to the betrothal rite, their silhouettes re-creating the ceremonial joining of hands (PL. 29).

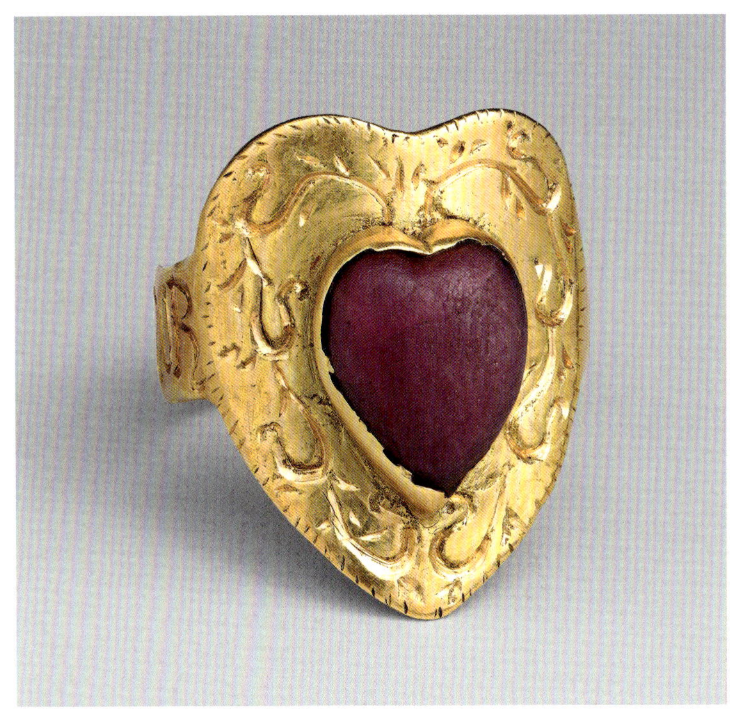

27. **Heart-shaped ring. Italian, 14th century. Gold and ruby**

Rituals of ring exchange presumed wedlock as being exclusively between a man and woman. Diane Wolfthal argues that Petrus Christus's renowned painting of an affianced couple shopping for a ring enlists the wonders of commerce and craft to endorse that stance (FIG. 20).[17] With its stacks of glittering jewels set among other wares, including purses, brooches, and double cups, the goldsmith's shop is presented as a nuptial emporium in the business of upholding the social order. Although the spouses-to-be focus their attention on the band they have selected, the goldsmith looks to the left, perhaps out to the street, at two men with a falcon whose reflection appears in the cracked mirror at right (FIG. 21). Wolfthal demonstrates that the pair are likely lovers, their affection for one another implied through the falcon, a classic symbol of courtship and eroticism. Excluded from the controlled and orderly spaces of societally sanctioned activities such as weddings and their preparations, the male couple is consigned to the unruly, unclean domain of the street. As a paragon of the sin of *sodomia*, a broad category of sins that included sex acts between people of the same gender, the couple in the mirror represents the antithesis of the bridal pair. The painting, seemingly intended for public display in Bruges, thus contributed to the stigmatization of so-called sodomites, whose persecution was particularly intense in that city at the very moment the painting was created.

For those who could marry, a wedding was a multistep process, and the gift economy was central to every stage, especially among the elite. Gifts expressed affection and aspirations for the marital pair, and their iconography commonly straddled two worlds: the fantasy of courtly love and the actual social expectations that husbands and wives needed to fulfill. Perhaps surprisingly, the former was understood as

28. **Ring with hunting scene. Spanish, probably 16th century. Gold**

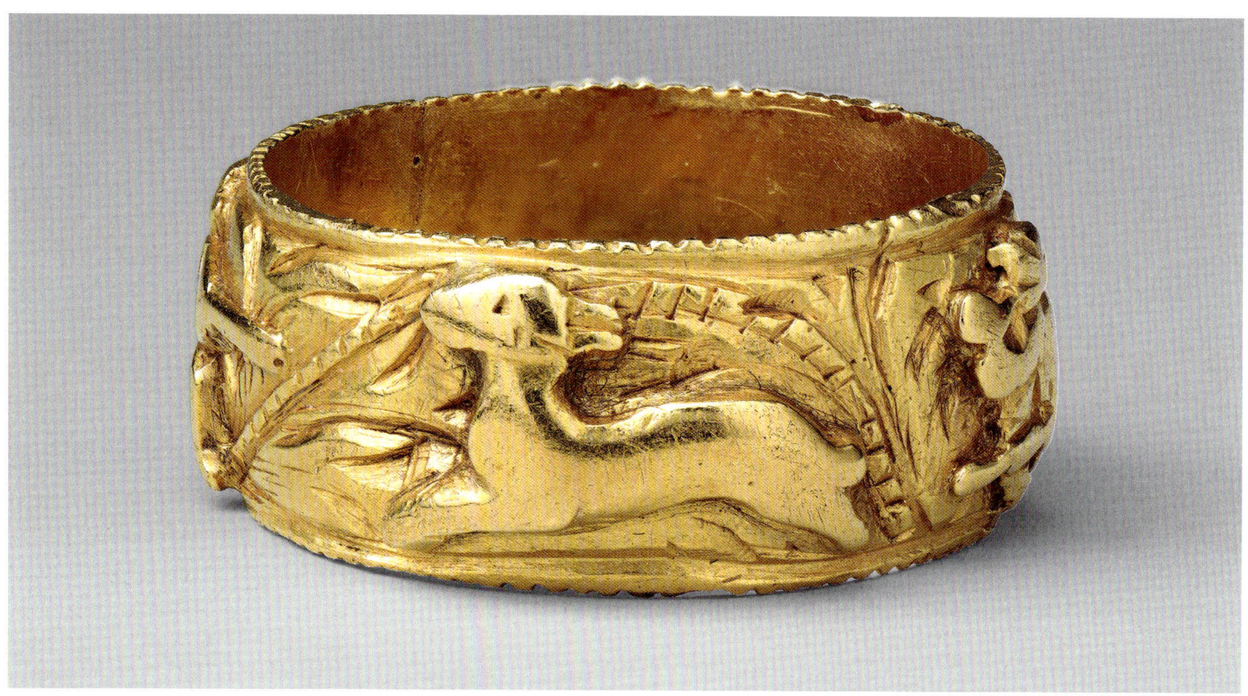

29. **Fede ring. Possibly British, 16th century. Gold**

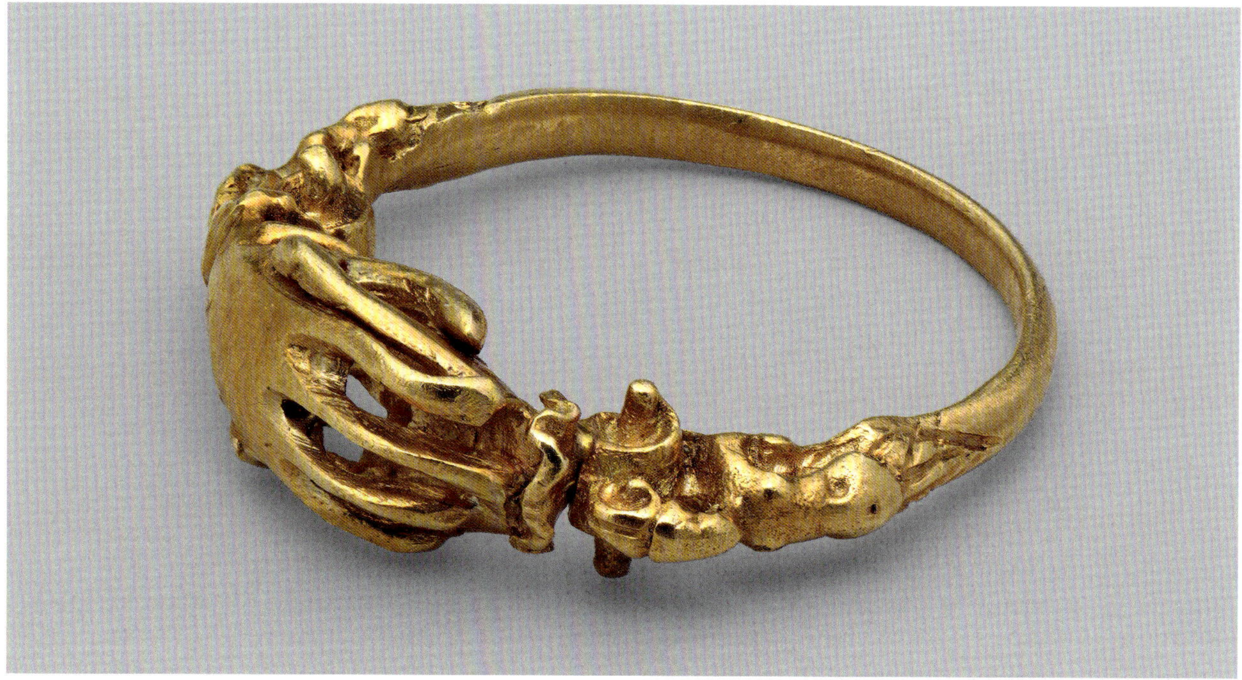

antithetical to the marital bond. For example, a saddle that may have been used in a procession from the bride's familial home to that of her new husband incorporated clichéd themes of romance into public ceremonials (PL. 30).[18] Made from the pelvic bones of a deer and lined with hide and birch bark, it depicts a series of vignettes. Men and women exchange gifts, clasp hands, grasp shoulders, and pull each other close, with women often acting as the aggressors. Allusions to sex are found throughout, as multiple men conspicuously handle their girdles; swords and arrows pierce the bodies of dragons and other hybrid creatures; and a male figure on the carved pommel thrusts his hand inside his conical hat. If Stephen Grancsay's proposal is correct that a male rider stood above the saddle rather than sat on it, he and others would have seen the carvings at the suggestive moment of mounting and dismounting.[19] Once the rider was astride, the message of sexual conquest was even more pronounced, as the pommel's vaguely penile form became an extension of his own body. With his backside resting against the cantle (the projecting rear element), he figuratively sits in the laps of the two women carved into it, their voluptuous skirts spilling out beneath him (FIG. 22). Then as now, the vocabulary of horseback riding provided ample material for the salacious double entendre.[20]

Other objects associated with weddings take aim at the bride, whether through paternalistic teachings, humorous jabs, or expressly violent imagery. An embroidered purse known as an *aumônière* (literally "alms bag") depicts a medieval model of wifely obedience, Patient Griselda, the protagonist of a popular narrative that is best known from Boccaccio's *Decameron* (1348–53) and Chaucer's *The Canterbury Tales* (ca. 1387–1400).[21] The *aumônière*, likely a wedding gift, held coins to be distributed to those in need at a specified moment during the ceremony.[22] The story of Patient Griselda resonates strongly with the marital context of the bag, as conduct literature presented her as an exemplary wife, daughter, and Christian.[23]

Boccaccio's version recounts that Gualtieri, an Italian marquis, decided to marry a shepherdess, Griselda, once she unconditionally agreed to remain

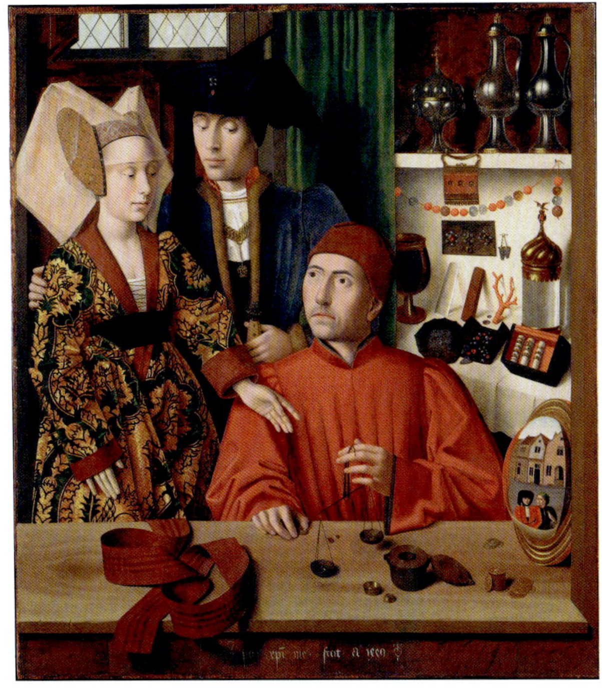

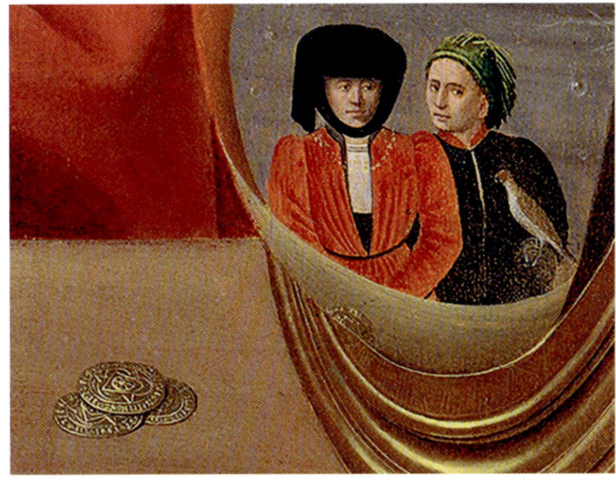

Fig. 20. ***A Goldsmith in His Shop*, 1449. Petrus Christus (Netherlandish, active by 1444–d. 1475/76). Oil on oak panel, 39 3/8 × 33 3/4 in. (100.1 × 85.8 cm). The Metropolitan Museum of Art, New York, Robert Lehman Collection, 1975 (1975.1.110)**

Fig. 21. **Detail of FIG. 20, depicting mirror with the reflection of a male couple with a falcon**

30. **Ceremonial saddle with suggestive scenes of lovers. Central European, ca. 1400–20. Bovine bone (body of saddle), deer antler and bone (decorative elements), limewood, rawhide, birchbark, and metal paint**

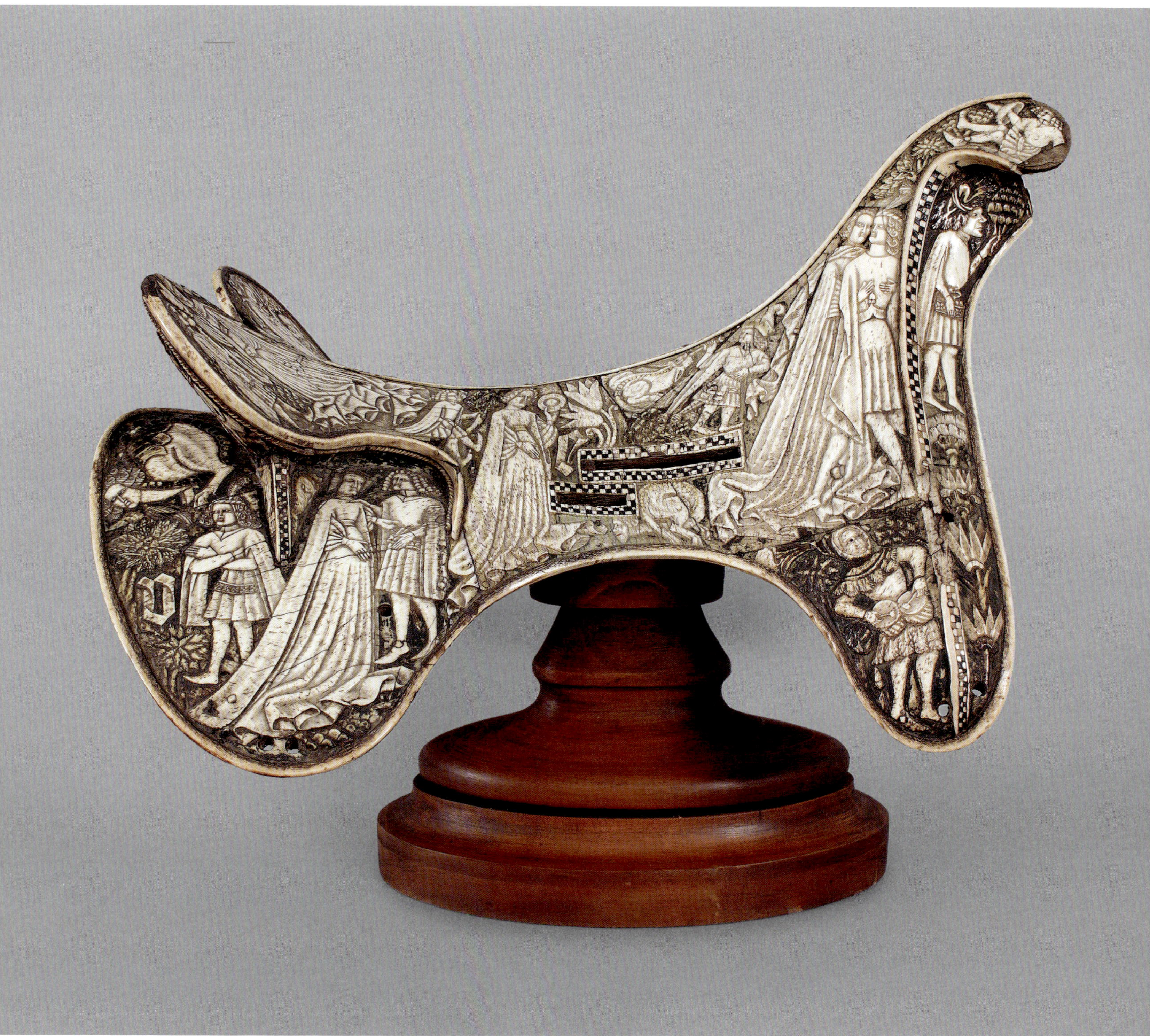

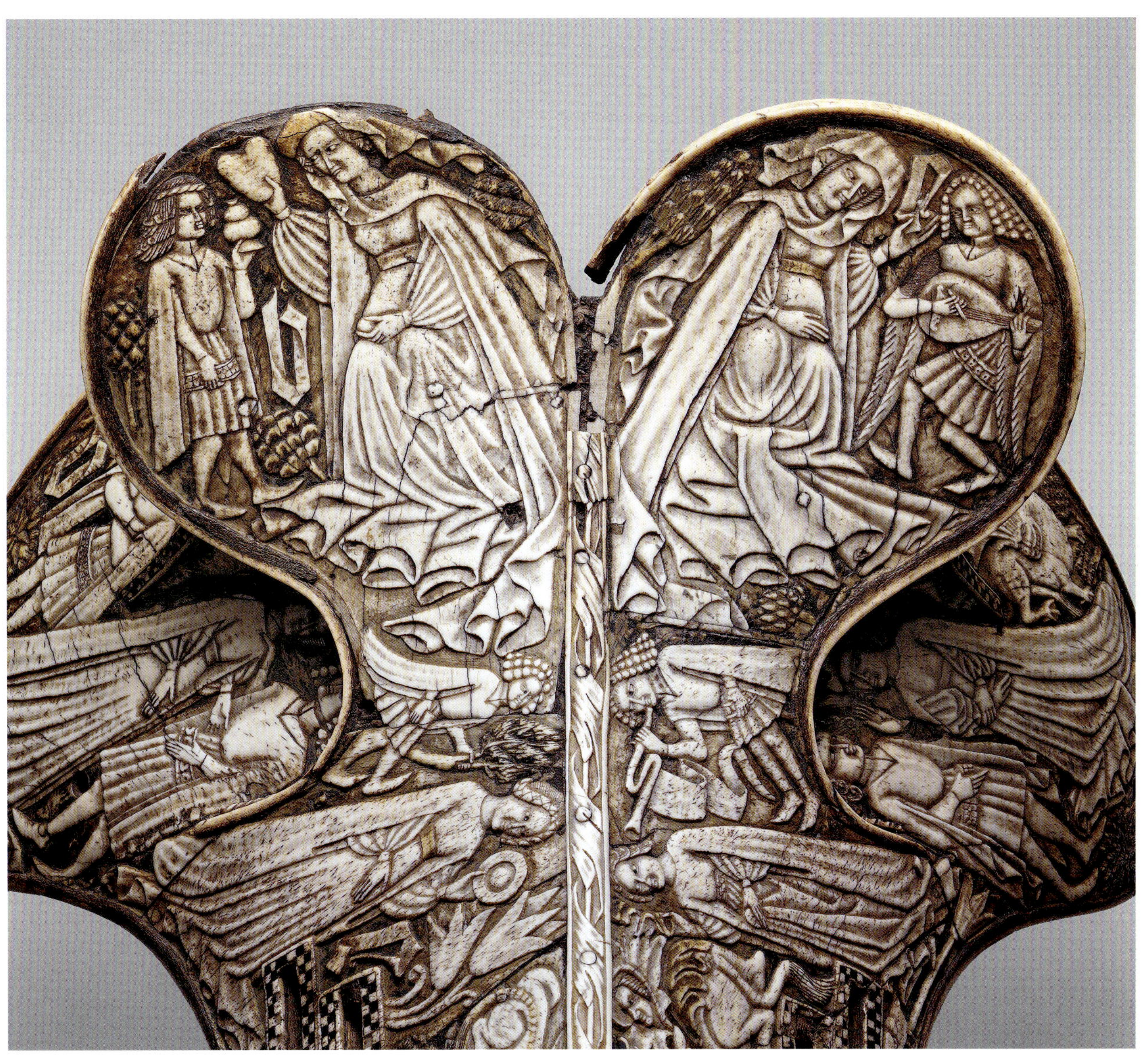

Fig. 22. **Top view of PL. 30 showing men giving gifts to and serenading women**

obedient to him.[24] For the wedding, he arranged for her to be dressed in rich bridal attire, comprising a "costly robe," "girdles and rings," and a "beautiful crown."[25] One side of the bag shows the newlyweds as they depart for Gualtieri's castle, with her father at left bidding farewell (PL. 31A). Griselda's elegant dress and stylish coiffure are the means of her transformation from lowly shepherdess into noblewoman, from maiden into bride. Once the pair are married, Gualtieri subjects Griselda to a series of terrible tests that include abducting their two children, allowing her to think they are dead, and pretending to take a new wife. In a reversal of her earlier sartorial metamorphosis, Griselda departs the castle in a coarse shift, leaving her ring, shoes, and bridal dress behind.[26] The scene on the other side of the purse could represent the beginning or end of the story (PL. 31B). The woman at right might be helping Griselda, depicted at center, put on or remove a sumptuous dress. She is also either taking away the spindle that marks Griselda's lowly status or returning it (PL. 31B). The purse's ambiguous iconography effectively conveys both the promise and potential consequences of married life.[27]

Though the story ends well for Griselda—Gualtieri reveals that their children are alive and that he will not, in fact, remarry—the happy ending is hardly the point. Gualtieri explains that his lies were concocted to teach her how to be a proper wife and to reassure himself of his decision to marry her.[28] The supposedly pedagogical value of Gualtieri's tests is in keeping with contemporary conduct literature, which provided lessons in proper behavior to husbands and wives. In his fourteenth-century treatise on marriage, Philippe de Mézières cites Griselda as an exemplary Christian wife.[29] Philippe's interpretation is allegorical, but for women at a wedding, the bag was a stark reminder of expectations that a wife submit to her husband.[30] Like Griselda, the bride also risked great suffering in her own relationship. Everything could be taken away—even the dress on her back—at her husband's whim.

Whereas the Griselda purse presents a model for brides to emulate, an Italian glass goblet offers a violent warning to women who scorn their male suitors (PL. 32).[31] Although its precise use remains unknown, the

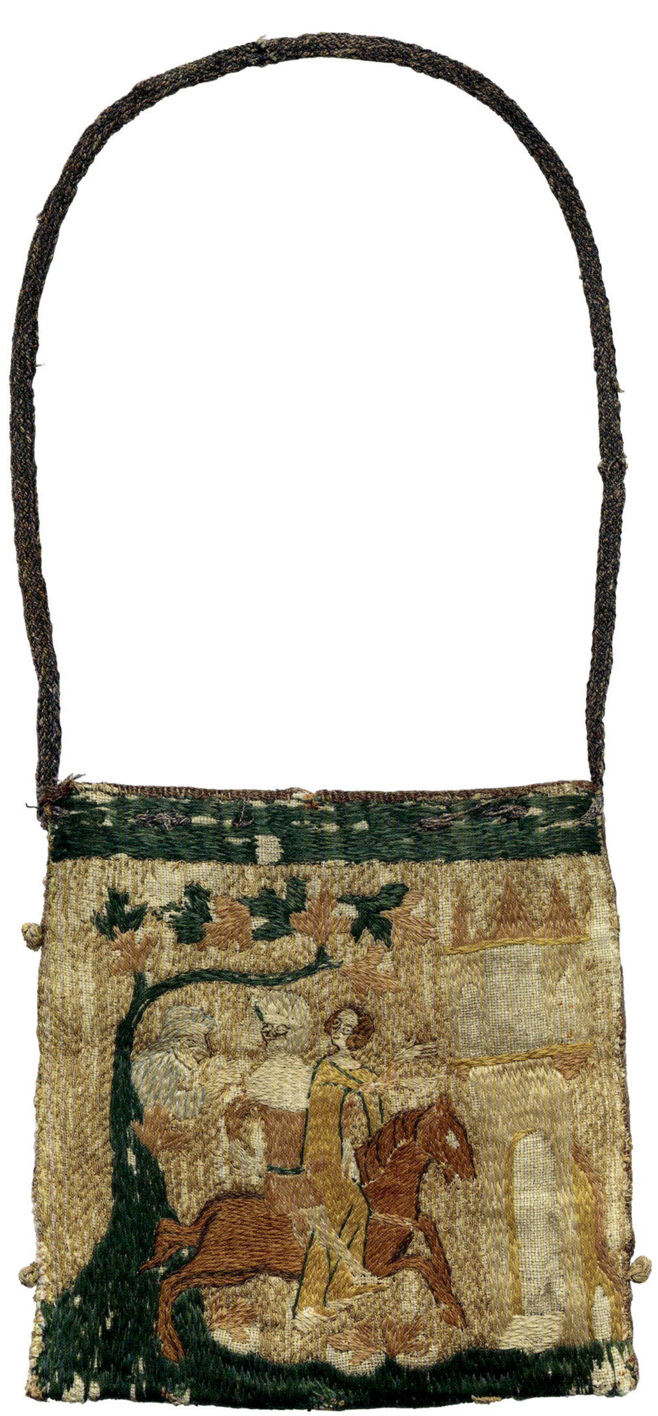

31A,B. **Front overall and back detail views of purse with the story of Patient Griselda. French, 14th century. Silk and metal thread on canvas**

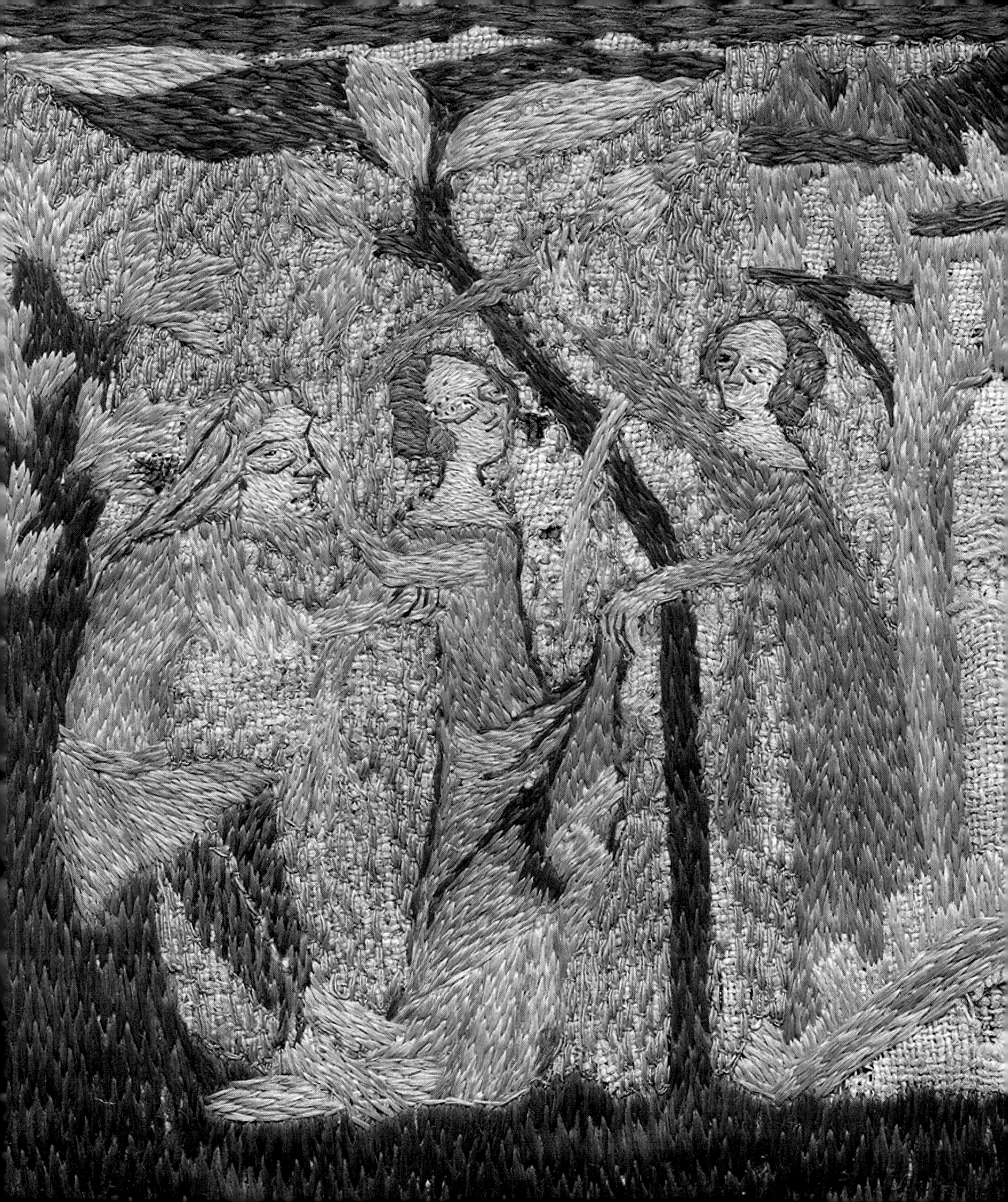

32. **Goblet with the story of Febilla and Virgil. Italian, ca. 1475–1500. Glass, enameled and gilded; modern foot**

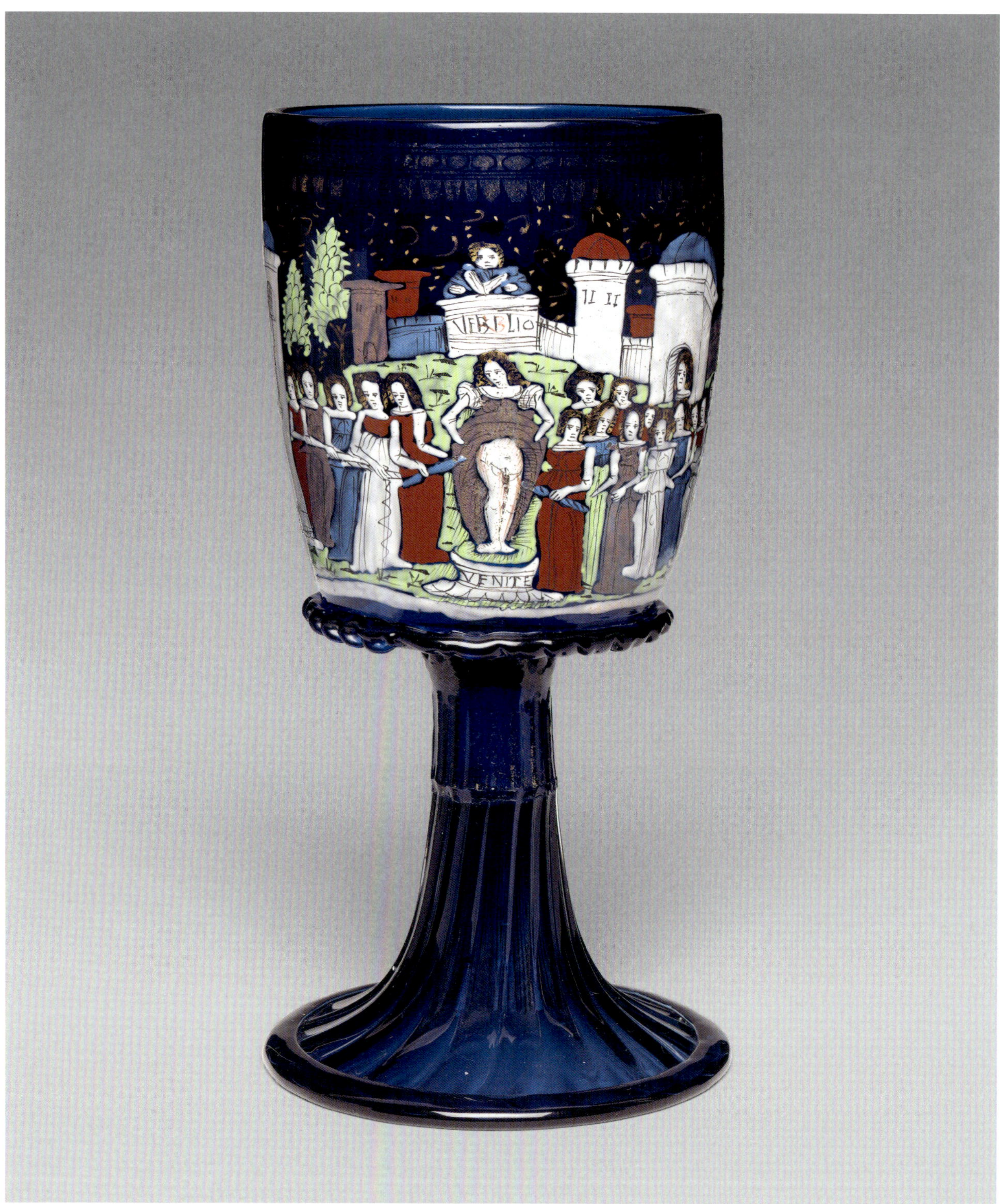

33. **Conjugal relations from *Le Régime du corps* (*The Regimen of the Body*). French, ca. 1440–50. Opaque watercolor, gold, silver and iron gall ink on parchment**

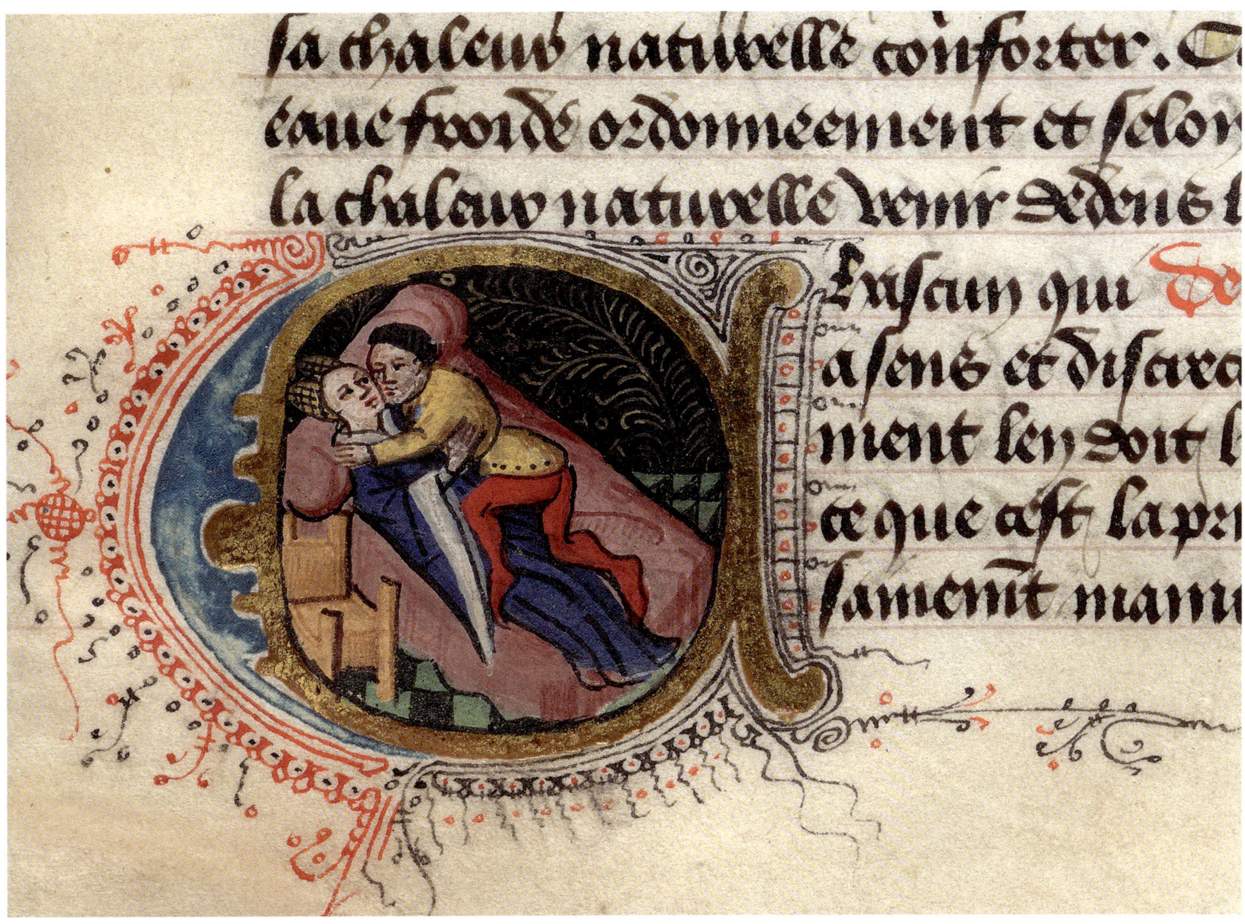

goblet is part of a group of objects associated with wedding banquets in northern Italy. Its message is dramatically different from that of a French ivory plaque of a century earlier that depicts the same story (SEE PL. 24). As discussed in the previous essay in this catalogue, the princess Febilla played a trick on Virgil, the poet-sorcerer, who then retaliates by extinguishing all the lights of Rome and placing a hot coal inside Febilla's body.[32] The goblet focuses on the supposed solution to the city's predicament: its citizens—here all women—must light their blue and white candles inside Febilla's vagina. Their gaze, collectively averted, implies they do so with reluctance. With her dress raised, Febilla stands atop a pedestal marked "venite" (come), as if beckoning the viewer, too, to participate in her violation. All are conscripted in what is presented as a civic obligation to shame an upstart woman.[33]

A male figure—perhaps Virgil, perhaps Febilla's father—stands above Febilla with book in hand, in the manner of a judge or doctor, and Febilla lifts her dress to allow inspection of her vagina and the blood that trickles down her legs. The blood may represent her loss of virginity, a reading that would align with the theme of virginity shown on other goblets of the same style, especially ones depicting the Greek goddesses Chastity and Hymen.[34] Unlike Griselda, Febilla is never presented as praiseworthy in conduct literature, but her image on the cup nonetheless offers up a similar paradigm of female passivity as she endures emotional and physical abuse at the hand of her would-be suitor.

Fig. 23. **Detail of PL. 14, showing the Prodigal Son performing a sex act with a naked woman**

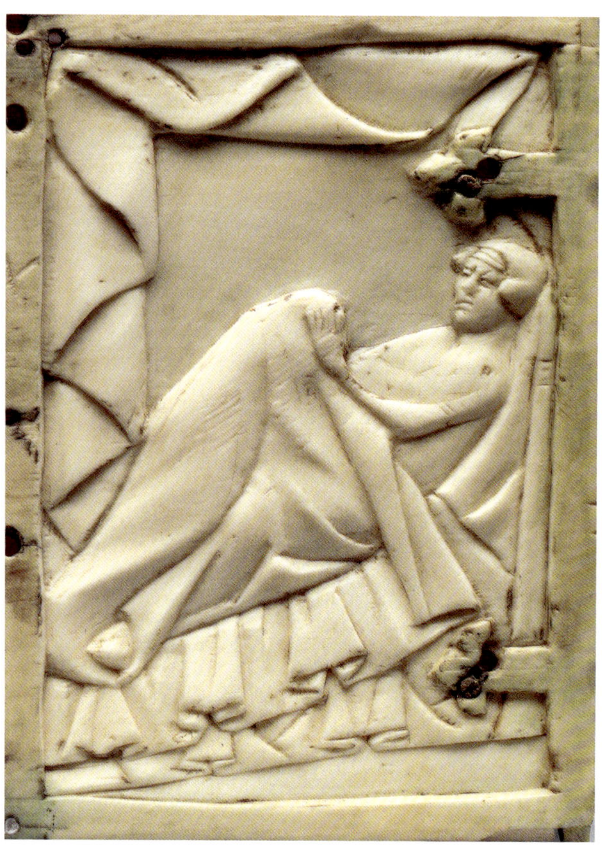

bedtime hug: according to medieval medical theory, he releases his "heat" into her cooler body and plants his "form" within her."[38] The empty crib at left clarifies the purpose of their sexual encounter.

The initial opens a chapter on sex that expounds on its mechanical and health-giving aspects. It addresses a male reader (although a woman may have owned and used the book) and instructs him to put "all of his efforts to learning how one should copulate with a woman, for it is a principal means of maintaining one's health and whoever does not do this . . . has a body that is good for nothing."[39] The text then describes when one should have sex (not when full from eating, not after sleeping), the risks of having too much sex (bad breath, weak kidneys), and its health benefits (reduce fatigue, clear the mind, and avoid disease).[40] The section concludes with the risks of not having enough sex: widows, religious men and women, and virgins "past their marrying age" could die suddenly as a result.[41] The fashionably dressed people in the manuscript thus model and teach the advantages of reproductive sex when properly performed.

In contrast to the medically approved coitus found in *Le Régime du corps*, an ivory box devoted to the biblical parable of the Prodigal Son pictures a sex act in which reproduction is not the end goal (FIG. 23). Here, the Prodigal Son lies on top of a woman who may be a sex worker. Textiles evocatively surround the scene: a curtain marks the space of the bedchamber; frilly blankets and a dust ruffle cover the bed's lower frame, and yet another cloth envelops the body of the Prodigal Son. Only his head peeks out from underneath the sheets, which otherwise obscure any specific sexual activity. The naked torso of the female lover, however, is plainly visible. The woman's body is misshapen and awkwardly rendered.[42] Her unveiled, unseemly appearance announces her lower-class status and points toward the illicit nature of the couple's encounter.[43] Though she is not positioned on top, her relative size and assertive grasp of the Prodigal Son's head indicate that she is the aggressor. His placement closer to her genitals than her face may even allude to oral sex, understood (and condemned) under canon law as *sodomia*.[44]

(NOT) SEEING SEX

Medieval artists generally shied away from explicit depictions of sexual intercourse.[35] More often, they represented sex obliquely, with textiles obscuring much of the activity. We find one such image tucked into an initial in *Le Régime du corps* (*The Regimen of the Body*), the popular late-medieval compendium of household medical knowledge (PL. 33).[36] There, a presumably married couple lies fully clothed and neatly coiffed upon a made bed. He lies on top, his bent leg slung over her, demonstrating the only acceptable position for intercourse according to medical doctors and the Church.[37] They wrap their arms around one another, as if to express mutual consent, but this is no

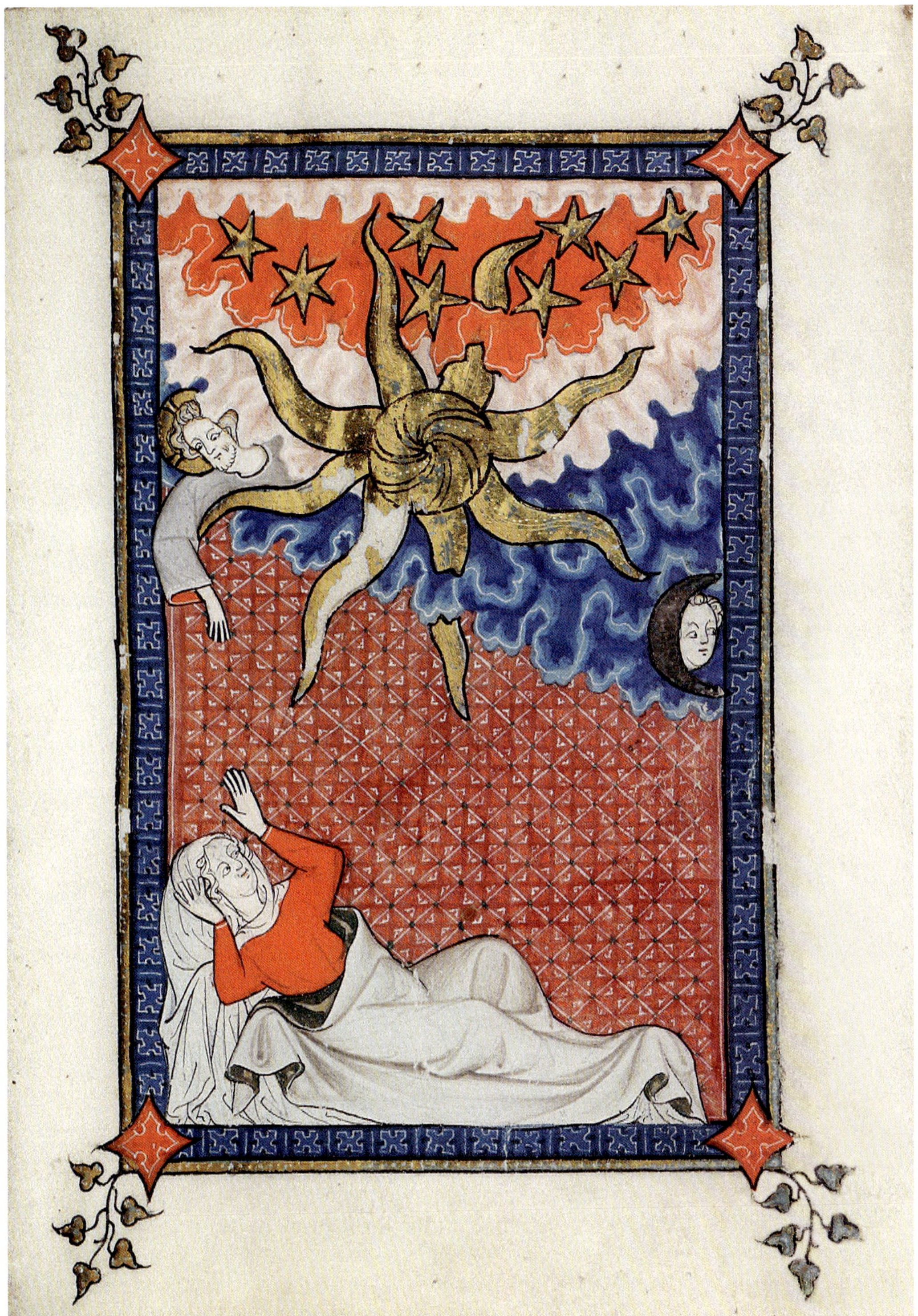

34. **The Sponsa in her spiritual bed from the Rothschild Canticles. French or Flemish, ca. 1300. Opaque watercolor, silver and gold leaf and iron gall ink on parchment**

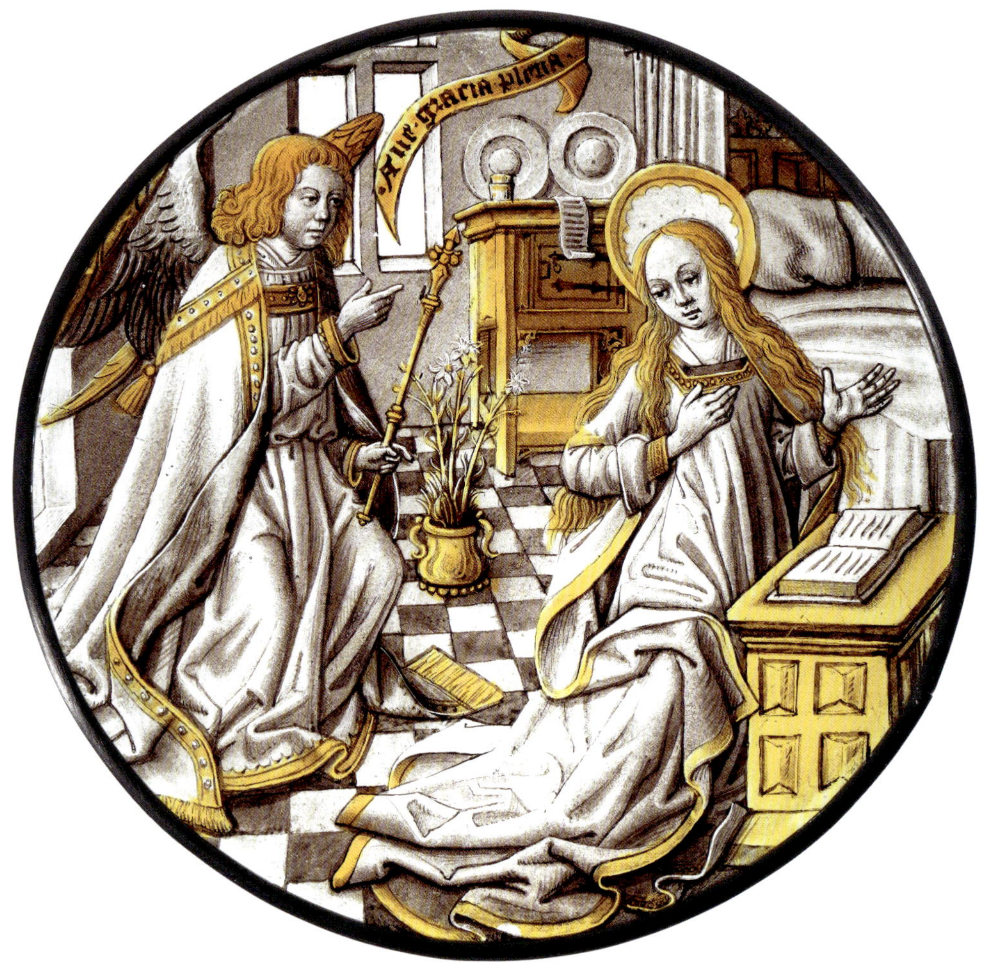

35. **Roundel with the Annunciation to the Virgin, showing a bed in the background. South Netherlandish, 1500–10. Colorless glass, vitreous paint and silver stain**

Not all beds carried the taint of carnality. The bed is an undeniable site of pleasure in the Rothschild Canticles, a devotional manuscript probably made for a nun in northern France around 1300 (PL. 34).[45] Here a single woman, the personification of the loving soul, enjoys a rapturous moment of mystical union with God. She lies simultaneously atop and beneath a rippling pile of white cloth, looking up at Christ, who extends his hand toward her from behind a radiant sun. The sun's tentacle-like rays pierce through the blue clouds and, echoing Christ's arms, reach for her body. With her eyes intent upon her lover and hands held aloft in delight, she conveys her willing and enthusiastic participation. The agitation of her legs outlined by the white blanket that covers her lower half adds to the sense of erotic thrill. Lying alone in bed, she enjoys a decidedly more exciting encounter than the woman in *Le Régime du corps*, who lies stiffly beneath her husband, or the woman on the ivory box, who manages the lovemaking of the errant son with little affect.

The painting was designed to prompt spiritual arousal, inviting the book's reader to aspire toward her own metaphysical encounter.[46] She would have been one of many such nuns, monks, priests, and even some laypeople (married or not) whose social identity and

36. **Virgin of the Annunciation. French, ca. 1300–10. Limestone with traces of paint**

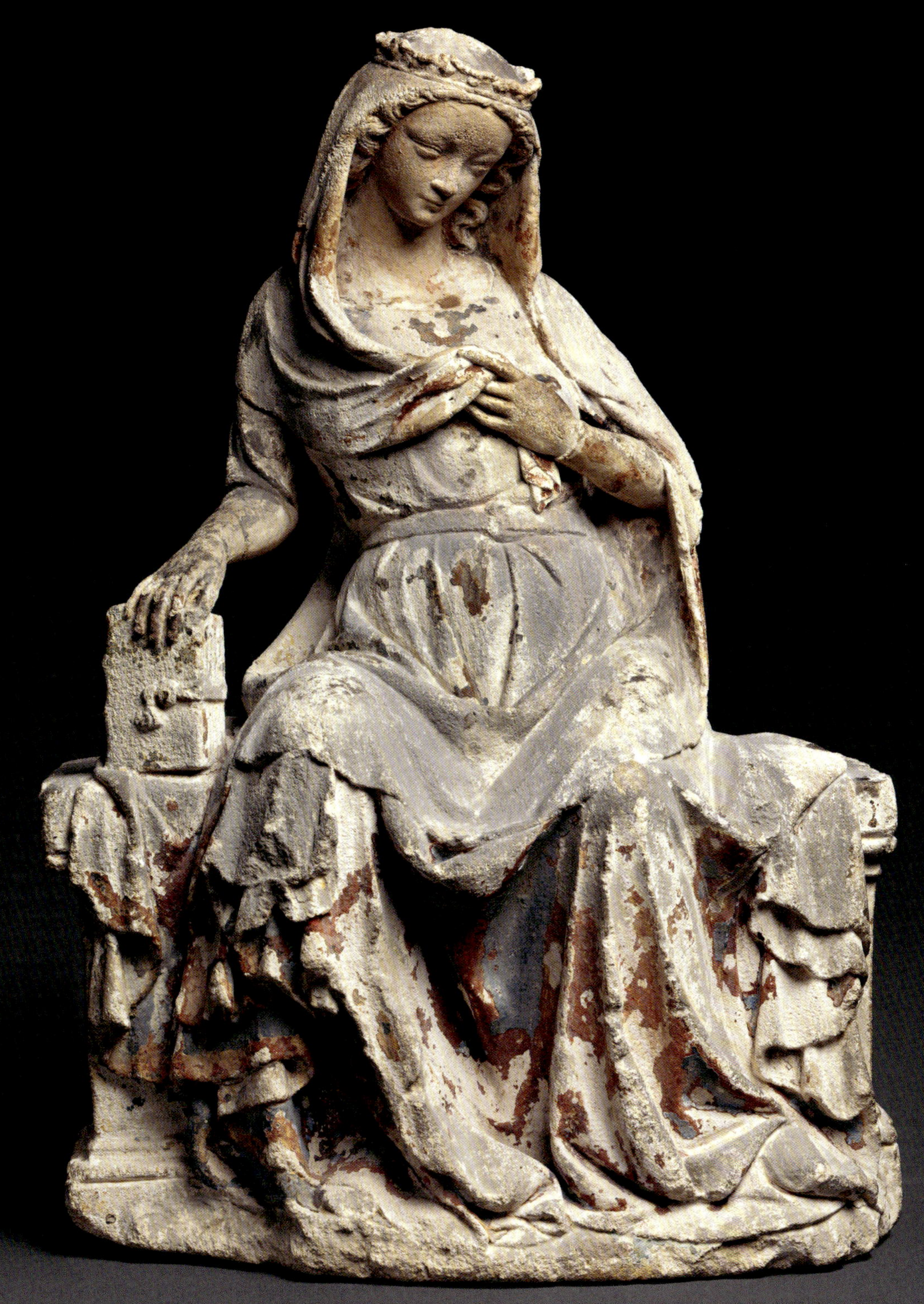

sense of self was tied to their decision to embrace abstinence. For Augustine, the relative valor was clear: "absence from all sexual union is better even than marital intercourse performed for the sake of procreation."[47] But not all forms of abstinence were equal. A hierarchy emerged in the Middle Ages, informed in part by what motivated the choice, whether devotees had ever experienced sex, and whether they felt sexual desire at all.[48] In some instances, refraining from sex was considered a kind of physical and spiritual ascent, leading to a state of perfection: it could make women more like men, and men more like angels, thus allowing them to transcend the gender binary altogether.

The Virgin Mary epitomized virtuous chastity. She set an impossible standard as one who remained untouched by a man but also conceived a child. That miraculous contradiction, a proof of Jesus's divinity, prompted theologians and artists to give concrete form to the simultaneity of the Annunciation, when the archangel Gabriel tells Mary that she will give birth to Christ, and the Incarnation, when God becomes flesh. Late-medieval scenes of the Annunciation usually take place within her private chambers, with a bed discreetly depicted in the background (PL. 35). A symbol of Mary's intact womb, the unused bed communicates the intimacy of this moment and the nuptial resonance of the incarnation.[49] Notably, she is generally depicted near but never *in* the bed at the moment of Christ's incarnation.

Even in the absence of provocatively crumpled sheets, the figure of Mary often conveys her willingness and even desire for this form of holy consummation—that is, her impregnation through the Holy Ghost.[50] A particularly poignant statue of the Virgin Mary that was once part of an Annunciation group signals both her surprise and consent (PL. 36). She clutches her veil, slightly bows her head, and pulls her torso away from the angel that likely once stood at right. The lower half of her body, however, conveys her submission to God: her legs are parted, and the V-shaped

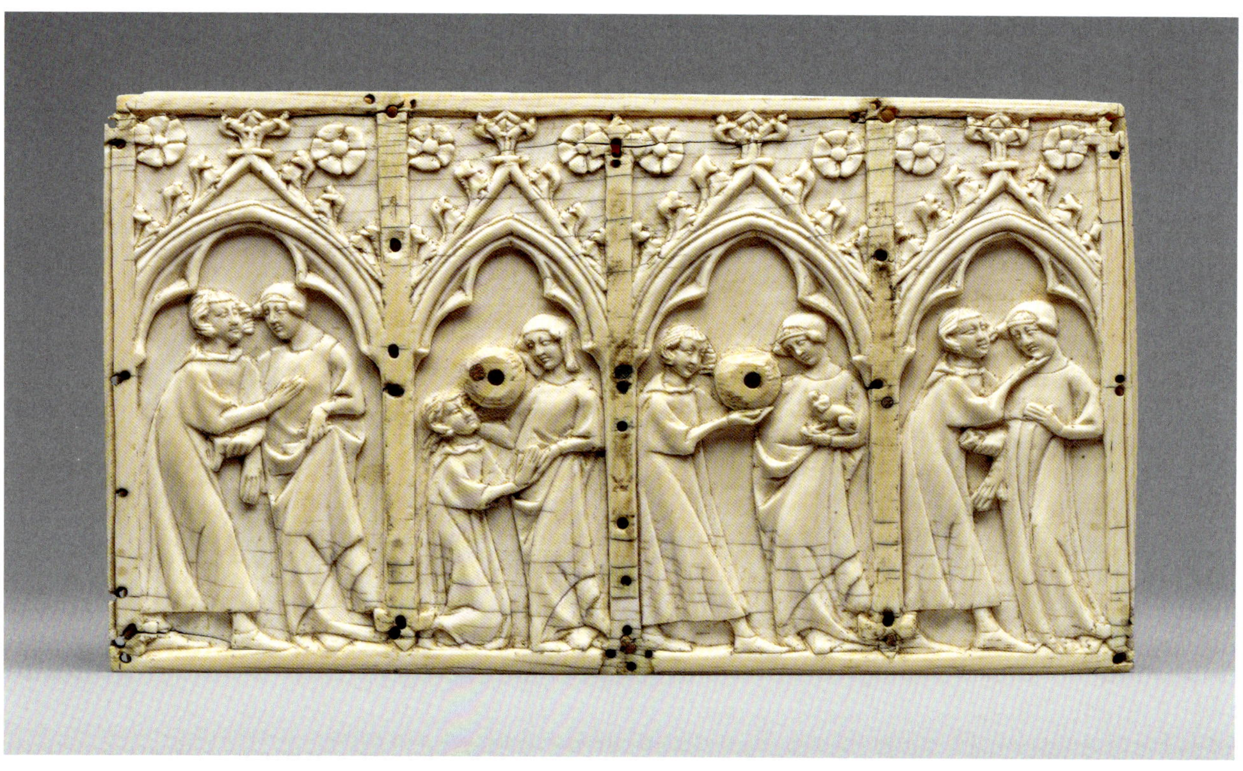

FIG. 24. **Lid of PL. 14 showing flirtatious couples**

Fig. 25. **Left side of PL. 22 showing a meeting of Tristan and Isolde, with her husband King Mark spying overhead and the capture of a unicorn lured by a maiden**

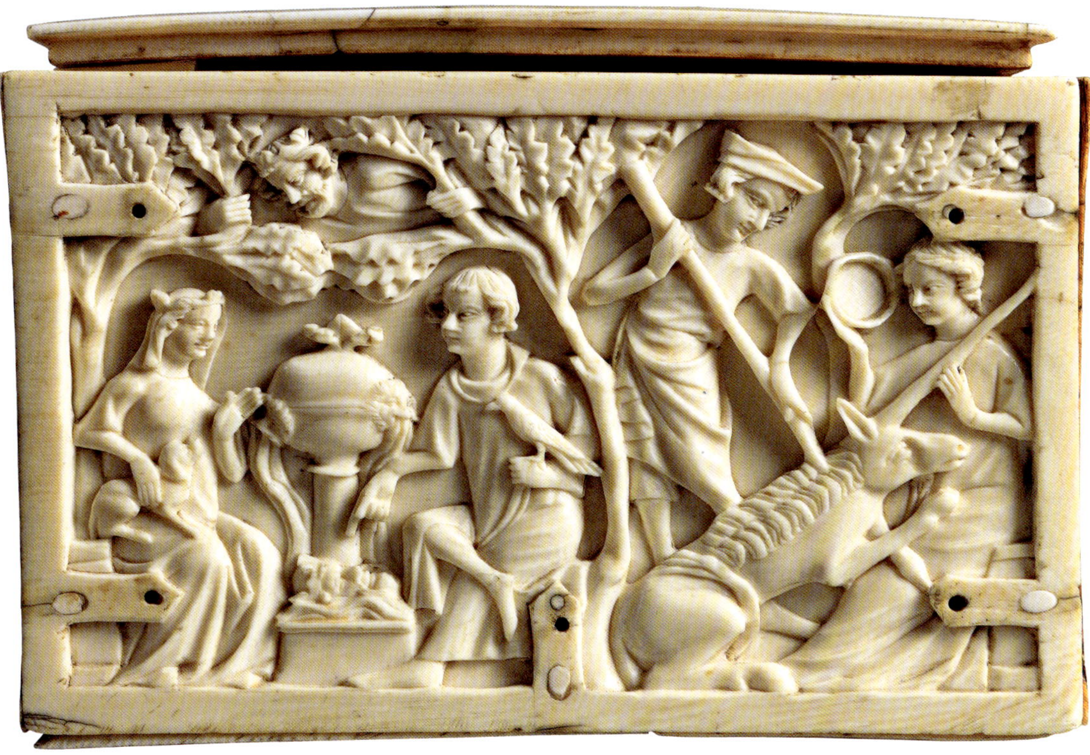

folds of drapery point toward her vagina and womb. The pose and drapery recall contemporaneous images of women on ivory carvings who perform the expressive choreography of courtship. We witness these back-and-forth, sometimes simultaneous gestures of restraint and desire on a number of ivories, including the lid of the Prodigal Son box (FIG. 24). One of the women, who holds a small dog, leans slightly back and directs her gaze downward. Deeply carved folds of fabric gather below her belly, insinuating the forms of her genitalia underneath. The visual language of sex and the desire for union—whether with a courtly lover or God—are remarkably similar.

ON PENETRATION

Medieval people viewed sexual intercourse as an act of penetration, whether expressed metaphorically as a pinprick of the heart or an assault on a fortress. It was a deed performed by one partner upon another, connoting possession of one over the other as much as absorption of one into the other.[51] This fundamental conception of sex informed gender roles, ideas of pleasure, understandings of same-sex erotic behavior, and even the grammar of sexual language. To read the image on an ivory box of a hunter thrusting his lance through a unicorn into the lap of a maiden as a scene of conquest and deflowering is not merely to impose modern, even Freudian sexual symbolism, but rather to see that which was plainly visible to medieval people (FIG. 25). It places the carving within the rich semantic and iconographic spheres of medieval discourse that regularly aligned the active role with men and the passive role with women. Writers and artists sometimes undermined or manipulated the binary logic of penetration, however, in order to heighten, or deliberately unsettle, gender norms.

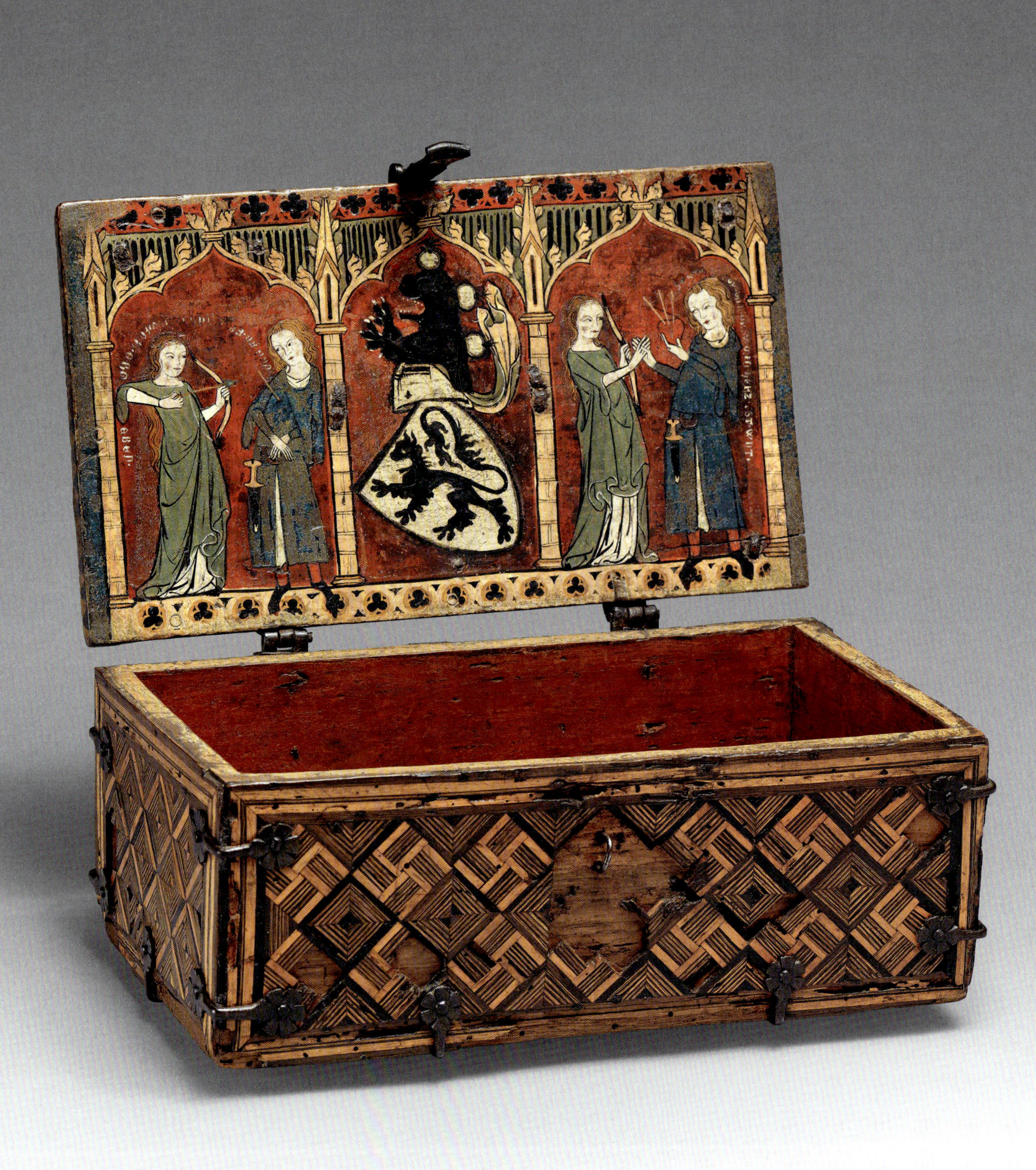

37. **Box with Lady Minne piercing the heart of a man. German, ca. 1325–50. Oak, tempera; wrought-iron mounts**

38. **Amors embracing Amant from the *Roman de la Rose* (*Romance of the Rose*), 1340. Jeanne de Montbaston (possible artist). Opaque watercolor, gold leaf, iron gall ink on parchment**

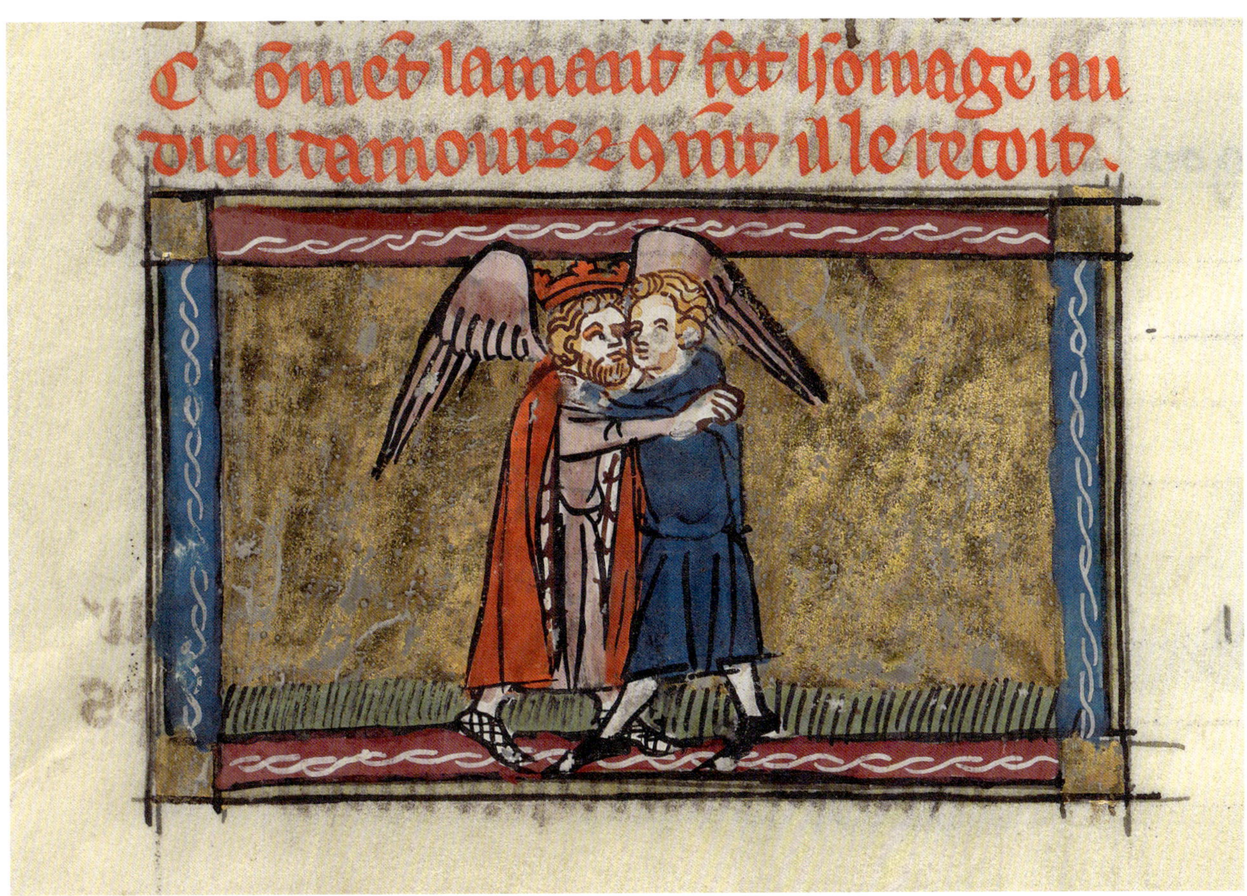

The unicorn vignette offers such an instance. Its imagery relied upon the widespread understanding that hunters could only succeed in capturing and killing a unicorn with the assistance of a virgin, whose purity lured and subdued the elusive beast.[52] The hunter may seem to us the paragon of a male pursuer, but who is his prey: the unicorn, with his priapic horn, or the maiden? The carved scene conveys a succession of penetrations, with the hunter first piercing the unicorn before driving the spear's tip into the lap of the maiden. The unicorn occupies a curious role, simultaneously capable of penetration and vulnerable to it. In the *Bestiary of Love*, the thirteenth-century writer Richard de Fournival compares himself to a unicorn vanquished by Love. Richard calls Love a "clever hunter," who is able to trap him by placing a maiden in his path. Like the unicorn, Richard is drawn to her "sweet smell," and in her lap, he dies the climactic "sort of death that is appropriate to love."[53] The possibility of active and passive positions is a prerogative of the male lover. Medieval codes of sexual behavior rarely allowed the same for women. The maiden remains at the conclusion of the penetrative sequence, her fondling of the horn's shaft an artist's effort to insinuate her willing submission to her limited role.

In other instances, the structure of language itself could allow the suggestive undoing of gender categories. In Germanic and Romance languages, grammatical gender does not need to be an indicator of sex, but medieval artists, when depicting allegorical figures,

39. **The Sponsa wounding Christ from the Rothschild Canticles. French or Belgian, ca. 1300. Opaque watercolor, silver and gold leaf and iron gall ink on parchment**

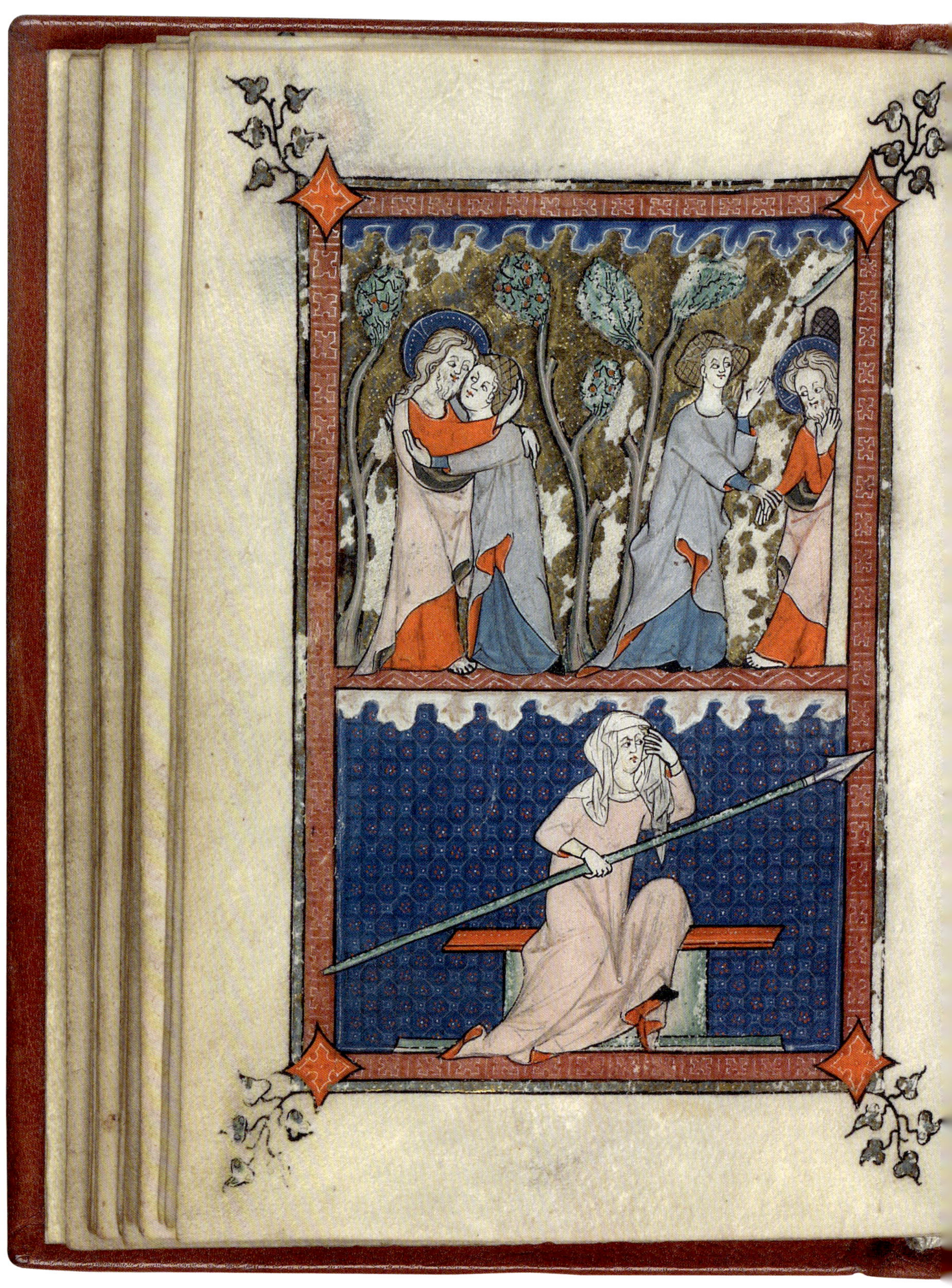

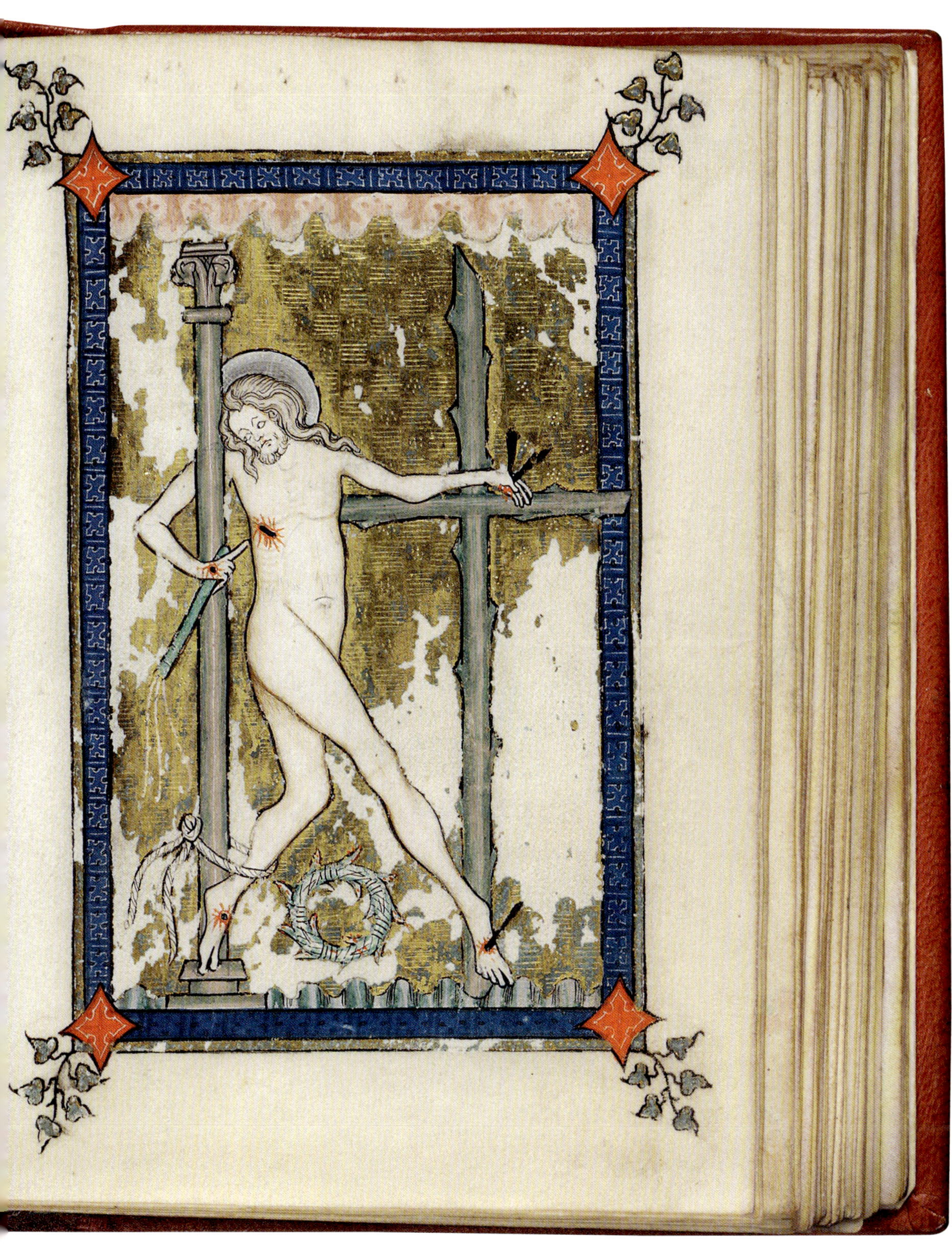

often made it so. In the German tradition, the deity of love assumed a feminine form in accordance with the grammatical gender of the word *Minne*. On a fourteenth-century painted box, Frau Minne (Lady Love) thus takes on the role of hunter, bending the bow that will propel her barbed arrows into a man's heart (PL. 37). Medieval French, however, gendered Amors, Love's personification, as male, following in the Roman tradition of Cupid. Amors's gender thus created an opening for homoerotic play within the dreamscape of the Old French story the *Roman de la Rose* (*Romance of the Rose*), otherwise dedicated to one man's quest to seduce a woman. Early in the thirteenth-century tale, the unnamed lover, whom scholars refer to as Amant, acknowledges that he can no longer resist the compulsion to seek the object of his desire. He then willfully surrenders to Amors's arrows, announcing, "I became his man." Amors rewards Amant for submitting to his fate by allowing him to kiss him on the mouth (PL. 38).[54]

Pain was a defining feature of penetration, the proof that it had occurred and the measure of its intensity. Amant in the *Roman de la Rose* barely has time to recover from one of Amors's arrows before another strikes. He falls, faints, wails, and sighs as arrows pierce his eyes and then his heart. He laments that there is "no hope of cure or relief." After an assault of five arrows, the points of which cannot be dislodged from the body, Love completely possesses Amant, who, in his wounded condition, is compelled to pursue the woman (represented by the rose). Only in uniting with her will he relieve his suffering.[55]

The concept that love hurts is a courtly notion from the Middle Ages that has retained its potency well into our era. Less familiar is the medieval idea that the language of pain, union, and eroticism could be a powerful expression of Christian religious experience.[56] Many Christian writers spoke of Christ as a kind of Cupid. An eleventh-century tract described Christ as "the arrow, the spear, the javelin of love that pierces... the petitioner's heart."[57] The twelfth century's great spiritual writer and monk Bernard of Clairvaux declared, "I would reckon myself happy if... I felt... the prick of the point of [Christ's] sword... I could say 'I am wounded with love.'"[58] The fourteenth-century Dominican chaplain Friedrich Sunder "desired to be pierced by the divine arrow of love, so that his heart would be... wounded."[59] Just as in courtly romance, love and pain go hand in hand.

The Rothschild Canticles makes use of a double-page opening to invite its monastic reader to imagine and contemplate a kind of spiritual penetration, in which a woman instigates the active role (PL. 39). On the lower half of the left page, a veiled woman directs her lance toward the naked body of Christ, pictured on the opposite page. With one leg extended behind her, the other stepping forward, she rises from her bench to lunge toward him, a Lady Minne with Christian intent. He awaits the thrusting weapon, meeting her eyes across the pages' gutter and pointing his finger to her target, the side wound he suffered from the Crucifixion and which spiritual leaders like Bonaventure described as the gateway to his heart.[60]

The losses in the patterned gold leaf that once covered the background of the right-hand miniature should not detract from the spectacle of splendid corporality that it portrays. Far from the bloodied, broken body that will appear in later medieval Passion imagery, this painting shows Christ as a lithe and perfect specimen. James Schultz may be right in noting that the conventions of romance literature do not permit noble bodies to be depicted naked. Nonetheless, Christ's contorted pose shows off the slender physique and shapely legs that courtly poets such as Wolfram von Eschenbach and Gottfried von Strassburg ascribed to young male aristocrats.[61] His notably white skin exemplifies the radiant ivory complexion that these writers praised as a feature of courtly beauty.[62]

The erotic tension of this pair of paintings fully accords with the biblical text to which they refer. They illustrate a verse (4:9) from the Song of Songs, appearing on the preceding page: "Thou hast wounded my heart, my sister, my spouse." A series of poems that celebrates the mystery and power of sexual love, the Song of Songs serves as an essential reference for the Rothschild Canticles, as it does for so many other mystical guides.[63] But the Rothschild Canticles stands out within this interpretive tradition for its complete

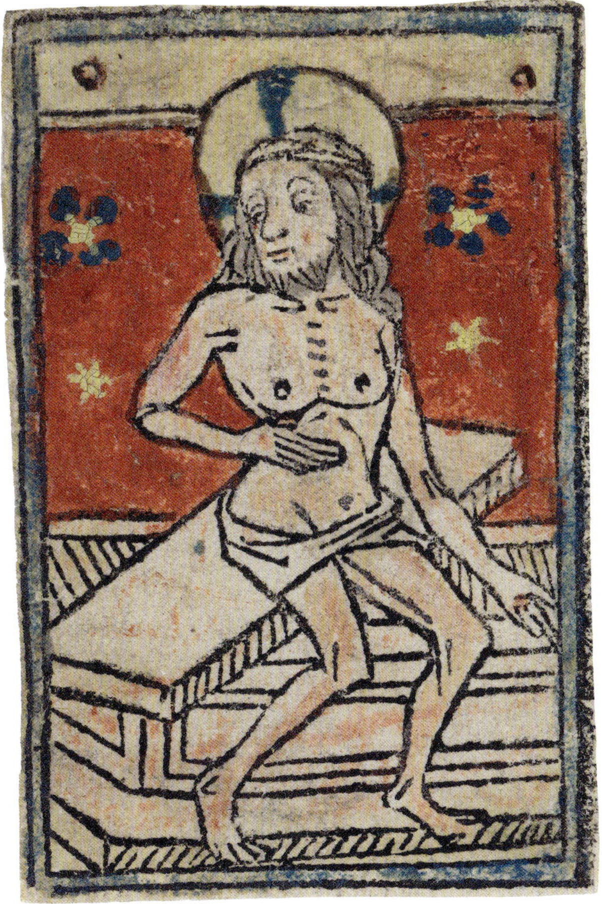

40. **Seated Man of Sorrows, showing his side wound. German, 15th century. Black printing ink with opaque watercolor on paper**

integration of visual images, which translated the heady ideas of the biblical text into a somatic experience for the manuscript's reader.

"Let him kiss me with the kiss of his mouth," begins the first Song. For a religion that directed its formidable legal and theological apparatus to the regulation and censure of sexual intercourse, the attention given by medieval exegetes (textual interpreters) to such highly eroticized poetry—no book of the Bible inspired more commentaries—might seem surprising.[64] Far from condemning its sensual language, these Christian thinkers used the text as the foundation for an elaborate allegorical architecture that accommodated multiple ideas of consummation. The passionate love professed by the poem's protagonists, the groom (*sponsus*) and bride (*sponsa*), was likened to the love between Christ and his Church, between Christ and Mary, and between Christ and the human soul. These various couplings were not mutually exclusive but built upon one another to affirm the bridal model as a means of achieving mystical ecstasy for men and women.

Jeffrey Hamburger has described the lavishly illustrated Rothschild Canticles as "an instrument [to initiate] its reader into transcendent mysteries."[65] Through an ordered sequence of images and texts, this hand-size devotional book was designed to transport its beholder to an ineffable realm, its pages urging her to identify with the bride depicted throughout. She is the reader and the soul. Her wounding of Christ launches a romance that transpires across several pages. The sequence of scenes draws from the Song of Songs, portraying the pursuit, withdrawal, and reconciliation that constitute the pulse of desire and represent the transformational journey of the soul itself. Christ and the soul play a game of hide-and-seek that culminates in her ecstatic surrender to him, the bridegroom, the Godhead. In no way suppressing feelings of sexual desire, the images encourage them, serving as an irresistible invitation to, and an indelible enactment of, a fully embodied spiritual experience.

The Rothschild Canticles spoke to a yearning that many medieval Christians, both cloistered and lay, felt for a deepening of religious experience. A focus on the site of penetration offered another way to satisfy those longings. Many small-scale devotional objects, made in an array of media, feature the near-naked Christ posed to draw attention to his side wound (FIG. 40). Others eschew the corporeal context and home in on the wound itself.[66] In a lavish prayer book for Bonne of Luxembourg, a Bohemian princess who married a member of the French royal family, one such image sits amid a lengthy meditation on the wound (SEE PL. 1).[67] Its lush depiction, achieved by dense and deft layering of paint, encourages visual and metaphorical absorption:

41. **Man of Sorrows, with a monk and flagellant.**
Italian, last quarter of the 14th century.
Champlevé enamel, gilded copper

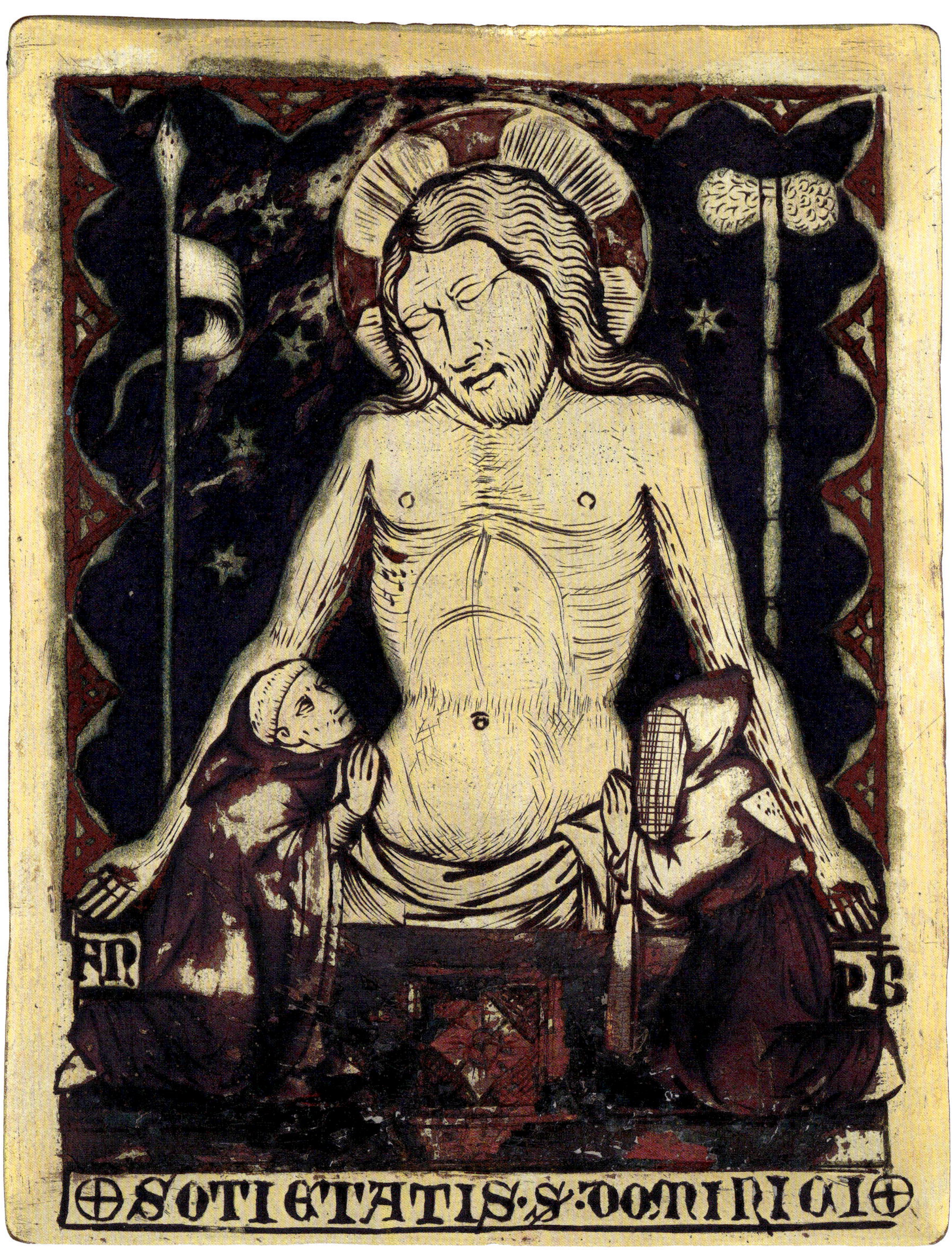

its colors grow darker and more concentrated as the eye is drawn into its center. At once fleshy and jewel-like, the image calls on tactile and visual modes of perception, further strengthening the bodily connection it was designed to forge. A caption indicates that the wound is in fact life-size.

Medieval devotion to the wound furthered the well-established association between pain and penetration, suffering and love. It is in this tradition that a member of a flagellant sect had himself pictured in prayer before the wounded Christ (PL. 41). The voluptuous lesion in the Bonne of Luxembourg manuscript is set against the sharp-edged instruments of Christ's passion and torture. These evocations of violence were meant to intensify, even eroticize, her meditative experience. Female mystics especially were encouraged to kiss, touch, drink from, enter, and be absorbed into the wound. As the work of Karma Lochrie and Martha Easton reminds us, it was the queerest of devotional prompts. Not only was its form explicitly vaginal but its symbolic properties also included the "bleeding, lactating and birthing functions associated with the female body."[68] To concentrate on two inches of Christ's damaged flesh was to unleash the spiritual imagination, to destabilize the very categories of gender and sexuality that undergird bridal mysticism, and to widen the understanding and experience of union.

MYSTICAL SEXUALITY

In a 1981 interview for the French magazine *Le Gai Pied*, Michel Foucault wondered aloud how homosexuality could open up a "multiplicity of relationships" that move beyond the "two readymade formulas of the pure sexual encounter and the lovers' fusion of identities."[69] For him, the gay movement was not about liberating one's desires, but rather "to make ourselves infinitely more susceptible to pleasure (*plaisirs*)."[70] Medieval mysticism, particularly within the context of cloistered life, permitted an imaginative rethinking of relational systems. It bypassed conventional lines of kinship and undermined legalistic understandings of consanguinity (blood relations) and inheritance. Marriage and family were reorganized and celebrated in new forms, and works of art stood at the center of this practice.

A dreamy, technicolor statue of Christ as a child offered a powerful point of meditative focus and encouraged multiform affective relationships with him (PL. 42).[71] The vivid paint, almost all of which is original, discloses the artist's desire to create a figure at once living and otherworldly, human and divine. His deeply flushed cheeks, rosy bottom, rounded belly, folds of flesh, pencil-thin eyebrows, and luscious head of curly, gilded hair resist a singular interpretation. Christ is at once a friendly tyke and a coquettish bridegroom, who stands in a confident pose and holds an apple, perhaps offering it to the viewer.[72] Even his genitals, pink and plainly on view, may have called attention to this duality. Schultz has noted the range of connotations that male genitalia—even that of a baby—imparted in medieval literature. In the case of the Arthurian hero Perceval, for instance, there is much ado about his penis shortly after he is born: on one occasion, his penis is a sign of "manly valor," and in another, it is a "penis of love" that communicates his future as a bridegroom and lover.[73] In the case of the sculpture of the infant Christ, his genitals, too, could telegraph his dual nature as child and future bridegroom.

The statue was likely owned by a nun, and it may have fostered visionary experiences of mystical union, maternal and marital, with Christ. Nuns identified with the Virgin Mary as Christ's mother and, after her assumption to heaven, his bride. Accounts of the nuns' visions of the youthful Christ—sometimes recorded in their own words—relate how such sculptures could self-animate and interact with them. In her auto-hagiography, the Dominican nun Margaretha Ebner (1291–1351) recalls how she received at the age of fifty-three a small statue of the young Jesus and a little bed for him from a friend in Vienna.[74] Not infrequently, the statue comes to life. Margaretha chastises him when he makes too much noise ("Why won't you be good and let me sleep? This certainly isn't how I ought to bring you up!"), and he demands to be fed ("If you don't give me to suckle, then I will take myself away at the moment you love me most").[75] Her account describes the infant Christ as unabashedly cheeky,

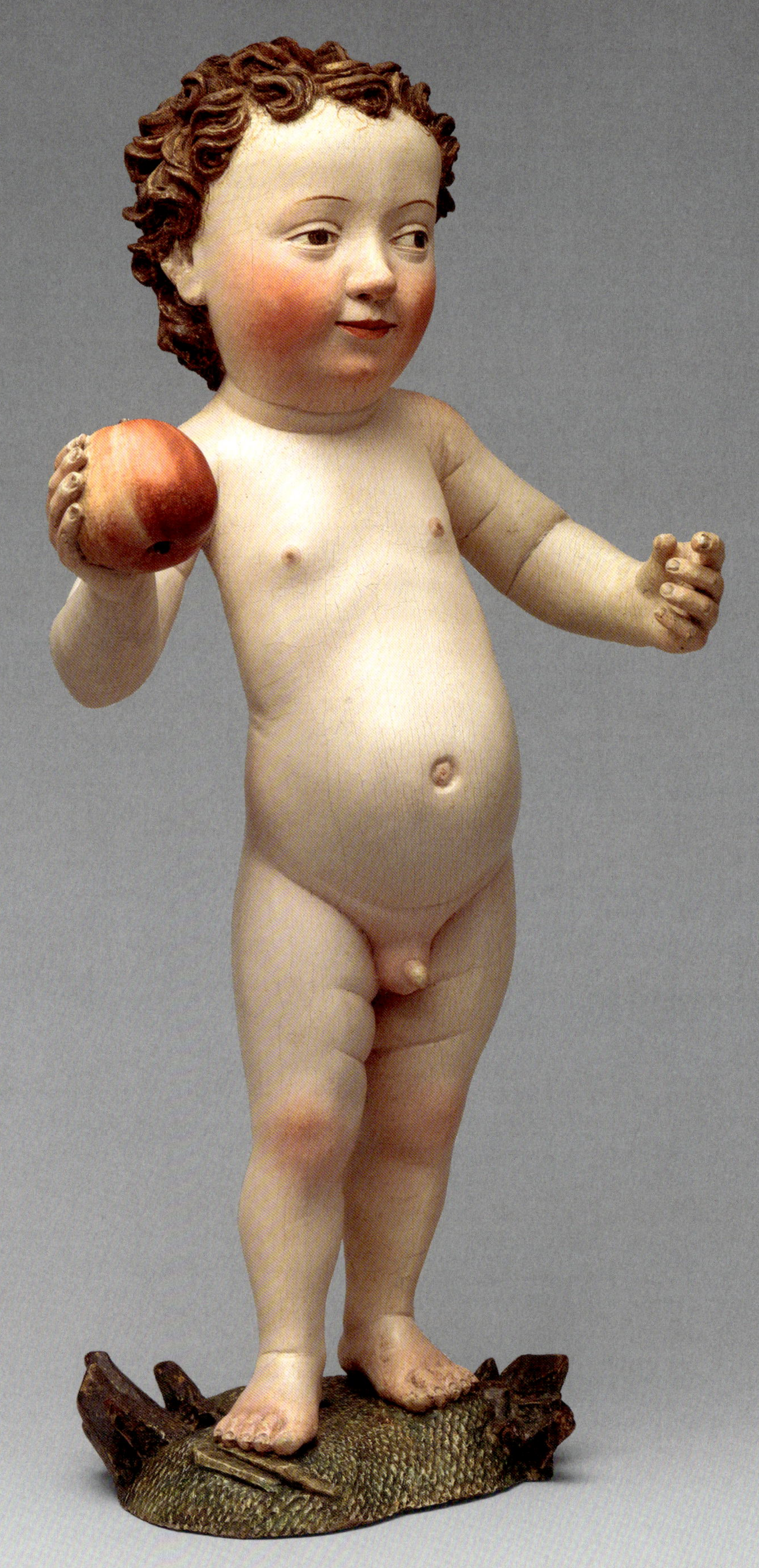

42. **Christ Child with an apple, ca. 1470–80. Circle of Michel Erhart. Willow with paint and gold**

possessing a demeanor that the artist of The Cloisters sculpture effectively evokes.

In other instances, maternal care is seemingly sidestepped, and Christ's beauty takes center stage. A fourteenth-century text recounts that the nun Gertrud von Herkenheim opened the monastery gate and saw "a most beautiful child, exceedingly handsome and comely, standing alone at the door. She looked at him closely [and] was most delighted in admiring his great beauty."[76] Gertrud is one of several nuns who admire Jesus as if he were a young lover.[77] Others are encouraged to move beyond looking and toward physical embrace. In the devotional text *Von Ihesus pettlein* (*On the Little Bed of Jesus*), a male pastor exhorts nuns to take Christ in their arms and "press him lovingly to you and kiss his sweet, rosy lips."[78] For some, these erotic encounters with the young Christ curbed more carnal desires.[79]

In at least one instance, the sculpture of the Christ child inspired parental tenderness and spousal desire for a male viewer. The medieval biography of Friedrich Sunder, the chaplain at the Dominican convent of Engelthal, describes how he experienced a powerful vision in which the infant Christ told him to "give me your right breast, so that I can suckle and be spiritually fed by it."[80] In another of Friedrich's visions, Jesus asks Mary to make a "joyous bed for me and my beloved spouse, [in] which I and my beloved bride can take our pleasure with each other."[81] The spouse here is Friedrich: he (or his soul) and the infant Christ unite in a bed prepared by Mary. Gender has seamlessly shifted in order to fit the marital model. In this bed, the two "had such loving joy and pleasure with one another of embraces and kisses with laughter with all divine pleasure."[82] As Andrea Pearson has shown, the eroticization of the Christ child in texts and images of mystical communion prompted some unease then, and even now.[83] This discomfort has prevented, at times, a recognition of the complex sensuality ascribed to the Christ child in the late Middle Ages, and in which The Cloisters statue likely took part.[84]

Among the configurations of bride and groom that medieval mystics and mystical thinkers imagined, perhaps none stretched gender and sexual identities more than the relationship between Jesus and his beloved disciple John, which was sometimes described in explicitly nuptial terms. A painted and gilded wood sculpture, now in the Cleveland Museum of Art, of John sleeping on Jesus's breast, is one of the finest of twenty-eight such sculptures—most in wood—that celebrate the theme (PL. 43).[85] The works are unique to the Upper Rhine/Lake Constance region (Swabia) of southwestern Germany, where numerous surviving illuminated manuscripts and devotional handbooks attest to the distinctive veneration of John, particularly within Cistercian and Dominican convents.[86]

The sculptor of the Cleveland work took pains to emphasize intimacy and tenderness. The figures mimic the standard pose of marriage, with the joining of right hands and Christ's protective reach around John's shoulder. Their serene facial expressions and the gentle points of contact between them give the impression that they share an easy trust. Still, Christ's greater stature, implied by the dimensions of his head, shoulders, and lap, conveys his superior role as John's mentor and elder, a notion further underscored by the contrast between their bearded and smooth-skinned faces. The rich gilding that once covered the mantles of both figures contributed to their allure. Combining the commanding power of one figure's direct address with the other's inviting passivity, the pairing encourages prolonged looking. Details large and small enticed viewers to contemplate Christ and John's polysemous, often paradoxical, and decidedly queer bond and to strive for its emulation.

John was widely revered in the Middle Ages as the writer of the Gospel that bears his name as well as of the Book of Revelation. He was the apostle whom the Bible claimed Jesus loved most and the one to whom he entrusted the care of Mary at the Crucifixion.[87] But for those who looked to John as an ideal mystic, two narratives in particular provided the biblical footings for his chosen status as Christ's bride. Both informed the sculpture's distinctive iconography and lent themselves to sexualized interpretations to underscore their extraordinary import.[88] The first was the Last Supper, during which John was said to have leaned upon Jesus's bosom, a crucial detail in the sculpture

43. **Christ and Saint John the Evangelist, the beloved disciple. German, 1300–20. Oak with paint and gold**

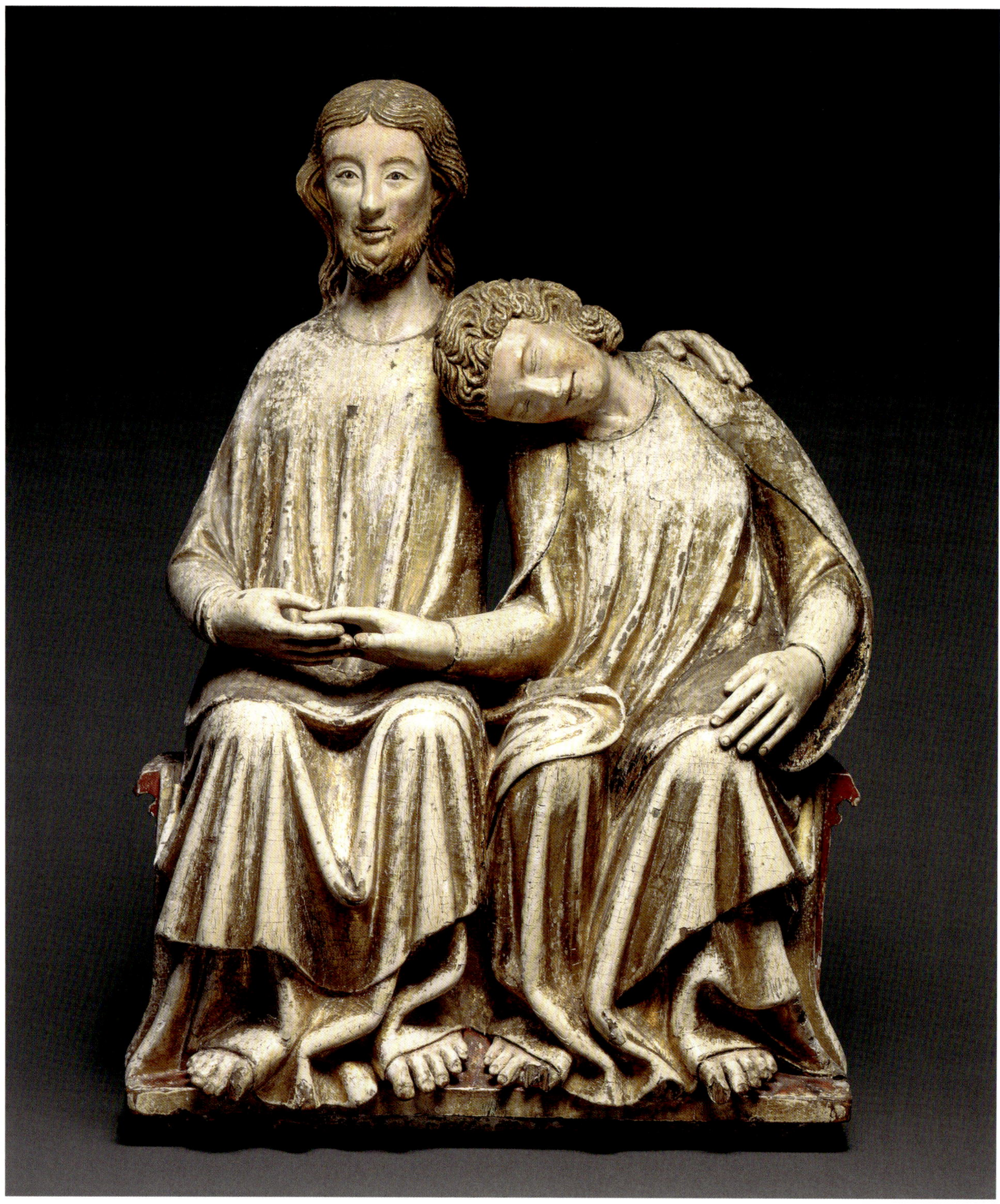

and one that early Christian and medieval interpreters seized upon as a moment of mystical rapture, linking it to the Song of Songs. They read the gesture as a form of intimacy reserved for lovers: the apostle metaphorically lay with Jesus. They also saw it as a moment of epiphany, with John "drinking" directly from Jesus's heart, a reference to the sultry line spoken by the Song's *sponsa* (1:1): "your breasts are better than wine." Through spiritual intercourse—some said he had indeed entered the Godhead at this moment—John received the theological wisdom that allowed him to write his Gospel.[89]

The second story explicitly spoke of nuptials. Popular legends beginning in late antiquity identified John as the anonymous bridegroom mentioned in the Gospel account of the wedding at Cana, where Jesus miraculously transformed water into wine. In these legends, John abandons his earthly bride at the altar in favor of a spiritual marriage to Jesus. A full-page painting in a Rhenish manuscript intended for the pastoral care of nuns feminizes him through a profusion of pattern and color, portraying John as a veritable queen with a glorious mane of golden locks and a flowery bridal chaplet (FIG. 26). In leaving a woman for a man (could God be anything other?), John assumed the role of bride, submitting to the binary logic of medieval wedlock. The Cleveland sculpture captures John's newly submissive state through pose and physical appearance.

We are witness here to an historically specific form of compartmentalization. No medieval theologian or pastoral leader understood these stories as condoning same-sex marriage or sexual relations between men, yet many extolled Jesus and John's relationship, with its rich nuptial and sexual dimensions, as the epitome of spiritual union.[90] Their bond was not sodomitical, to use their term, but it was queer, to use ours, in that it operated outside of normative relational models. For medieval thinkers, there was no more effective way to evoke the rare and intoxicatingly beautiful epiphany that they sought. The Jesus-John bond certainly reinscribed the gendered power dynamics of medieval marital and religious experience, but it also promoted unpredictable gender identities and fluid forms of kin-

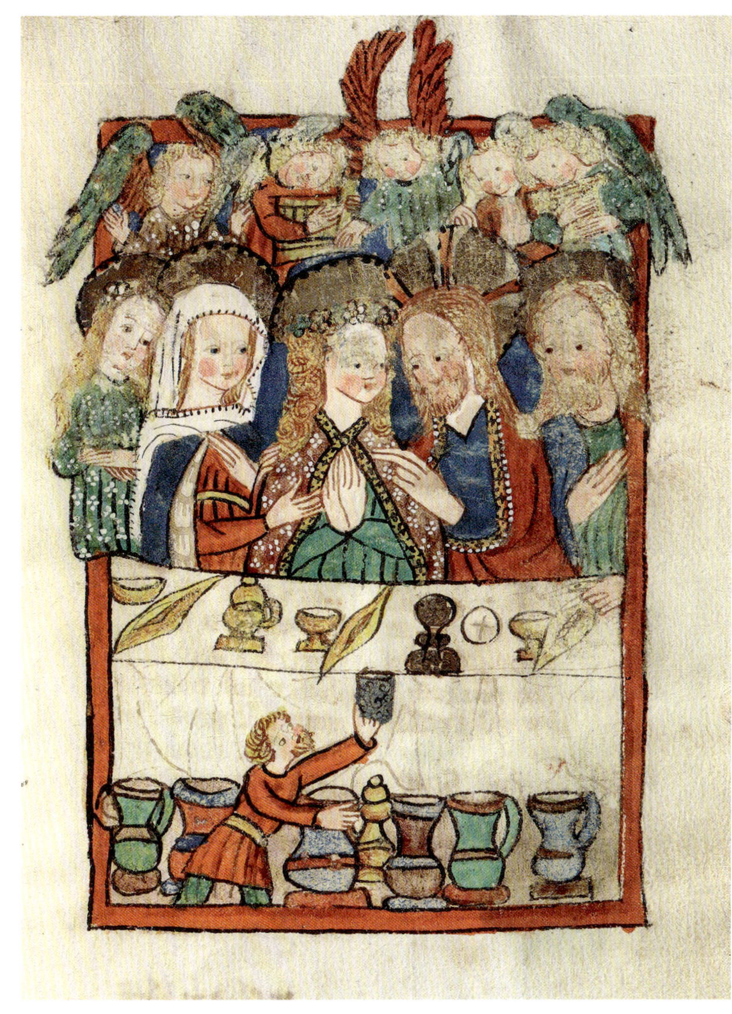

Fig. 26. **Marriage of Christ and John the Evangelist at the Wedding of Cana from the Libellus of John the Evangelist. Upper Rhenish, before 1493. Opaque watercolor, silver and gold leaf, iron gall ink, 8 ⅛ × 5 5⁄16 in. (20.5 × 13.5 cm). University Library, Basel (MS A VI 38, fol. 4r)**

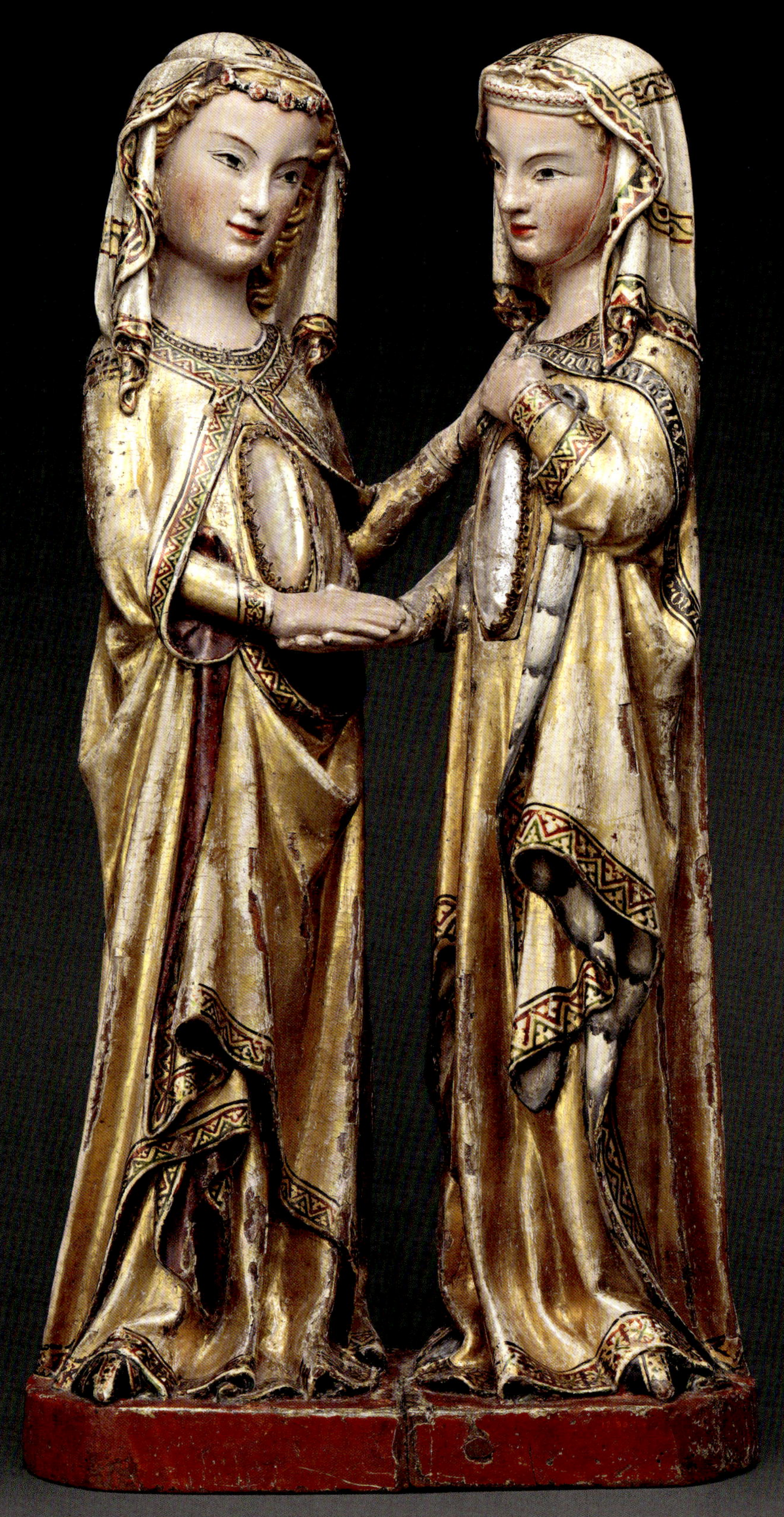

44. The Visitation, ca. 1310–20. Attributed to Master Heinrich of Constance. Walnut with paint, gold, and rock-crystal cabochons inset in gilded silver mounts

ship that empowered both men and women in their spiritual, and presumably identificatory, quests.

The interpretation of Jesus and John as marital partners did not prevent some medieval Christians from also describing John as Jesus's brother. In that siblings were understood to share flesh and blood, this kinship offered another mode of conjuring the idea of physical communion.[91] So complete was the melding of Jesus and John that the latter achieved a deified state. In certain contexts, John could even substitute for Jesus. Bride, brother, friend, the Man himself. That John could occupy all of these roles helps us understand why he above all others embodied the contemplative life and exemplified mystical ecstasy. The special devotion that many nuns had for John, one could argue, stemmed in part from the creative possibilities his person and his relationship with Jesus opened up for them as gendered and sexualized subjects. When Mechthild von Magdeburg (ca. 1208–ca. 1282/1290) had a vision in which she slept with John "in heart-felt love on the bosom of Jesus Christ," she imagined a threesome of soaring delights, both directed by and unbound from limiting medieval constructions of the body: "I saw and perceived such wonderful marvels there that my body frequently became separated from my self."[92]

John's multivalent role also helps to explain the power of images that attempted to capture the extraordinary convergence of what might seem contradictory affinities. We know that the Dominican nuns in the Katharinenthal convent praised the beauty of a sculpture they owned that was similar to the Cleveland statue and also that one of the sisters, Adelhait Pfefferhartin, was so overcome when praying before it that light streamed from her body and she floated above the ground.[93] Anne von Ramsvag, another nun from Katharinenthal, glowed "like a crystal" as she regarded the sculpture, while her fellow contemplative Mechthild von Eschenz became "as clear as crystal, so that [a companion] saw straight through her" as she turned away from it.[94]

If such sculptures allowed religious women to be absorbed into new relations with the divine, they likely also enriched the women's relationships with each other. A statue of the Visitation also from Katharinenthal and made by the same workshop that created their own Jesus and John sculpture, enshrines female-centric care, sisterhood, and maternity (PL. 44).[95] Mary and her cousin Elizabeth join their right hands in a gesture resonant of betrothal, and their left hands meet at Mary's heart. This is the moment when they exchange the news of their respective pregnancies: Mary will give birth to Christ, and Elizabeth will give birth to John the Baptist. Their similar countenances, matching attire, and shared manifestations of their pregnancy further indicate their bond.[96] Mary and Elizabeth were put forth as exemplars for nuns as brides, mothers, and instead more. The statue's quiet allusion to the marital bond ultimately disrupts it, offering up homosocial community, spiritual kinship, and even potentially homoerotic desire as a point of reference.[97] As such, it worked in tandem with the Christ and John sculpture to offer thrilling alternatives to the normative bonds available to them outside the convent.

As Jacqueline Jung has noted, the Visitation sculpture seems to have a ready analogue in the writings of the aforementioned mystic Mechthild von Magdeburg. Though describing the joining of soul and bridegroom, Mechthild captures the sweet synergy expressed in the sculpture:

> eye gleams into eye,
> and there spirit flows into spirit,
> and there hand grasps hand,
> and there mouth speaks to mouth,
> and there heart greets heart.[98]

Mechthild died shortly before the Visitation group was made, but the sculpture and text emerge from a time and context that allowed feminine desire and sexuality to shape notions of erotic union, at once amplifying, confounding, and reimagining its terms. For the nuns at Katharinenthal, their bodies reverberating with pleasure, works of art proved conducive to express physical and spiritual ecstasy. Sarah Salih has rightly claimed that devotional love spawned "some of the most exciting and powerful...erotic texts" of the Middle Ages.[99] One could say the same about medieval images, if we are open to the vision of eroticism that they construct.

TOUCHING SAINT SEBASTIAN

KARL WHITTINGTON

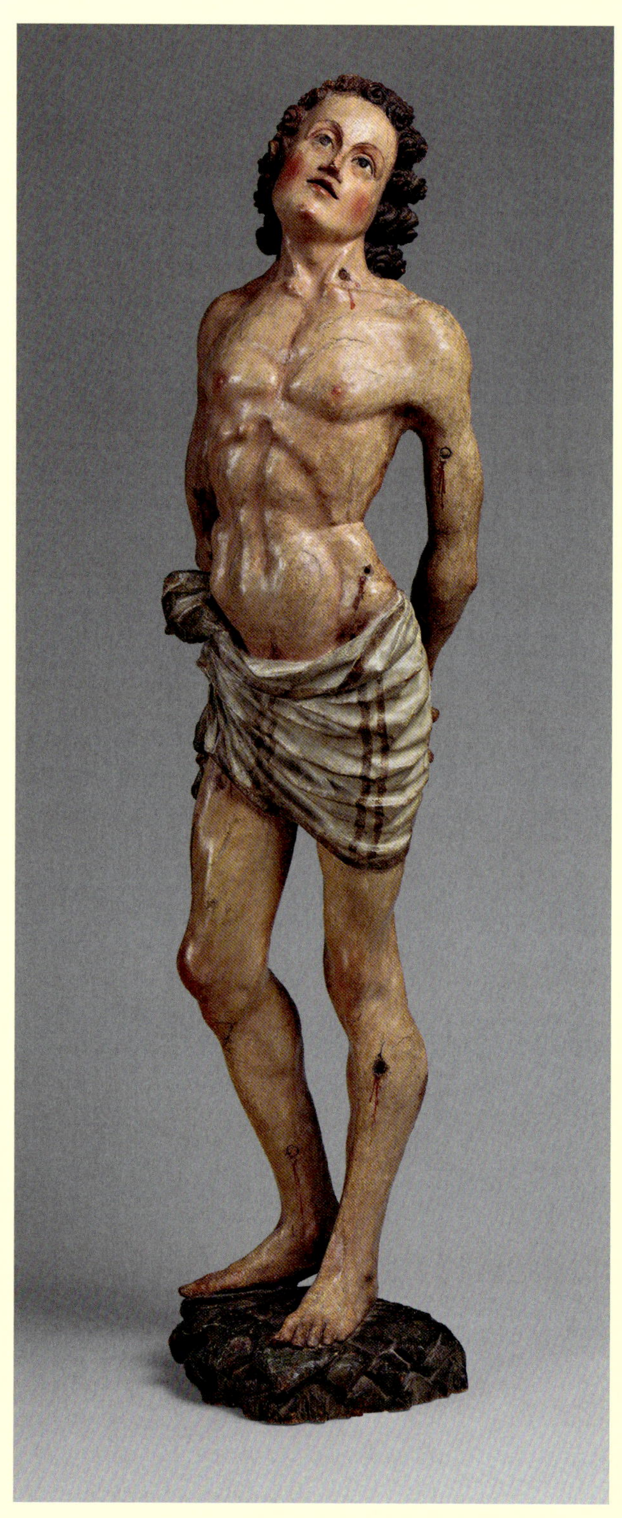

45. Saint Sebastian. Austrian(?), late 15th century. European poplar with paint and gold

SAINT SEBASTIAN HAS BECOME A CONTEMPORARY gay icon, a popular emblem of queer beauty and erotic vulnerability. His story began as that of a Christian martyr who was clubbed to death during the persecutions of Diocletian in the third century after surviving an assault with arrows, and the earliest representations of him in the visual arts contain few hints of what his image would ultimately become. The history of how this remarkable transformation from mainstream Catholic saint to LGBTQ symbol took place, has begun to be told by scholars, who point to the saint's connection to illness and suffering (which found renewed meaning for queer viewers during the AIDS Crisis), the opportunities his representation presented for depictions of the male nude, and the harnessing of his image by a century of queer modern artists.[1]

Central to this history is Sebastian's seduction of his viewers through works of art, a power in beauty that artists embraced and the Church approved, though not without reservations. This erotic reception of Sebastian is communicated most famously by Giorgio Vasari, who reported in the sixteenth century that a particularly beautiful and lifelike painting of Saint Sebastian by Fra Bartolommeo had to be removed from a church because its allure was causing women to "sin at the sight of it" (interestingly, Vasari tells us that it was removed to the chapter-house, where it would only have been seen by monks).[2]

Paintings of the nearly nude Sebastian by artists such as Bartolommeo, Giovanni Antonio Bazzi (often called Il Sodoma), Perugino, Mantegna, and Guido Reni created a canon of works that emphasize Sebastian's beauty and vulnerability, favorites of both modern and premodern viewers. Scholars argue that as Sebastian's popularity as a saint associated with plague and healing grew, it became more important to show the triumph and imperviousness of his body, palpably present before the viewer in works of art.[3] And the saint's isolation in these works, typically depicted without his torturers, allowed viewers unimpeded access to his body.[4]

But sight was not the only sense through which medieval and early modern people engaged with the saint. The polychrome wood Sebastian in The Met, believed to have been sculpted in the Tyrol (a region in the eastern Alps in modern-day Italy and Austria) in the years just before 1500, provides an opportunity to think about the artwork not only through the viewer's gaze but also through the artist's touch (PL. 45). Carved from a single poplar trunk, the work is typical of the saint's representation in some ways and unusual in others. As in many depictions, Sebastian is here rendered nearly nude, with a slender, youthful body. His bare chest is thrust forward and the cloth wrapped around his groin slips down as far as possible, revealing a delicately painted trail of body hair, part of the statue's original polychromy. His vulnerability is emphasized by the placement of his hands behind his back. The wrists were likely once tied with an actual rope, perhaps to a sculpted tree trunk whose outline we see at the back of the statue's base. His head leans far back, yielding to the torture and tilting upward toward God. The face is more conventional when viewed from below at an angle, appearing courtly and androgynous; from closer range, however, the paint on the face, which is original, appears almost like drag makeup, with exaggerated orange-red cheeks, pink eyelids, and sweeping dark brows (FIG. 27).[5]

The sculptor has seized the opportunity to do something that painters could not: create a striking dissonance between the front and back of the saint's body.[6] While his front conforms to at least some of the standards of Sebastian's typical submissive beauty, the back of the sculpture emphasizes emaciation, contortion, and suffering (FIG. 28). With skin stretched across prominent bones, shoulder blades bulging and a deep crease down the spine, the figure more resembles Christ's tormented, broken body in many late-medieval crucifixes than the calm heroic bodies popular in Italian Renaissance depictions of Sebastian. The conventional beauty of the statue's front would also have been disrupted by the arrows that originally pierced the body; now broken off, the remains of these arrows can be seen on the figure's front and back in the lower leg, groin, biceps, neck, and chest. Sticking out in all directions and encasing the statue in a frenzy of lines, the arrows would likely have tamed the work's eroticism for many viewers, shifting the balance toward suffering, foregrounded as well by the painted blood that drips from the wounds.

These dissonant effects, details both soft and hard, eroticized and violent, emerged through the touch of the artist's hands and tools. Like other large wood sculptures in the late-medieval and early modern periods, this work would have been created with the figure stretched out horizontally, probably clamped to a workbench to keep the wood still so that it could withstand the pressure of the tools. The artist would thus hover over the work, rather than in front of it, asserting the pressure of their body on the material. As the chisel cut, the artist's hand would rest on the statue's emergent form, their body bracing against that of Sebastian. The acts of smoothing and polishing the statue in preparation for a layer of paint would have begun with firm strokes of abrasive tools and ended with gentler caressing by the artist. Their touch would be mirrored in later years by handling of the statue when it was cleaned, moved, or restored. Such a wide range of artisanal nearness can be read in many ways. We can see how the artist had a kind of physical access to the statue that viewers could only imagine. For sculptors trained primarily in the creation of draped bodies, this could have been a charged experience, either uncomfortable or exciting.[7] Alternatively, however, the artist could envision themselves as the saint's torturer. Just as the saint was clubbed to death by his torturers,

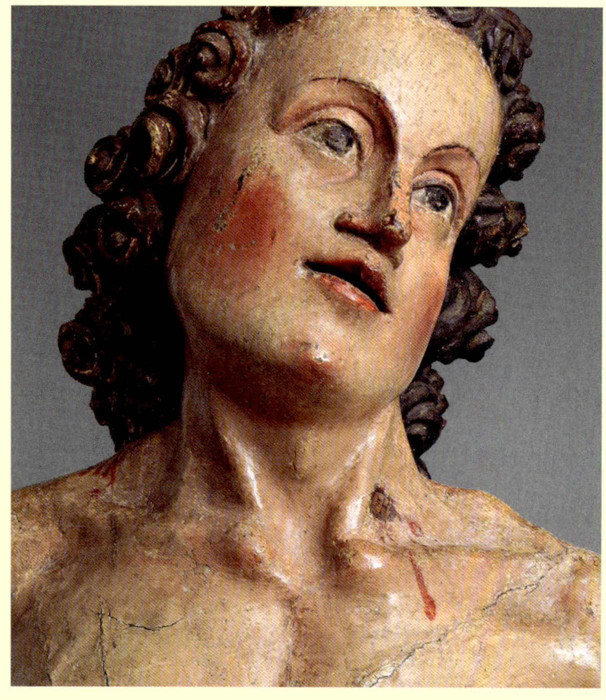

Fig. 27. **Detail of PL. 45**

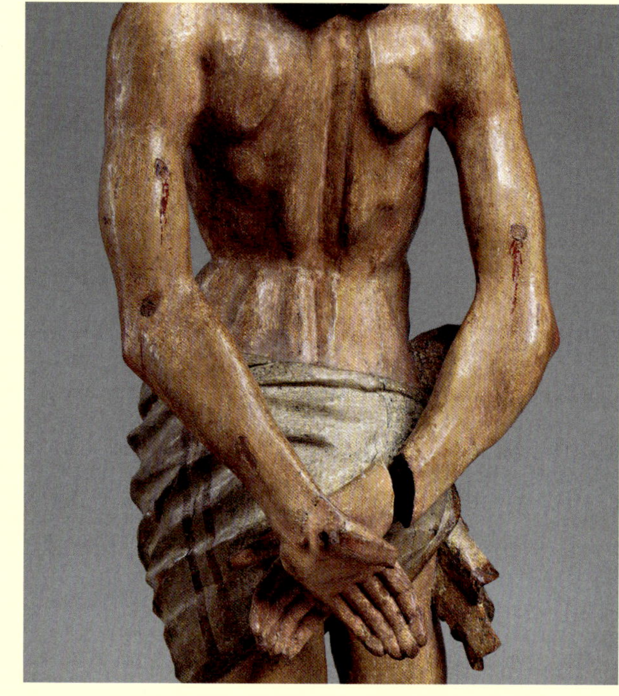

Fig. 28. **Back of PL. 45**

so too the artist struck the body with thousands of blows; just as he was shot with arrows, the artist bored into his body with a drill and thrust carved arrows into the resulting holes. Placing oneself in the role of a torturer of Christ or a saint was a popular devotional exercise in fifteenth-century Europe, one that the artist of this work came to enact far more literally.

Where does queer desire enter this picture, if at all? It is difficult to say. While many depictions of Saint Sebastian in art conform to a more conventional type of male homoeroticism, their smooth, muscular bodies and passive expressions offering little challenge to a viewer's desiring gaze, this Sebastian is queerer and more disruptive. Foregrounding awkward pain as much as yielding pleasure, the artist's choices and touch render the figure enigmatic (much like an artwork that others have argued is similarly queer, Donatello's bronze *David*). We know nothing of the work's artists or original viewers and their own specific desires or reactions. But the touch of the artists' hands on Sebastian's body, through gestures both gentle and violent, are another site where desire could have erupted in dialogue with the saint's body.

FLIRTATION, VIOLENCE, AND DOMINATION ON AN IVORY CASKET

EMMA LE POUÉSARD

MEN, WOMEN, AND ANIMALS CONVERSE, CAVORT, and confront each other on this handsomely carved fourteenth-century elephant ivory casket (SEE PL. 22). The lively scenes playing out across its five panels draw from widespread chivalric texts like Chrétien de Troyes's *Knight of the Cart* and popular oral and visual tropes such as the Capture of the Unicorn. The lid depicts a clever combination of the attack on the Castle of Love and a scene of jousting in a culmination of the strands explored on the casket's side panels: flirtation, domination, duplicity, and masculine prowess (FIG. 29). Used to store intimate belongings like jewelry, cosmetics, and other trinkets, such caskets gave viewers a diverting and varied picture of relations between the sexes that drew directly from the manuscripts and oral tradition so avidly consumed by courtly society.

The Castle of Love, a theme with unclear origins, was a favorite of ivory carvers, undoubtedly because the erotically charged scene of conquest resonated with the sensuousness of ivory. In turn, the whiteness of the ivory recalled the white skin of elite men and women that had been idealized as the desired standard of beauty.[1] This iconography, with its many vignettes, gave ivory artisans free rein to demonstrate their wit and "narrative agency" in creating subtle variations on the theme.[2] On the lid of the casket, women are seen enthusiastically reciprocating the knights' advances—kissing on horseback and in a boat on the left panel—as well as mounting a spirited defense against them, throwing flowers at their assailants on the right panel. Other interactions are more ambiguous. The wimpled woman on the battlements at right may be preparing to crown the clambering knight below with the garland in her right hand in a gesture of affection, or rather, about to throw the flower in her left hand at him. Below her, a knight climbs a rope ladder that must have been lowered by the women standing above him, and yet the strength with which they prepare to attack him with flowers is apparent and may hint at their inner conflict. Rendered in ivory, the Castle of Love trope embodied the idea expounded in chivalric literature that women's resistance must be overcome with perseverance (in some cases physical assault): ivory, initially cold to the touch, becomes warmer the longer one touches it.[3]

The lid's jousting scene, however, focuses on masculine bravado: in chivalric iconography, the homosocial bonds between men take precedence. Knights were primarily motivated in their pursuit of quests (including romantic ones) by a desire to prove themselves to one another. The casket lid, by giving pride of place to the jousting scene, firmly centers relationships between men. The back panel of the casket makes this point emphatically clear (FIG. 30). Three of four registers depict Lancelot and Gawain performing heroic tasks, whether battling a lion, crossing a treacherous bridge, or surviving the night on a deadly mechanized bed. Swords and armored bodies fill the space. The final register shows three women eagerly observing the prowess on display, but unlike in the joust scene on the lid, there is no culminating show of adoration. One of the two casket ends depicts a knight rescuing a woman from a wild man. The woman serves the narrative function of being the object of the knight's gallantry and courage but, once rescued, she disappears from the scene as the knight is granted the key to a castle. The casket thus makes clear the role of women in chivalric literature primarily as conduits through which masculine heroism is exercised.

The front of the box, meanwhile, emphasizes the irrationality of love (FIG. 31). Aristotle is made to look like a fool when, having cautioned Alexander the Great not to let his lover Phyllis distract him, Aristotle himself

Fig. 29. **Lid of PL. 22 showing the attack on the Castle of Love and a jousting tournament**

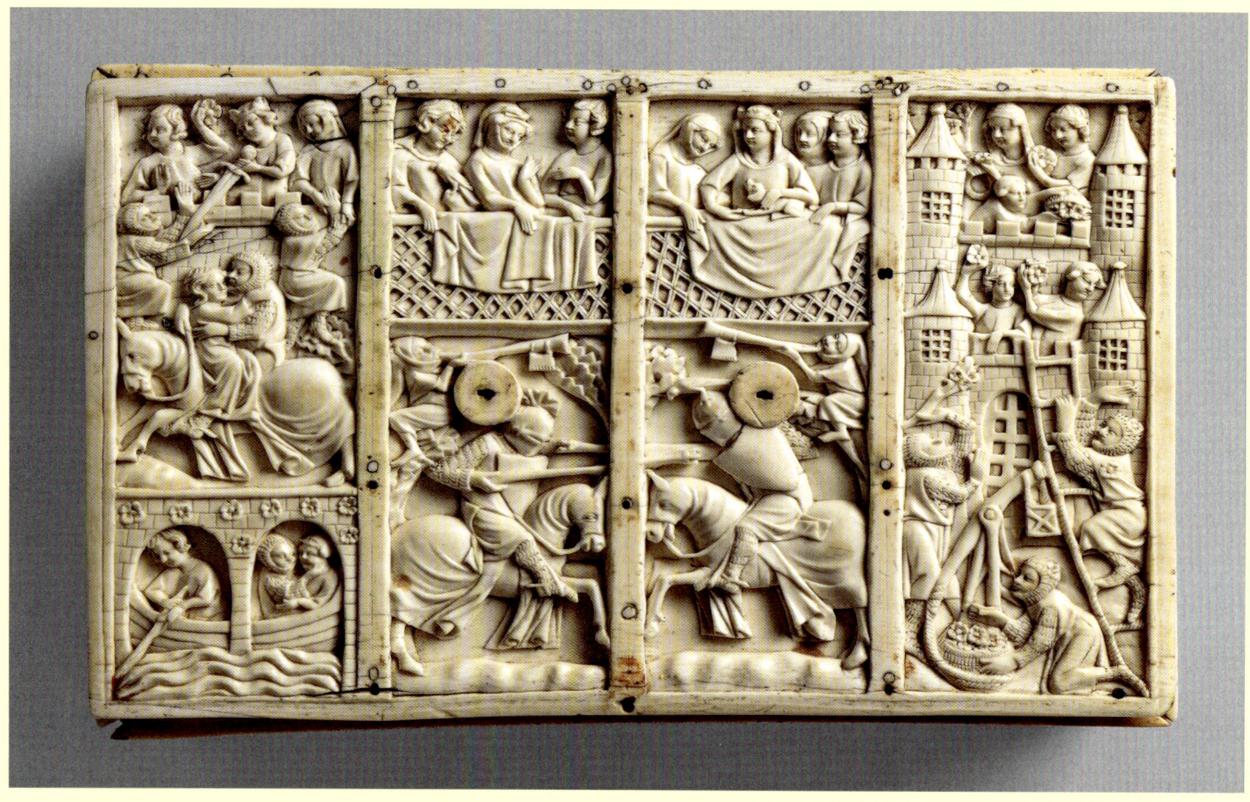

succumbs to her charms and lets her ride him like a horse. As Alexander looks on from the battlements, Phyllis placidly mounts Aristotle, spurring him on with a whip and steering him via reins grasped between his teeth. The fascinating gender dynamics at play are interwoven with complex ideas about the difference between, and the alliance of, human and nonhuman animals. Phyllis's excessive sexuality by virtue of her femininity is part of what makes her, in medieval thought, closer to the animal world.[4] And yet, in succumbing to her, it is Aristotle who becomes beastlike, sedately bearing his punishment. The materiality of ivory and its effective depiction of supple flesh convey slippages between human and nonhuman animality. The story depicted emphasizes the nature of femininity as contagiously bestial, making a quadruped of Aristotle.

Animals recur on the casket, serving as proxies for the erotic games being negotiated by their human counterparts. On one of the narrow ends of the casket lid, Isolde snuggles her dog Petitcreiu on her hip, their nearness hinting at Isolde's illicit relationship with Tristan.[5] Opposite her, Tristan holds a falcon on his wrist, a common metaphor for the capture and taming of a lover. On the lid, falcon and dog reappear among the groupings of men and women atop the latticed balcony overlooking the joust. Nestled to the breast, the animals display the physical closeness sought through courtship.

Over the course of five panels, their numerous compositions economically laid out and expertly carved, the casket depicts a riot of human and nonhuman relationships and power dynamics.[6] Displayed within the intimate space of the bedchamber, it bore witness to the range of relationships enacted in that space. The casket's elite viewers, who owned copies of illustrated Arthurian romances and enjoyed oral performances of these tales at court, would have brought

Fig. 30. **Back of PL. 22 showing Lancelot or Gawain attacking the lion, Lancelot on the sword bridge, Gawain on the deadly, mechanized bed, and maidens watching**

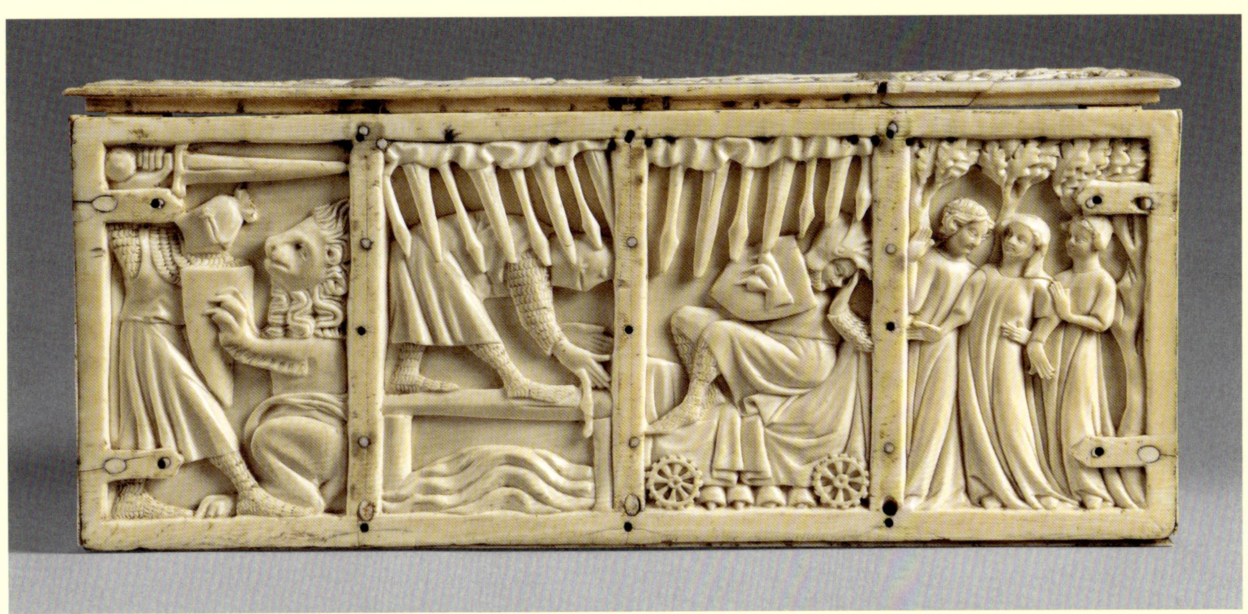

Fig. 31. **Front of PL. 22 showing Phyllis riding Aristotle and doomed lovers Pyramus and Thisbe**

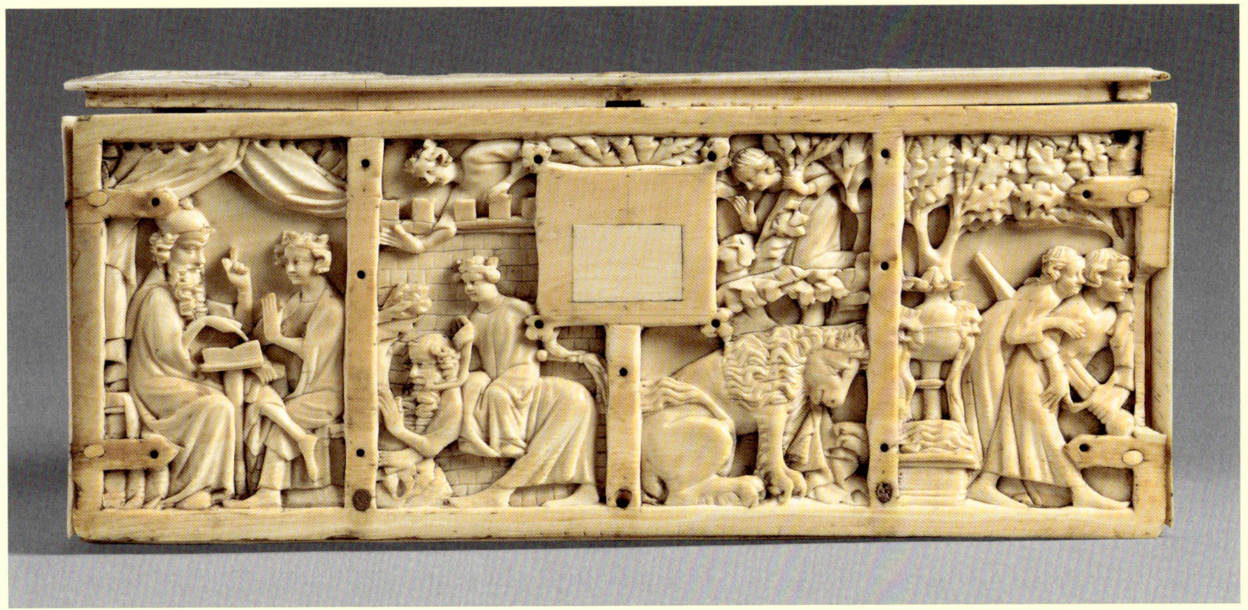

this knowledge to bear upon its carved narratives. Containing personal items, like jewelry, grooming utensils, or cosmetics, the casket participated in the construction of its owners' gendered selves. The activities depicted on the casket's panels gave the viewers an opportunity to reflect on how they negotiated all manner of relationships—heterosexual, homosocial, and even with the animal world through rejection, granting favors, or allyship.

QUEER CONNECTIONS WITH CHRIST'S BODY

BRYAN C. KEENE

THE BODY OF CHRIST, BLOODIED FROM A VIOLENT beating and torturous death, is on display for both Saint Francis and the viewer in Michele Giambono's panel painting from around 1430 (PL. 46). The subject of Christ as the Man of Sorrows has long provided artists with opportunities for depicting naked or partially clothed flesh within a spiritual dimension of meditation on pain, suffering, compassion, and salvation.[1] Similarly, the figure of Saint Francis (1181/82–1226) appears in art in various states of dress or undress, with an emphasis on his body or the skin of others.[2] Francis is another Christ—an *alter Christus* in theological terms—because of the marks of the stigmata that both bodies bear on their hands, feet, and sides. Medieval and Renaissance audiences, especially Franciscans, felt these connections between the two individuals and their own bodies in myriad ways. For example, art historians have noted qualities in representations of Christ and Francis that are potentially seductive (aesthetically and spiritually) and sensual (appealing to the senses).[3] Queer and trans contemporary artists have also drawn inspiration from this sacred imagery for commentaries on gender identity and sexuality, offering a dialogue between art historical theory and artistic practice.

The Venetian artist Giambono treated the Man of Sorrows iconography on no fewer than five occasions.[4] The painting in The Met is unique in the combination of figures and tactile elements, which would have elicited many possible associations for Franciscan viewers. Notably, Giambono used painted and sculpted gesso for the crown of thorns and for the blood that drips from the nails on the Cross and flows from Christ's head, hands, and side wound and down his arms, chest, and above his groin (FIG. 32). Red lines connect the stigmata on Francis with the corresponding marks on Christ, encouraging the viewer to likewise connect directly with both figures (FIG. 33). The Franciscan author of the late thirteenth-century devotional text known as the *Supplicationes variae* speaks of Christ's posture in this moment: "Christ's hand is extended to you so that you might do as he did; his side, so that you might feel what he felt." The writer tells readers to guard the falling drops of blood as the very state of one's soul.[5] Saint Bonaventure (ca. 1217–1274) drew more specific attention to the side wound, expressing a goal of entering it to touch the heart of Christ.[6] At the time, devotion to the gash at Christ's side used evocative language of touch together with words and images suggestive of a vulva, allusions that prompt considerations of the role of such images for female-identifying viewers in relation to menstruation and childbirth, as much as for those who identify as male.[7] Saint Claire, for instance, had a vision in which Christ fed her from his side wound.[8] The allure of Christ's body comes with a warning from Saint Bernardino of Siena (1380–1444), who condemns the act of an individual masturbating to the crucified Christ in one of many tirades against "sodomy" (a term that was categorically vast in its meanings throughout the Middle Ages).[9]

Giambono also simulated various material textures, from the grain of the Cross to the wooden architectural frame elements and columns (possibly in collaboration with a carpenter); from the stone of the sepulcher itself to the painted porphyry on the back of the panel; and from the white-and-gold embroidered textile draped in the tomb to the blue-and-gold patterned fabric resembling Islamic weaving hung as a cloth of honor. The columns measure about 30 centimeters, double the traditional lengths used to determine the height of Christ (when multiplied by the biblically symbolic number 12) in the *Supplicationes variae*

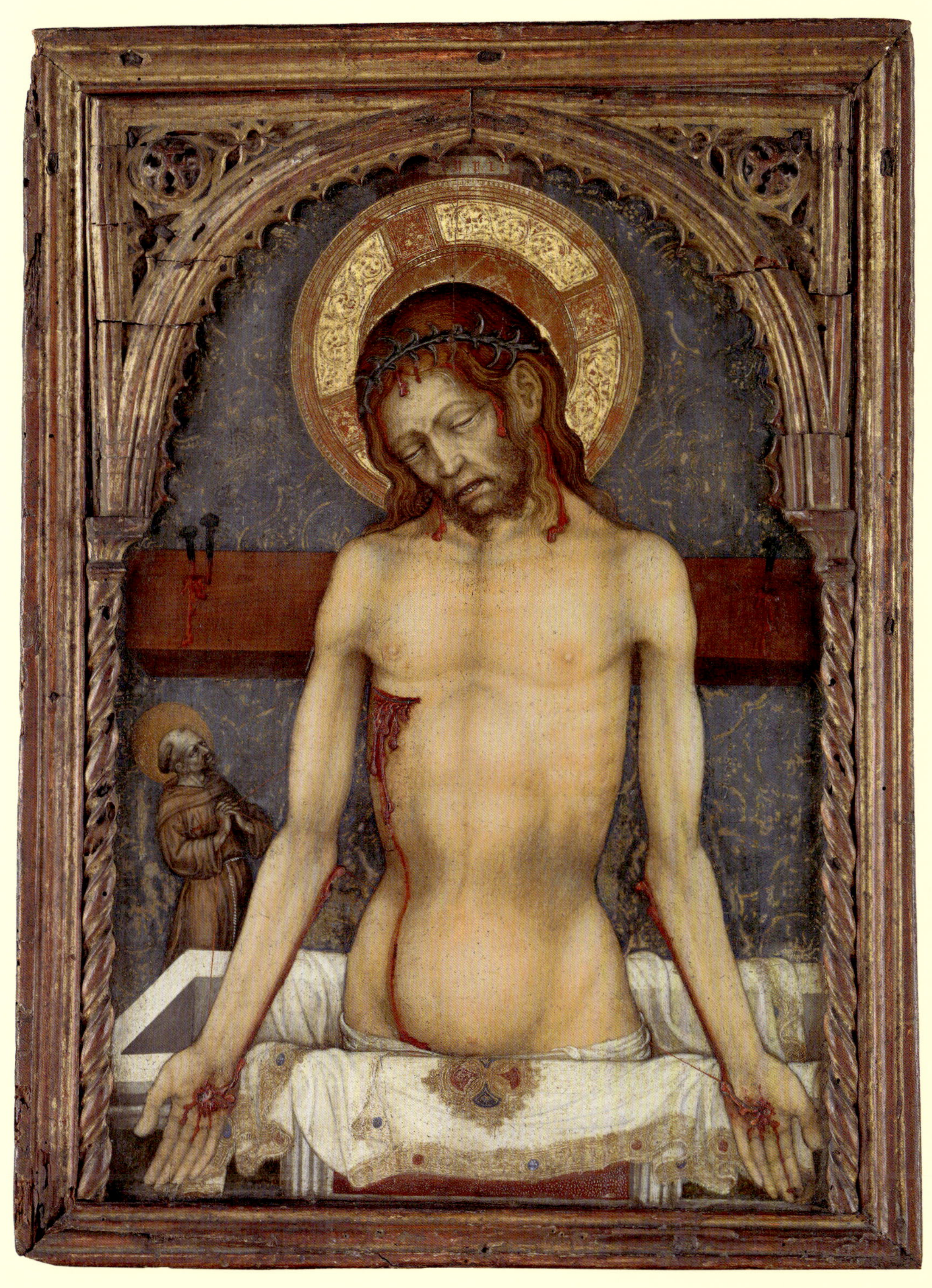

46. Man of Sorrows, ca. 1430. Michele Giambono (Michele Giovanni Bono) (Italian, 1420–62). Tempera and gold on wood

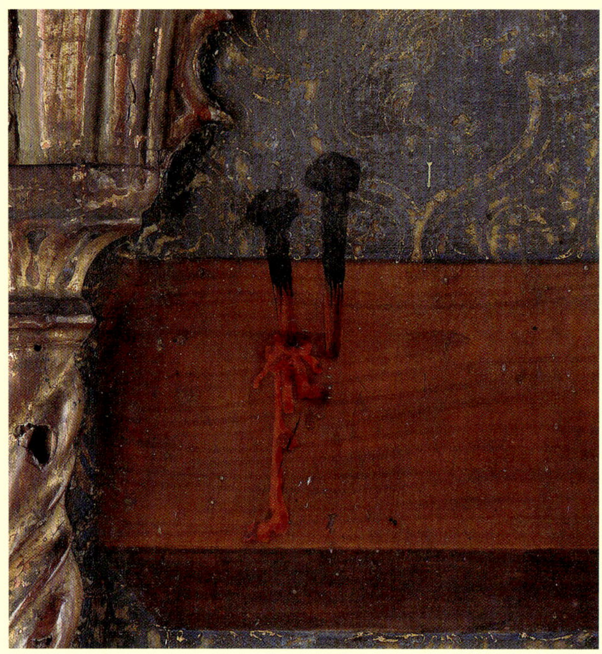

Fig. 32. **Detail of PL. 46 showing blood dripping from the nails of the cross**

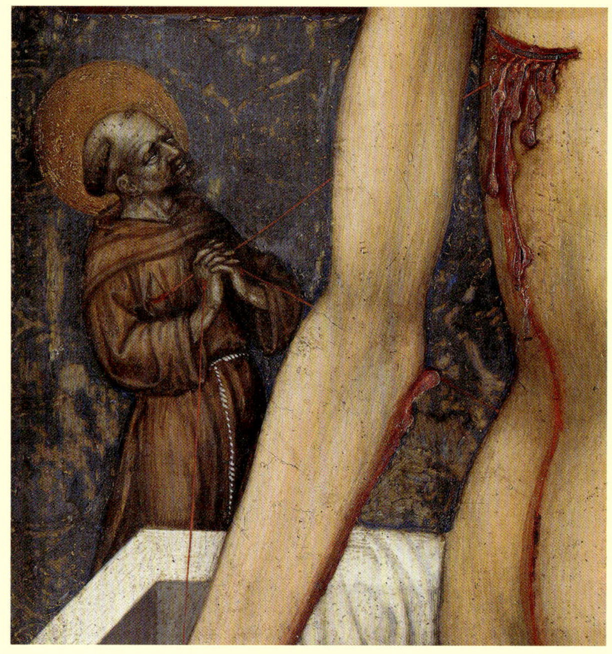

Fig. 33. **Detail of PL. 46 showing Saint Francis behind Christ's gaping wound**

(which often featured miniatures of the Man of Sorrows). A mendicant viewer could have fingered the length on the panel similar to instructions for doing so in manuscripts.[10] The evocation of porphyry on both sides, but specifically on the back, could be a reminder of the relic of the Stone of Unction on which Christ's body was prepared for burial.[11] The wooden panel's weight, temperature, and texture would feel quite different than those of stone, while at the same time the wood could be a textural reference to the True Cross itself, so carefully depicted behind Christ's body. The Franciscan friar and theologian Ugo Panziera (ca. 1260–1330) described the ways painters worked up the body of Christ to produce a flesh-like relief image that leads one's mind from the material to the divine world.[12] Some scholars emphasize the "feminine" body types in Man of Sorrows paintings, while others point out "masculine" features (specifically noting the penis, at times seemingly erect).[13] Giambono depicted a bearded Christ with hair around the nipples, under the arms, and visible above the groin, possibly suggesting a "masculine" portrayal according to gender conventions of the period.[14]

The historical and religious considerations of how artists depict nude bodies and physical states of suffering inform the work of Catherine Opie. Grids of immersive-scale photographs in Opie's *Vatican: Blood* (2023) (FIG. 34) frame details of blood detached from their narrative contexts in medieval and Renaissance frescoes, paintings, and tapestries in the Vatican. Several of the wounds are clearly on the bodies of Christ and various saints. By isolating the wounds in celebrated masterpieces of art history, Opie exposes the ways cultural institutions—both religious and artistic—frame violence, suffering, and sanctity. Blood has been a consistent element throughout Opie's

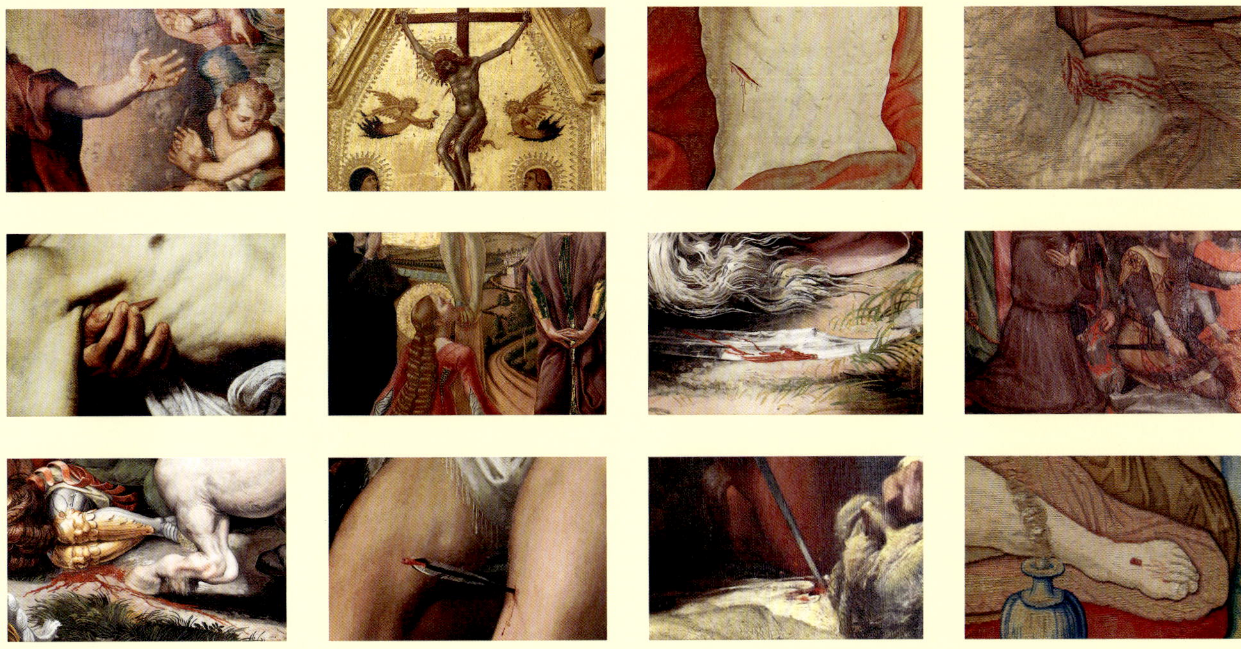

Fig. 34. **Catherine Opie (American, b. 1961). *Blood Grid #2*, 2023. Pigment print (edition of five), twelve prints, each 11 × 16 ½ in. (27.9 × 41.9 cm). Lehmann Maupin, New York, Los Angeles, Seoul, and London**

career. The grid recalls her earlier, provocative photographs that showcase cutting, flesh wounds, and HIV+ individuals bleeding as part of her commentary on harm, pain/pleasure (specifically bondage and sadomasochism, or BDSM), and AIDS. Opie notes that museums often display trigger warnings for her photographs due to the putative offensive or uncomfortable content, but during her 2021 residency at the American Academy in Rome she visited the Vatican galleries and felt surrounded by images of violence and conquest in Catholic art. "Why would my blood be perverted, but this blood acceptable?," she asks.[15] Opie has spoken about wanting viewers to deconstruct the systems that govern our world—including museums—and the role of art in those processes.[16] From the small scale of a medieval devotional painting to immersive gallery displays, images of nude bodies can be at once spiritual, sensual, and seductive.

MASCULINITIES AND TRANSGENDER EXPRESSION IN *THE BELLES HEURES* OF JEAN DE FRANCE, DUC DE BERRY

CLOVIS MAILLET

IN ONE OF THE MOST EXQUISITELY CONFOUNDING miniatures in *The Belles Heures* of Jean de France, duc de Berry, we see a monk at right placing a feminine cotte (a formfitting garment), dyed a beautiful lapis blue, next to another monk as he sleeps. Upon awakening, the bearded and tonsured figure—lantern in hand and awkwardly dressed in the feminine costume—prepares to attend Matins, at left, where the monks look at him and whisper to one another (PL. 47). This monk is Saint Jerome, the Church Father and staunch advocate of the renunciation of wealth and sexuality. The text below the miniatures explains that Jerome was the victim of a prank by a fellow brother who, by placing the feminine garment at his bedside, sought to falsely accuse him of having engaged in sexual relations with a woman. This episode marks a pivotal moment in Jerome's life, prompting him to leave the monastery for the desert.

Following the death of Pope Liberus, it is said that Jerome was judged very worthy of the highest priesthood, and was acclaimed by all, but he was shamefully mocked by someone who slipped a woman's habit into his home, and in the morning he was mocked. Seeing such folly among them, he left.[1]

The meaning of the scene has been notoriously difficult to parse.[2] The miniature was painted by the brothers Herman, Paul, and Jean de Limbourg, who were known for blending artistic virtuosity with humorous double entendre. The artists were also probably involved in sexual misconduct in their own lives (Paul was allegedly an accomplice in the abduction of a young girl).[3] Their influential patron, Jean de France, was not only a trendsetter in clothing styles and painting but was also accused of inappropriate sexual behavior. Hagiographic narrative, costume innovations, and sexual innuendo contribute to the scene's multiple layers of meaning.

Clothing in the miniatures by the Limbourg Brothers is highly varied, but it is always possible to distinguish between feminine and masculine garments. Fashion underwent enormous changes between the 1330s and the 1350s.[4] Before then, men and women wore nearly identical pieces of clothing, namely a robe made of a shirt (*chainse*), a tunic (cotte), and an overcoat (*surcote*), albeit decorated differently. Christian women wore veils and sashes, and their garments extended over their ankles, whereas men's costumes were somewhat shorter and could end above the ankles. The subsequent shift in fashion originated with the padded paltock (*pourpoint*), a short jacket designed as a combat garment and adapted for civilian use, accompanied by close-fitting breeches that showed the outline of the legs from the ankle to just below the buttocks. Women continued to cover their legs but emphasized the waist and bosom by wearing tight bodices with deep necklines. The "daring tunic" (*cotte hardie* or *cottardie*) could be worn without an overcoat.

The story of Jerome dates to the fourth century, but the Limbourg Brothers dressed the protagonist in fifteenth-century clothing. This practice was common, but it has particular consequences for cross-dressing narratives. In the fourth century, women's dress consisted of a large tunic with a veil; in the fifteenth century, the *cottardie* clung to the body. In late antiquity, only veils and other specific adornments like necklaces or earrings, distinguished women from men. The Life of Saint Matrôna, a near contemporary of Saint Jerome, offers a strong example of what a gender transition and change in clothing could entail. They (Matrôna) dressed as a eunuch and called themselves Babylas to enter the monastery of Bassianos. Their

47. **Saint Jerome in a woman's dress from *The Belles Heures* of Jean de France, duc de Berry, 1405–1408/1409. The Limbourg Brothers (Franco-Netherlandish, active in France by 1399–1416). Opaque watercolor, silver, gold, and iron gall on parchment**

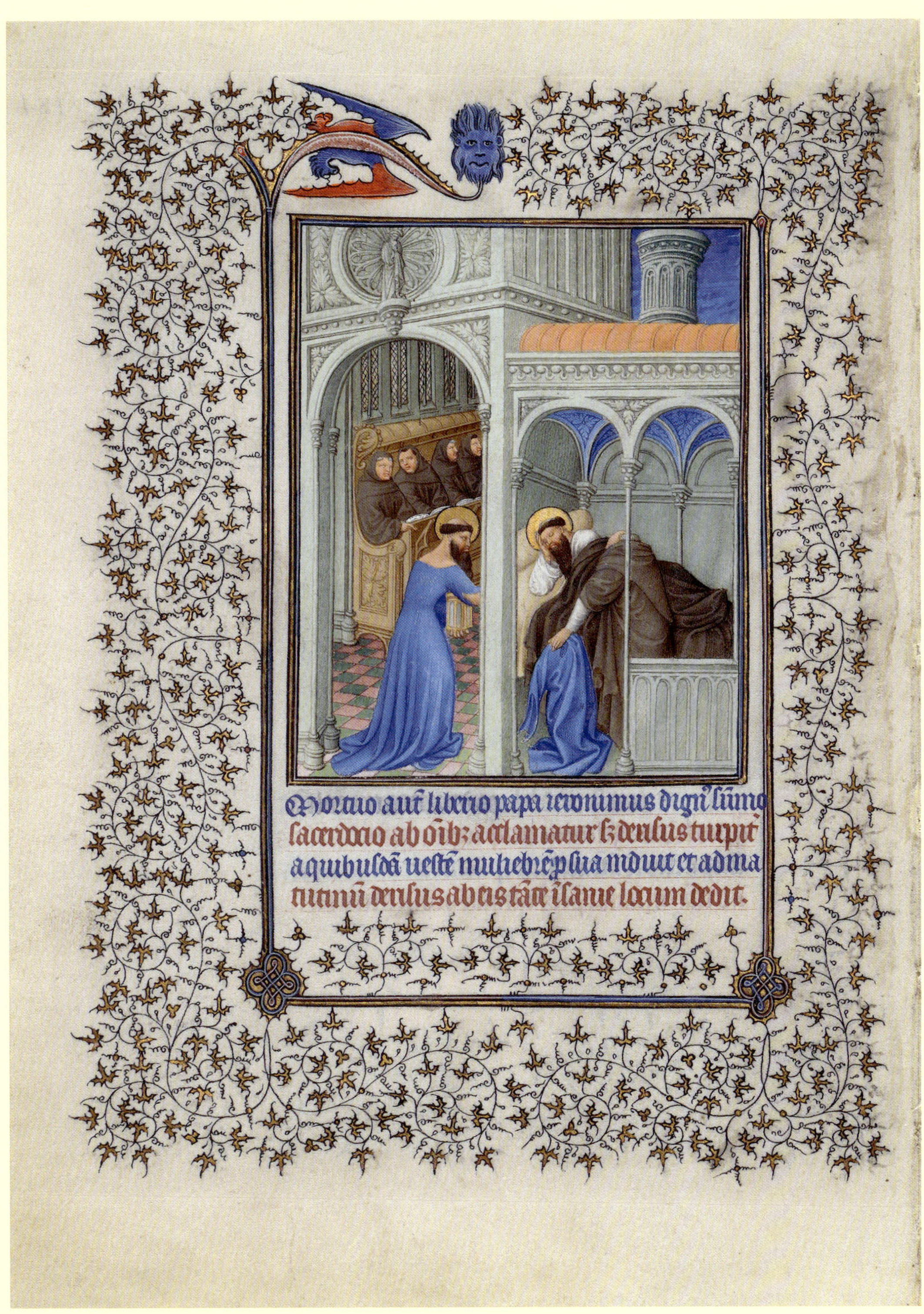

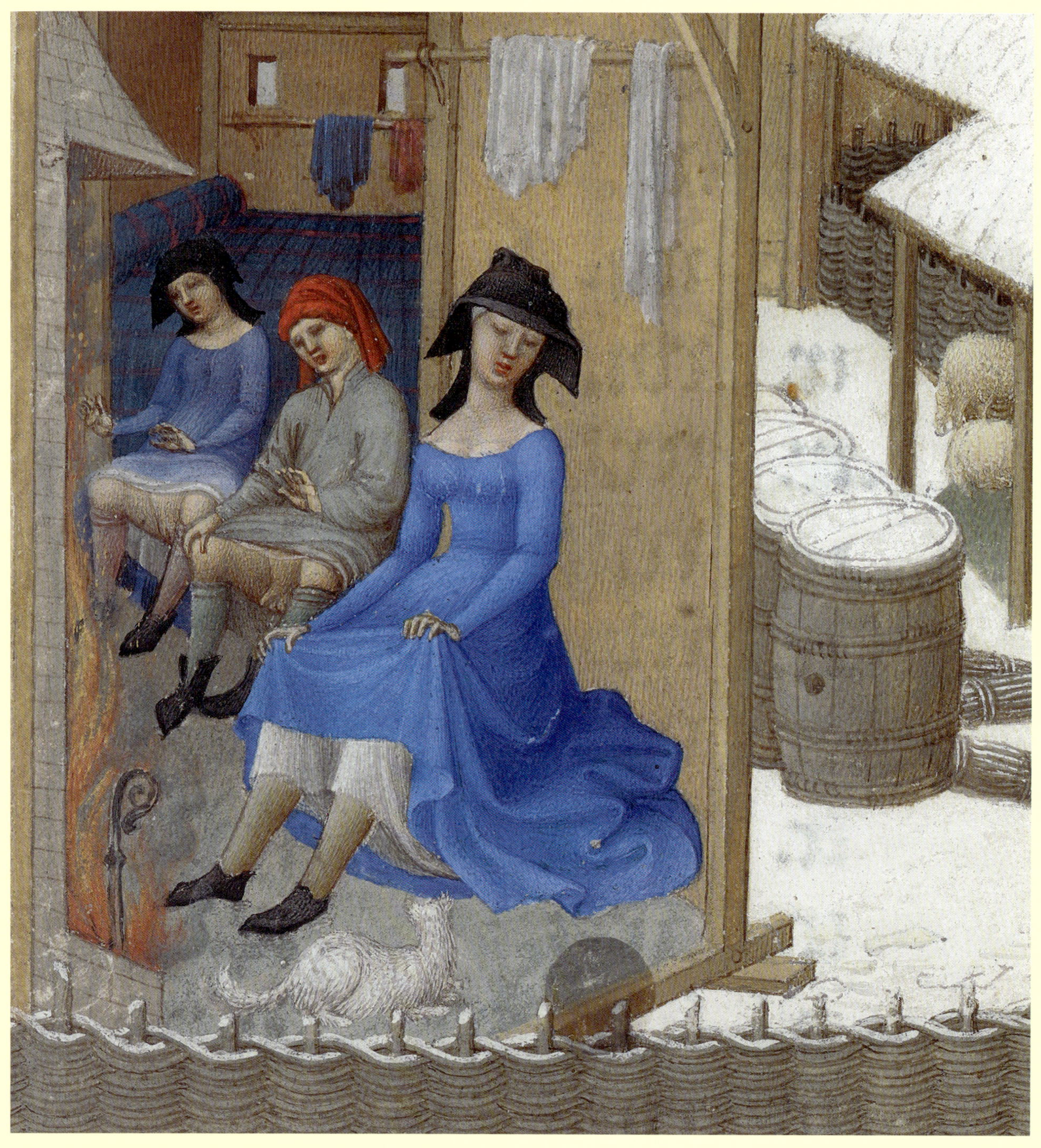

Fig. 35. *February*, from the *Très Riches Heures* of Jean de France, duc de Berry. Paris and Bourges, 1411–86. The Limbourg Brothers (Franco-Netherlandish, active in France by 1399–1416). Tempera, gold, and ink on parchment, 11 ⅜ × 8 ¼ in. (29 × 21 cm). Musée Condé, Chantilly (ms 65, fol. 2v)

transition only required readjusting their existing garment "in the manner of a man," by removing the girdle and veil.[5]

In the *Belles Heures* miniature, Jerome wears a fitted lapis blue *cottardie* with bare lower arms, while the other monks wear shirts underneath their brown frocks. In contrast, women depicted in the manuscript—such as the duchess on folio 91v or the dancers on folio 186r—typically wear both an undergarment and an overgarment with their cotte. Jerome is therefore not fully dressed, appearing in essentially women's underwear. The historic Jerome was close to the holy women Paula, Eustochium, and Marcella, whose lives he chronicled, as a confessor, friend, and advisor.[6] The notion that he might have been mocked for wearing women's clothes did not emerge until the High Middle Ages (seventh to eighth century), probably because at that time the separation between genders was institutionalized, and proximity to women became all the more suspicious. Gender was more fluid in early Christendom, when abstinence was a more important distinction than gender, the boundaries of which were not firm. Not only could holy men and women live close together (there were no monasteries), their genders could be obscured: Jerome himself praised the masculinization of women: "[women] should stop being women and become men, because everything that is perfect is in men."[7] As depicted by the Limbourg Brothers from their vantage point in the fifteenth century, the ill-fitting costume—with its partial sleeves and lack of undershirt—no longer symbolized a saint's renunciation of worldly wealth or association with saintly women but rather conveyed a sense of eroticized clumsiness.

Herman, Paul, and Jean de Limbourg worked in the service of a princely court whose customs they knew intimately, given that their uncle Jan Maelwael (Jean Malouel) was a renowned Flemish painter in the Burgundian court. Arrested at a border for trespassing, they were incarcerated but released after interventions first from their guild and then from the Duke of Burgundy. In exchange for their liberation, they began working for Philip the Bold and later for his brother, Jean de France. Engaging with Jean de France's love for beautiful objects, the Limbourg Brothers demonstrated playful wit, such as when they gifted him a fake book that was a wooden trompe l'oeil.[8]

In the *Belles Heures*, the brothers infused eroticism into various contexts, including martyrdom. Saint Catherine heals her wounds with angels as if she were a courtesan at the bath (fol. 17v).[9] Beautiful men transform scenes of flagellation into appealing displays of the male form (fol. 74v). In the *Très Riches Heures* of Jean de France, duc de Berry, which they painted in 1413–16, this erotic undertone extended to both devotional and everyday scenes, such as in the February folio, where peasants are shown raising their dresses to warm themselves by the fire. Their genitalia—vulvas and penises—are shown in detail beneath their clothing, with exaggerated body proportions that overemphasize these intimate parts (FIG. 35).

The only explicit example of gender ambiguity in their work is the miniature of Saint Jerome in a dress, offering one of the few existing visual depictions of a form of transfemininity in the fifteenth century. This queer moment is a rare instance of gender blurring, rendered in bright colors, and taking place in isolation within an otherwise highly masculine community, all dressed in brown. Jerome's arrival at mass in what resembles female undergarments is countered by the mockery of the monks, who whisper among themselves, creating a clear instance of transmisogynistic reaction. The miniature remains a flamboyant gender performance, clumsy as it may be.

LOVE IN MORTAL TIME

SCOTT D. MILLER

LONGING, REGRET, AND THE RELENTLESS CHANGE OF time seem a world away to the young couple in this oil-on-panel painting from around 1470 (PL. 48). These adolescent courtiers wear opulent, formfitting clothing, abundant jewelry, and long, flowing hairstyles.[1] Absorbed in each other's gaze, they touch delicately as the man reaches across to offer the lady a flower (FIG. 36). She clutches the folds of her dress to her abdomen, her posture closed and hesitant. She has yet to accept the gift, but raises her right hand to touch it.

The floral imagery that embowers the couple—the cherry and apple trees above them, the shrubby eglantine and flowering currant on either side, and the meadow at their feet aglow with buttercup, cowslip, lily of the valley, dandelion, and forget-me-not—all place the action in the middle of spring. This scenery evokes metaphors of youth and poetic genres such as the *pastourelle* that explored the tumultuous and often violent sexuality attributed to young men against a backdrop of spring verdure. Late-medieval intellectuals like the theologian Jean Gerson characterized the erotic impulses of women and young men as too intense and changeable to be trusted.[2] Yet the gift of the flower puts forth a gesture of enduring love. It is a forget-me-not, a flower whose Middle French name, "*ne m'oubliez mye*," and Middle German name, "*vergisz mein nit*," encode claims to remembrance and steadfastness in love.[3] The youth also wears the flower in his diadem, where it is poised as a badge publicly announcing his personal desire.[4] Similar emblems were exchanged during courtly Maying celebrations, where parties dressed in green clothing, created crowns and belts out of plant material like green branches and flowers, and entertained themselves in the woods. Popular festivities of Maying included acts of sexual license, but scholar Susan Crane has called attention to a distinct strand of courtly maying lyric and ritual that emphasized restraint and the sublimation of sexual desire, assimilating the custom with the ideals of courtly love and asserting the social distinctiveness of the ruling class.[5] In the painting of a bridal couple, the young man's gentle touch and the woman's cautious manner may be read as an expression of the young couple's class affiliation as much as of their gender or sexuality.

Authors of courtly love lyric often express ambivalence about its ideals, but the painter leaves little ambiguity about the ultimate value of courtly love and its promises. This panel is one side of a double-sided *memento mori* painting and serves as a warning about the transience of earthy pleasures. Its correspondent, now in the Musée de L'Oeuvre Notre-Dame, Strasbourg, depicts the couple after the changes of a long life (FIG. 37).[6] The figures are now rotting corpses standing in

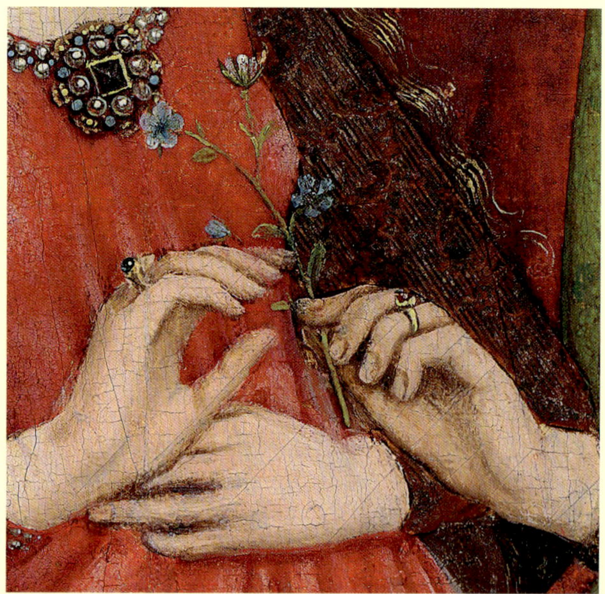

Fig. 36. **Detail of PL. 48 showing the gift of a forget-me-not**

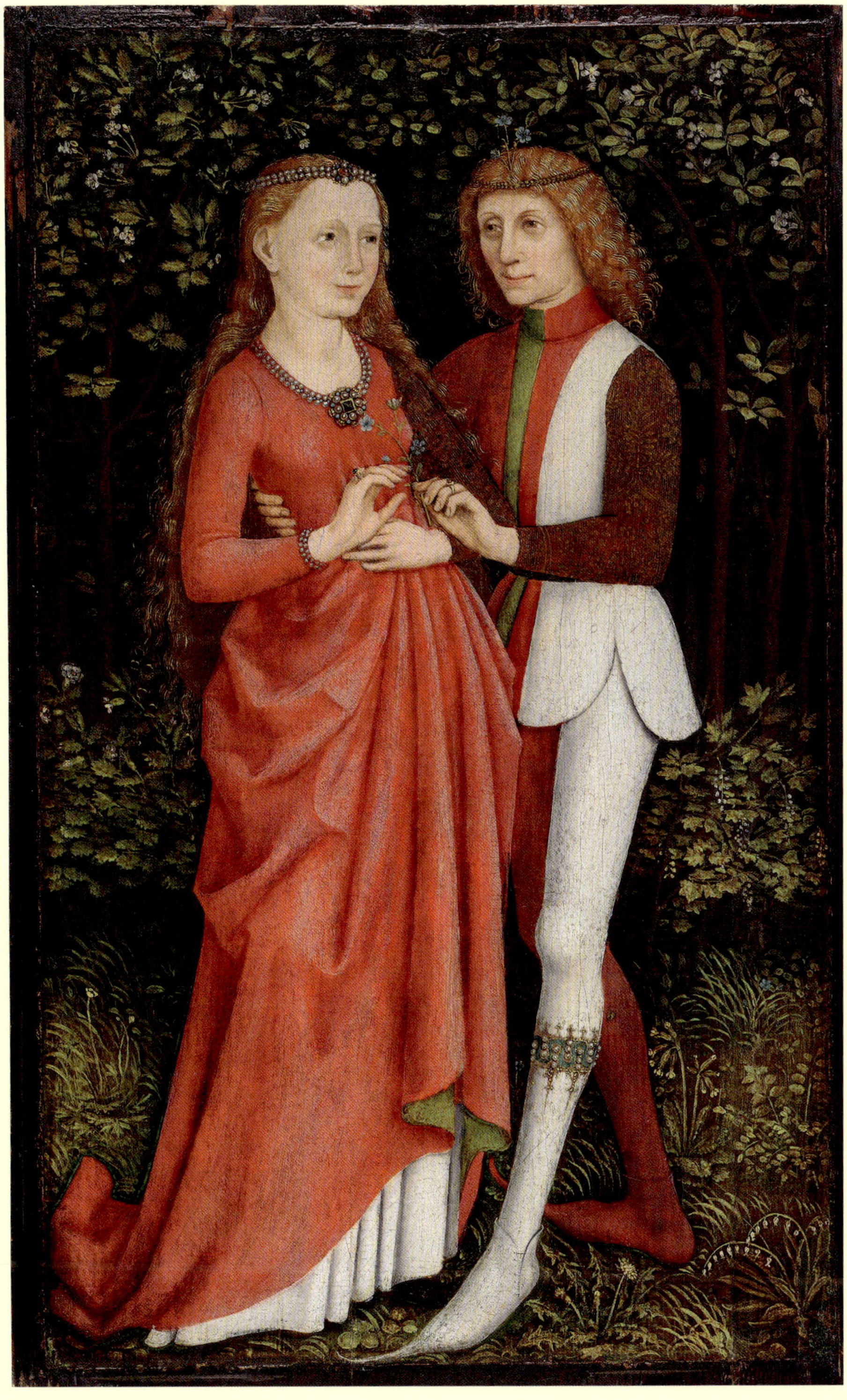

48. **A bridal couple. German, 1470. Oil on panel**

Fig. 37. The rotting pair. South German, ca. 1470. Oil on panel, 24 ⅝ × 15 ¾ in. (62.5 × 40 cm). Musée de L'Oeuvre Notre-Dame, Strasbourg (MBA 1442)

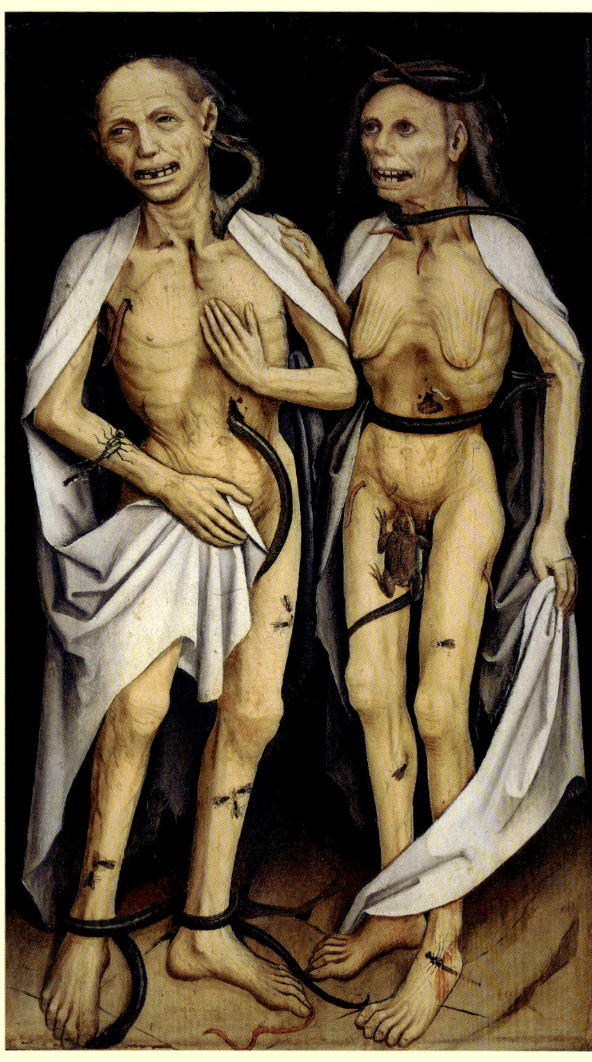

a dark, shallow space that resembles a grave. Their hair has thinned and whitened, their teeth have fallen out, their faces and bodies have wrinkled and shriveled, and their bodies are now the sites of regeneration in a cracked and barren soil. Of the fauna populating on the corpses, only the earthworms and the unseen larvae of the flies eat flesh. The other animals—the toads, dragonflies, and snakes—have been included to inject a sense of disgust into the process of aging and death and to imply the moral corruption of the jewelry they replace. The couple's position is reversed, and so the roles of coaxing and hesitancy, active and passive, have reversed. The figures are both draped in shrouds, but the woman throws hers back to reveal her body, now naked save for the frog clutching her vulva. A symbol of *luxuria*, the frog supplants pleasure with disgust and shields the woman's genitals from view. For his part, the man covers himself with a fold of cloth and averts his eyes from the sight of the body he once pursued. In a pose reversing the female resistance to sexual overtures seen in an ivory tablet (SEE FIG. 13), now he recoils from the woman's touch, extending a sharp elbow to create space between them.

This rejection enacts a common medieval narrative around sexuality in later life. Humor theory suggested that men lost interest in sex as the heat of their bodies cooled. Women, by contrast, retained a high sex drive as age progressed on account of their cooler, wetter bodies.[7] In Chaucer's *The Canterbury Tales* (ca. 1387–1400), the Wife of Bath contrasts the sexual failings of her elderly husbands with her increased erotic agency and fulfilment past middle age, and attributes misogyny to male frustration over their own sexual incapacity.[8] Christine de Pisan likewise argued in her book *City of the Ladies* (1405) that misogyny is the solace of men who despair over their loss of sexual prowess.[9] Viewed in this light, the rejection of older women can be read as a projection of self-loathing.

If the paintings set up old age and death as times when male and female libidos are out of sync, it does not depict the pair of youths as quite ideal. The mismatch of the aged resulted from the overzealous promises of youth, after all, and if the bodies of the old were not up to the challenge of loving well, the young lacked the temperament. It is a narrative in which no one can win, and in which earthly joy leads unvaryingly to abjection. In this structure, people cannot face time with gratitude or age with dignity, and a woman's appeal may not grow from experience or agency. This construction also discourages the belief that bonds between partners will deepen over time or that life goes on after heartbreak. It is a reductive, pessimistic view of sexuality in the human life cycle that other medieval narratives such as *The Wife of Bath's Prologue and Tale* resisted.

LIST OF PLATES

INTRODUCTION

1
The wound of Christ
from the Prayer Book of Bonne of Luxembourg, Duchess of Normandy, before 1349
Attributed to Jean Le Noir (French, active 1331–75) and workshop
Opaque watercolor, silver, gold, and iron gall ink on parchment, $4\frac{15}{16} \times 3\frac{9}{16}$ in. (12.6 × 9 cm)
The Metropolitan Museum of Art, New York, The Cloisters Collection, 1969 (69.86, fol. 331r)
MS M.805

2
Cover of a writing tablet with lovers and the god of love
French, ca. 1325–50
Elephant ivory, $3\frac{11}{16} \times 2\frac{5}{16} \times \frac{5}{16}$ in. (9.3 × 5.9 × .8 cm)
The Metropolitan Museum of Art, New York, The Cloisters Collection, 2003 (2003.131.3a, b)

3
Saint Catherine of Siena receiving the stigmata, ca. 1447–65
Giovanni di Paolo (Giovanni di Paolo di Grazia) (Italian, 1398–1482)
Tempera and gold on wood, $11 \times 7\frac{7}{8}$ in. (27.9 × 20 cm)
The Metropolitan Museum of Art, New York, Robert Lehman Collection, 1975 (1975.1.34)

4
Crucifixion scene with a Carthusian monk, 14th century
Jean de Beaumetz (French, ca. 1335–1396)
Oil on oak panel, framed $25 \times 20\frac{11}{16} \times 2\frac{5}{8}$ in. (63.5 × 52.5 × 6.7 cm); unframed $22\frac{5}{16} \times 18$ in. (56.6 × 45.7 cm)
The Cleveland Museum of Art, Ohio, Leonard C. Hanna Jr. Fund, 1964 (1964.454)

5
Pax with the Crucifixion
South German, ca. 1360–70 (ivory); 15th century (frame)
Elephant ivory and gilded copper, $3\frac{3}{4} \times 3\frac{1}{8} \times \frac{15}{16}$ in. (9.5 × 7.9 × 2.4 cm)
The Metropolitan Museum of Art, New York, The Cloisters Collection, 1970 (1970.324.9)

BODIES IN FLUX

6
Two riddles of the Queen of Sheba
Upper Rhenish, ca. 1490–1500
Linen warp; wool, linen and metallic wefts, $31\frac{1}{2} \times 40$ in. (80 × 99.7 cm)
The Metropolitan Museum of Art, New York, The Cloisters Collection, 1971 (1971.43)

7
Creation with Adam and Eve from *Le Régime du corps* (*The Regimen of the Body*), said to be compiled by Aldobrandino of Siena (Italian, d. 1296/1299?), 1256
French, ca. 1440–50
Opaque watercolor, gold, silver and iron gall ink on parchment; 129 folios, $10\frac{1}{4} \times 7\frac{1}{16}$ in. (26 × 18 cm)
The Morgan Library & Museum, New York, Purchased by J. Pierpont Morgan (1837–1913) in 1902 (MS M.165, fol. 5r)

8
Base for a statuette
Netherlandish, 1470–80
Boxwood, $3\frac{1}{2} \times 4\frac{7}{8} \times 3\frac{3}{8}$ in. (8.9 × 12.4 × 8.6 cm)
The Metropolitan Museum of Art, New York, The Cloisters Collection, 1955 (55.116.2)

9
Saint Wilgefortis on the Cross
from a Book of Hours
Netherlandish, ca. 1500
Opaque watercolor, gold, silver and ink on parchment; 192 folios, $7\frac{7}{8} \times 5\frac{5}{16}$ in. (20 × 13.5 cm)
Manuscripts Division, Princeton University Library (MS Garrett 59, fol. 161r)

10
Judgment of Saint Marinos; Death of Saint Marinos
from *The Golden Legend,* written by Jacobus de Voragine (Italian, ca. 1230–1298), ca. 1259–66
Belgian, 1445–65
Opaque watercolor, gold leaf, silver and ink on parchment, 124 folios, $14\frac{15}{16} \times 10\frac{5}{8}$ in. (37.9 × 27 cm)
The Morgan Library & Museum, New York (MS M.672–5 III, fol. 279v)

11
Philip the Deacon baptizes Simeon Bachos (the "Ethiopian Eunuch")
from a Book of Hours, 1533
Master of Charles V (Flemish, active 1505–1533)
Opaque watercolor, gold leaf, silver and ink on parchment; 71 folios, $5\frac{5}{8} \times 3\frac{1}{8}$ in. (14.3 × 8 cm)
The Morgan Library & Museum, New York, Purchased by J. Pierpont Morgan (1837–1913) in 1912 (MS M.491, fol. 129r)

12
Ethiopians of Jerusalem
from *Peregrinatio in Terram Sanctam* (*Pilgrimage to the Holy Land*), published in Mainz, 1486
Bernhard von Breydenbach (German, 1440?–1497?), author
Erhard Reuwich (German, ca. 1455–ca. 1490), artist
Peter Schöffer the Elder (German, 1425–1503), publisher
Black printing ink with watercolor on paper, 12 5/8 × 9 1/16 × 1 3/8 in. (32 × 23 × 3.5 cm)
The Metropolitan Museum of Art, New York, Rogers Fund, 1919 (19.49.3, fol. 72v)

13
Plaque with the Fountain of Youth
French, ca. 1320–40
Elephant ivory, 4 7/16 × 2 5/8 × 3/16 in. (11.2 × 6.6 × .4 cm)
The Metropolitan Museum of Art, New York, The Cloisters Collection, 2003 (2003.131.4)

MEDIEVAL EROTICA

14
Box with the parable of the Prodigal Son and scenes of lovers
French, 14th century
Elephant ivory, 3 3/16 × 7 3/16 × 4 1/8 in. (8.1 × 18.3 × 10.5 cm)
The Metropolitan Museum of Art, New York, Gift of George Blumenthal, 1941 (41.100.159a, b)

15
Box with scenes of lovers
Flemish, 14th century
Leather, walnut, gold, paint, copper alloy and iron fittings, 4 5/16 × 8 5/16 × 7 in. (11 × 21.1 × 17.8 cm)
The Metropolitan Museum of Art, New York, Gift of George Blumenthal, 1941 (41.100.194)

16
Belt
North Italian, ca. 1330–50
Silver, with traces of gilding and enamel; modern textile support, 65 3/8 × 1 5/16 × 9/16 in. (166 × 3.3 × 1.4 cm)
The Metropolitan Museum of Art, New York, The Cloisters Collection, 2015 (2015.705a, b)

17
Hair combing
from *Le Régime du corps* (*The Regimen of the Body*), said to be written by Aldobrandino of Siena (Italian, d. 1296/1299?), composed 1256
French, ca. 1440–50
Opaque watercolor, gold, silver, and iron gall ink on parchment, 129 folios, 10 1/4 × 7 1/16 in. (26 × 18 cm)
The Morgan Library & Museum, New York, Purchased by J. Pierpont Morgan (1837–1913) in 1902 (MS M.165, fol. 49v)
This folio is not shown in the exhibition.

18
Comb with scenes from a hunt
French or Italian, 15th or 16th century
Elephant ivory, paint, and gold, 3 7/16 × 5 1/16 × 3/16 in. (8.8 × 12.9 × .4 cm)
The Metropolitan Museum of Art, New York, Gift of J. Pierpont Morgan, 1917 (17.190.245)

19
Writing tablet with lovers
French, 14th century
Elephant ivory, 4 9/16 × 3 1/16 × 3/16 in. (11.7 × 7.8 × .6 cm)
The Metropolitan Museum of Art, New York, Gift of Ann Payne Blumenthal, 1938 (38.108)

20
Drawings of five half-figures including wild men
from a sketchbook, ca. 1400
Circle of Jacquemart de Hesdin (French, ca. 1355–ca. 1414)
Metalpoint on prepared ground with dilute watercolor washes on boxwood, 2 3/4 × 5 1/16 in. (7 × 12.9 cm)
The Morgan Library & Museum, New York, Purchased by J. Pierpont Morgan (1837–1913), 1906 (MS M.346, fol. 3v)

21
Drawings of four figures, including a king
from a sketchbook, ca. 1400
Circle of Jacquemart de Hesdin (French, ca. 1355–ca. 1414)
Metalpoint on prepared ground with dilute watercolor washes on boxwood, 2 3/4 × 5 1/16 in. (7 × 12.9 cm)
The Morgan Library & Museum, New York, Purchased by J. Pierpont Morgan (1837–1913), 1906 (MS M.346, fol. 2r)

22
Box with romance scenes
French, ca. 1310–30
Elephant ivory, 4 5/16 × 9 15/16 × 6 1/4 in. (10.9 × 25.3 × 15.9 cm)
The Metropolitan Museum of Art, New York, Gift of J. Pierpont Morgan, 1917; The Cloisters Collection, 1988 (17.190.173a, b; 1988.16)

23
Aquamanile in the form of Aristotle and Phyllis
South Netherlandish, late 14th or early 15th century
Copper alloy, 12 13/16 × 7 1/16 × 15 1/2 in. (32.5 × 17.9 × 39.3 cm)
The Metropolitan Museum of Art, New York, Robert Lehman Collection, 1975 (1975.1.1416)

24
Cover of a writing tablet with the story of Febilla and Virgil
French, 1340–60
Elephant ivory, 3 ¾ × 2 1⁄16 × 3⁄16 in. (9.5 × 5.2 × .6 cm)
The Walters Art Museum, Baltimore, Maryland, Acquired by Henry Walters, 1902 (71.267)

MARITAL AND MYSTICAL UNIONS

25
Manuscript leaf with marriage scene from the *Decretals* of Gregory IX
Italian, ca. 1300
Opaque watercolor, gold leaf, and iron gall ink on parchment, 18 ⅛ × 11 ⅝ in. (46.1 × 29.6 cm)
The Metropolitan Museum of Art, New York, Gift of Harry G. Friedman, 1955 (55.18.3)

26
Meeting of Saints Joachim and Anne at the Golden Gate, ca. 1515–20
Benedikt Dreyer (German, active Lübeck, ca. 1500–1525)
Oak with paint and gold, 23 × 19 ¼ × 4 ⅞ in. (58.4 × 48.9 × 12.4 cm)
The Metropolitan Museum of Art, New York, Gift of J. Pierpont Morgan (1837–1913) in 1916 (16.32.213)

27
Heart-shaped ring
Italian, 14th century
Inscribed: *Corta Porta Amor* (*The heart brings love*)
Gold and ruby, 13⁄16 × ¾ × ⅞ in. (2.1 × 1.9 × 2.2 cm)
Griffin Collection

28
Ring with hunting scene
Spanish, probably 16th century
Gold, 13⁄16 × 13⁄16 × ⅜ in. (2.1 × 2.1× .95 cm)
Griffin Collection

29
Fede ring
Possibly British, 16th century
Gold, 15⁄16 × ⅞ × ¼ in. (2.4 × 2.2 × .64 cm)
Griffin Collection

30
Ceremonial saddle with scenes of lovers
Central European, ca. 1400–20
Bovine bone (body of saddle), deer antler and bone (decorative elements), limewood, rawhide, birchbark, and metal paint, 13 ½ × 16 × 21 ¾ in. (34.3 × 40.6 × 55.2 cm)
The Metropolitan Museum of Art, New York, Harris Brisbane Dick Fund, 1940 (40.66a, b)

31A,B
Purse with the story of Patient Griselda
French, 14th century
Silk and metal thread on canvas, 6 × 5 ⅝ in. (15.2 × 14.3 cm)
The Metropolitan Museum of Art, New York, Gift of Mrs. Edward S. Harkness, 1927 (27.48.2)

32
Goblet with the story of Febilla and Virgil
Italian, ca. 1475–1500
Glass, enameled and gilded; modern foot, 6 ⅞ × 3 7⁄16 in. (17.5 × 8.7 cm)
The Metropolitan Museum of Art, New York, Gift of J. Pierpont Morgan, 1917 (17.190.730a, b)

33
Conjugal relations from *Le Régime du corps* (*The Regimen of the Body*), said to be compiled by Aldobrandino of Siena (Italian, d. 1296/1299?), 1256
French, ca. 1440–50
Opaque watercolor, gold, silver, and iron gall ink on parchment, 129 folios, 10 ¼ in × 7 1⁄16 in. (26 × 18 cm)
The Morgan Library & Museum, New York, Purchased by J. Pierpont Morgan (1837–1913) in 1902 (MS M.165, fol. 17r)

34
The Sponsa in her spiritual bed from the Rothschild Canticles
French or Flemish, ca. 1300
Opaque watercolor, silver and gold leaf, and iron gall ink on parchment, 4 ⅝ × 3 5⁄16 in. (11.8 × 8.4 cm)
General Collection, Beinecke Rare Book & Manuscript Library, Yale University, New Haven (MS 404, fol. 66r)

35
Roundel with Annunciation to the Virgin
South Netherlandish, 1500–10
Colorless glass, vitreous paint, and silver stain, Diam. 8 ⅞ in. (22.5 cm)
The Metropolitan Museum of Art, New York, The Cloisters Collection, 1972 (1972.245.1)

36
Virgin of the Annunciation
French, ca. 1300–10
Limestone with traces of paint, 16 11⁄16 × 11 ⅝ × 7 ⅜ in. (42.4 × 29.6 × 18.8 cm)
The Metropolitan Museum of Art, New York, Gift of J. Pierpont Morgan, 1917 (17.190.739)

37
Box with Lady Minne piercing the heart of a man
German, ca. 1325–50
Oak, tempera; wrought-iron mounts, 4 ¾ × 10 ¾ × 6 ½ in. (12.1 × 27.3 × 16.5 cm)
The Metropolitan Museum of Art, New York, Rogers Fund and The Cloisters Collection, by exchange, 1950 (50.141)

38
Amors embracing Amant
from the *Roman de la Rose* (*Romance of the Rose*), 1340, written by Guillaume de Lorris (French ca. 1200–ca. 1240), ca. 1230, with additions by Jean de Meun (French, ca. 1240–ca. 1305), ca. 1275
Jeanne de Montbaston (French, active ca. 1320–1355) (possible artist)
Opaque watercolor, gold leaf, iron gall ink on parchment, $8\frac{1}{4} \times 11\frac{13}{16}$ in. (21 × 30 cm)
The Morgan Library & Museum, New York, Purchased by J. Pierpont Morgan (1837–1913) in 1912 (MS M.503, fol. 14v)

39
The Sponsa wounding Christ
from the *Rothschild Canticles*
Possibly French or Belgian, ca. 1300
Opaque watercolor, silver and gold leaf, and iron gall ink on parchment, $4\frac{5}{8} \times 3\frac{5}{16}$ in. (11.8 × 8.4 cm)
General Collection, Beinecke Rare Book & Manuscript Library, Yale University, New Haven (MS 404, fols. 18v-19r)

40
Seated Man of Sorrows
German, 15th century
Black printing ink with opaque watercolor on paper, $2\frac{1}{16} \times 1\frac{5}{16}$ in. (5.2 × 3.3 cm)
The Metropolitan Museum of Art, New York, The Elisha Whittelsey Collection, The Elisha Whittelsey Fund, 1966 (66.529.10)

41
Man of Sorrows
Italian, last quarter of the 14th century
Champlevé enamel, gilded copper, $4\frac{1}{8} \times 3\frac{1}{8} \times \frac{1}{16}$ in. (10.4 × 8 × .2 cm)
The Metropolitan Museum of Art, New York, Gift of Georges Seligmann, in memory of his wife, Edna, his father, Simon Seligmann, and his brother, René, 1982 (1982.480)

42
Christ Child with an apple, ca. 1470–80
Circle of Michel Erhart (German, active 1464–1522)
Willow with paint and gold, $14\frac{15}{16} \times 7\frac{1}{2} \times 4\frac{3}{4}$ in. (38 × 19.1 × 12.1 cm)
The Metropolitan Museum of Art, New York, The Cloisters Collection, 2012 (2012.449)

43
Christ and Saint John the Evangelist
German, 1300–20
Oak with paint and gold, $36\frac{1}{2} \times 25\frac{3}{8} \times 11\frac{5}{16}$ in. (92.7 × 64.5 × 28.7 cm)
The Cleveland Museum of Art, Ohio, Purchase from the J. H. Wade Fund (1928.753)

44
The Visitation, ca. 1310–20
Attributed to Master Heinrich of Constance (German, active in Constance, ca. 1300)
Walnut with paint, gold, and rock-crystal cabochons in gilded silver mounts, $23\frac{1}{4} \times 11\frac{7}{8} \times 7\frac{1}{4}$ in. (59.1 × 30.2 × 18.4 cm)
The Metropolitan Museum of Art, New York, Gift of J. Pierpont Morgan, 1917 (17.190.724)

TOUCHING SAINT SEBASTIAN

45
Saint Sebastian
Austrian(?), late 15th century
European poplar with paint and gold, $49\frac{1}{4} \times 12\frac{3}{8} \times 9\frac{7}{8}$ in. (125.1 × 31.4 × 25.1 cm)
The Metropolitan Museum of Art, New York, The Cloisters Collection, 1961 (61.15.2)

QUEER CONNECTIONS WITH CHRIST'S BODY

46
Man of Sorrows, ca. 1430
Michele Giambono (Michele Giovanni Bono) (Italian, 1420–1462)
Tempera and gold on wood
Overall, with engaged frame $21\frac{3}{4} \times 15\frac{3}{4}$ in. (54.9 × 38.7 cm); painted surface $18\frac{1}{2} \times 12\frac{1}{4}$ in. (47 × 31.1 cm)
The Metropolitan Museum of Art, New York, Rogers Fund, 1906 (06.180)

MASCULINITIES AND TRANSGENDER EXPRESSION IN *THE BELLES HEURES* OF JEAN DE FRANCE, DUC DE BERRY

47
Saint Jerome in a woman's dress
from *The Belles Heures* of Jean de France, duc de Berry, 1405–1408/1409
The Limbourg Brothers (Franco-Netherlandish, active in France by 1399–1416)
Opaque watercolor, silver, gold, and iron gall ink on parchment, $9\frac{3}{8} \times 6\frac{11}{16}$ in. (23.8 × 17 cm)
The Metropolitan Museum of Art, New York, The Cloisters Collection, 1954 (54.1.1a, b, vol. 2, fol. 184v)

LOVE IN MORTAL TIME

48
A bridal couple
German, 1470
Oil on panel, framed $30\frac{1}{2} \times 20\frac{1}{16} \times 3\frac{3}{16}$ in. (77.5 × 51 × 8.1 cm)
The Cleveland Museum of Art, Ohio, Delia E. Holden and L. E. Holden Funds (1932.179)

EXHIBITION WORKS NOT ILLUSTRATED

Comb
Possibly French, 15th–16th century
Boxwood with bone and silk, 3 ⅞ × 6 ½ × ⅜ in. (9.8 × 16.5 × 1 cm)
The Metropolitan Museum of Art, New York, The Cloisters Collection, 1982 (1982.357)

Man of Sorrows between two angels
German, 15th century
Black printing ink with opaque watercolor on paper, sheet, 3 9⁄16 × 2 ½ in. (9 × 6.4 cm)
The Metropolitan Museum of Art, New York, Bequest of James Clark McGuire, 1930 (31.54.122)

Pair of altar angels
French, ca. 1275–1300
Chestnut with traces of paint, 29 ½ × 6 ½ × 7 in. (75 × 16.5 × 17.8 cm) and 29 × 7 ⅝ × 8 in. (73.7 × 19.4 × 20.3 cm)
The Metropolitan Museum of Art, New York, The Cloisters Collection, 1952 (52.33.1, 2)

Roundel with the Temptation of Saint Anthony
German, 1532
Colorless glass, vitreous paint and silver stain, 8 in. (20.3 cm)
The Metropolitan Museum of Art, New York, The Cloisters Collection, 1982 (1982.433.5)

Roundel with Saint Catherine of Alexandria
South Netherlandish, ca. 1500
Colorless glass, vitreous paint and silver stain, 8 1⁄16 in. (20.5 cm)
The Metropolitan Museum of Art, New York, The Cloisters Collection, 1984 (1984.338a, b)

Amatory brooch
German, ca. 1340–60
Gold and freshwater pearl, 1 ¼ × ⅞ × 1 ½ in. (3.2 × 2.2 × 3.8 cm)
The Metropolitan Museum of Art, New York, The Cloisters Collection, 1986 (1986.386)

Cusped ring
North European, 15th century
Gold, garnet; bezel, ¾ × ½ in. (1.9 × 1.3 cm)
Griffin Collection

Ring brooch
British or French, 1250–1300
Gold, sapphire, garnet, 15⁄16 × 3⁄16 in. (2.4 × .4 cm)
The Metropolitan Museum of Art, New York, Gift of Tobias Meyer and Mark Fletcher, 2013 (2013.453)

Ring brooch
French or British, 13th century
Gold and garnet, ⅝ × 13⁄16 × 3⁄16 in. (1.6 × 2.1 × .5 cm)
The Metropolitan Museum of Art, New York, Purchase, Diane Carol Brandt Gift, in memory of her husband, Martin Lewis, 2018 (2018.355)

Plate with wife beating husband
South Netherlandish, ca. 1480
Copper alloy, 3 ⅞ × 20 ¼ in. (9.8 × 51.5 cm)
The Metropolitan Museum of Art, New York, Gift of Irwin Untermyer, 1964 (64.101.1499)

Narcissus at fountain
from the *Roman de la Rose* (*Romance of the Rose*), 1340, written by Guillaume de Lorris (French ca. 1200–ca. 1240), ca. 1230 with additions by Jean de Meun (French, ca. 1240–ca. 1305), ca. 1275
Possibly Jeanne de Montbaston (French, active ca. 1320–1355)
Opaque watercolor, gold leaf, iron gall ink on parchment, 8 ¼ × 11 13⁄16 in. (21 × 30 cm)
The Morgan Library & Museum, New York, Purchased by J. Pierpont Morgan (1837–1913) in 1912 (MS M.503, fol. 11v)

Marriage of Saint Theodora; Saint Theodore enters the monastery
from *The Golden Legend,* written by Jacobus de Voragine (Italian, ca. 1230–1298), ca. 1259–66
Belgian, 1445–65
Opaque watercolor, gold leaf, silver and ink on parchment, 124 fol, 14 15⁄16 × 10 ⅝ in. (37.9 × 27 cm)
The Morgan Library & Museum, New York (MS M.672–5 III, fol. 310r)

NOTES TO THE ESSAYS

A QUEER MIDDLE AGES

1 Many modern scholars have discussed the similarity. See especially Caroline Walker Bynum, *Christian Materiality: An Essay on Religion in Late Medieval Europe* (Zone Books, 2011), 195–208; Martha Easton, "The Wound of Christ, the Mouth of Hell: Appropriations and Inversions of Female Anatomy in the Later Middle Ages," in *Tributes to Jonathan J. G. Alexander: The Making and Meaning of Illuminated Medieval & Renaissance Manuscripts, Art & Architecture*, ed. Susan L'Engle and Gerald B. Guest (Harvey Miller, 2006), 395–409; Karma Lochrie, "Mystical Acts, Queer Tendencies," in *Constructing Medieval Sexuality*, ed. Karma Lochrie, Peggy McCracken, and James A. Schultz (University of Minnesota Press, 1997), 180–200; Maeve K. Doyle, "Mysticism and Queer Readings of Christ's Side Wound in the Prayer Book of Bonne of Luxembourg," in *Smarthistory*, June 29, 2020, https://smarthistory.org/jean-le-noir-bourgot-miniature-of-christ-wound-passion-prayer-book-bonne-luxembourg/; Michelle M. Sauer, "Queer Time and Lesbian Temporality in Medieval Women's Encounters with the Side Wound," in *Medieval Futurity: Essays for the Future of a Queer Medieval Studies*, ed. Will Rogers and Christopher Michael Roman (De Gruyter; Medieval Institute Publications, 2020), 199–219. For a note of caution, see Ruth Mazo Karras and Katherine E. Pierpont, *Sexuality in Medieval Europe: Doing unto Others*, 4th ed. (Routledge, 2023), 77–78.

2 The text indicates that the charm should be placed in the woman's hand to effect its protective powers. See Mary Morse, *English Birth Girdles: Devotions for Women in "Travell of Childe"* (Medieval Institute Publications, 2024), 271–300; Katherine Storm Hindley, "'Yf A Woman Travell Wyth Chylde Gyrdes Thys Mesure Abowte Hyr Wombe': Reconsidering the English Birth Girdle Tradition," in *Continuous Page: Scrolls and Scrolling from Papyrus to Hypertext*, ed. Jack Hartnell (Courtauld Books Online, 2020), https://courtauld.ac.uk/research/research-resources/publications/courtauld-books-online/continuous-page-scrolls-and-scrolling-from-papyrus-to-hypertext/9-reconsidering-the-english-birth-girdle-tradition-katherine-storm-hindley/; Eleanor Jackson and Julian Harrison, eds., *Medieval Women: Voices and Visions*, exh. cat. (British Library, 2024), 54–55.

3 Easton, "The Wound of Christ, the Mouth of Hell," 402; Jeffrey F. Hamburger, *The Rothschild Canticles: Art and Mysticism in Flanders and the Rhineland circa 1300* (Yale University Press, 1990), 72–82.

4 Easton, "The Wound of Christ, the Mouth of Hell," 401.

5 Joni M. Hand, *Women, Manuscripts and Identity in Northern Europe, 1350–1550* (Ashgate, 2013), 12–16.

6 Ann Marie Rasmussen, *Medieval Badges: Their Wearers and Their Worlds* (University of Pennsylvania Press, 2021); Ben Reiss, "Pious Phalluses and Holy Vulvas: The Religious Importance of Some Sexual Body-Part Badges in Late-Medieval Europe (1200–1550)," *Peregrinations: Journal of Medieval Art and Architecture* 6, no. 1 (2017): 151–76; Jos Koldeweij, "'Shameless and Naked Images': Obscene Badges as Parodies of Popular Devotion," in *Art and Architecture of Late Medieval Pilgrimage in Northern Europe and the British Isles*, ed. Sarah Blick and Rita Tekippe (Brill, 2005), 1:493–510, 2:figs. 232–57; Malcolm Jones, "The Sexual and the Secular Badges," in *Heilig en profaan 2: 1200 laatmiddeleeuwseinsignes uit openbare en particuliere collecties*, ed. H. J. E. van Beuningen, A. M. Koldeweij, and D. Kicken, Rotterdam Papers 12 (Stichting Middeleeuwse Religieuze en Profane Insignes, 2001), 196–206.

7 James A. Brundage, *Law, Sex, and Christian Society in Medieval Europe* (1987; pbk. ed., University of Chicago Press, 1990).

8 For a helpful overview of the linguistic range of desire in the Middle Ages, see James A. Schultz, *Courtly Love, the Love of Courtliness, and the History of Sexuality* (University of Chicago Press, 2006), 64–77, with the caveat that he curiously omits *desiderium* from his discussion.

9 Schultz, *Courtly Love*, 69.

10 Schultz, *Courtly Love*, 71.

11 Medieval Occitan, Old French, Middle English, or Middle High German, respectively.

12 We thank Barbara Drake Boehm for directing us to this image.

13 Raymond, of Capua, *The Life of St. Catherine of Siena*, trans. George Lamb (P. J. Kenedy and Sons, 1960), pt. 1, chap. XI, pp. 99–100. On the discrepancy between biographers' accounts and Catherine's own, see Caroline Walker Bynum, *Holy Feast and Holy Fast: The Religious Significance of Food to Medieval Women* (University of California Press, 1987), 174–75.

14 The choice is in contrast to rays that often figure in images of Saint Francis's stigmatization. On the visual and textual polemics of Catherine's invisible stigmata, see Diega Giunta, "The Iconography of Catherine of Siena's Stigmata," in *A Companion to Catherine of Siena*, ed. Carolyn Muessig, George Ferzoco, and Beverly Mayne Kienzle (Brill, 2012), 259–94; David Ganz, "The Dilemma of a Saint's Portrait: Catherine's Stigmata between Invisible Body Trace and Visible Pictorial Sign," in *Catherine of Siena: The Creation of a Cult*, ed. Jeffrey F. Hamburger and Gabriela Signori (Brepols, 2013), 239–62.

15 *Lancelot do Lac: The Non-Cyclic French Prose Romance*, ed. Elspeth Kennedy (Clarendon Press, 1980), 1:568. For an abridged English translation of this thirteenth-century Old French text, see *Lancelot of the Lake*, trans. Corin F. V. Corley (Oxford University Press, 2000); this quotation, 409.

16 *Lancelot do Lac*, 1:350; Corley, *Lancelot of the Lake*, 324. On the nuances of their shared bed, see Peggy McCracken, "The Love of the Dead: Heroic Love and Heroic Masculinity in the *Prose Lancelot*," in *Entre Hommes: French and Francophone Masculinities in Culture and Theory*, ed. Todd W. Reeser and Lewis Carl Seifert (University of Delaware Press, 2008), 54–56.

17 *Lancelot do Lac*, 1:568; Corley, *Lancelot of the Lake*, 408.

18 For a sampling of views, see McCracken, "The Love of the Dead," 51–66; Carol R. Dover, "Galehot and Lancelot: Matters of the Heart," in *The World and Its Rival: Essays on Literary Imagination in Honor of Per Nykrog*, ed. Kathryn Karczewska and Tom Conley (Rodopi, 1999), 119–35; Gretchen Mieszkowski, "The Prose *Lancelot*'s Galehot, Malory's Lavain, and the Queering of Late Medieval Literature," *Arthuriana* 5, no. 1 (1995): 21–51.

19 *Lancelot do Lac*, 1:348–49; Corley, *Lancelot of the Lake*, 321–23.

20 *Lancelot do Lac*, 1:568; Corley, *Lancelot of the Lake*, 409.

21 Our method is indebted to Eve Sedgwick's definition of queerness: the "open mesh of possibilities, gaps, overlaps, dissonances and resonances, lapses and excesses of meaning when the constituent elements of anyone's gender, of anyone's sexuality aren't made (or *can't be* made) to signify monolithically"; Eve Kosofsky Sedgwick, *Tendencies* (Duke University Press, 1993), 8.

22 Sherry C. M. Lindquist, *Agency, Visuality and Society at the Chartreuse de Champmol* (Ashgate, 2008), esp. 138, 165.

23 Jeffrey F. Hamburger, "The Writing on the Wall: Inscriptions and Descriptions of Carthusian Crucifixions in a Fifteenth-Century Passion Miscellany," in Jeffrey F. Hamburger and Anne S. Korteweg, eds., *Studies in Painting and Manuscript Illumination of the Late Middle Ages and Northern Renaissance: Tributes in Honor of James H. Marrow* (Brepols, 2006), 231–52, esp. 236–37; for the entire text in Latin, see Appendix 2b, 251–52.

24 On this iconography, see Carol M. Schuler, "The Sword of Compassion: Images of the Sorrowing Virgin in Late Medieval and Renaissance Art" (PhD diss., Columbia University, 1987).

25 See Further Reading in this catalogue.

26 Jonathan Weinberg, "Things Are Queer," *Art Journal* 55, no. 4 (1996), 11–14; Teresa de Lauretis, "Queer Theory: Lesbian and Gay Sexualities: An Introduction," *differences: A Journal of Feminist Cultural Studies* 3, no. 2 (1991): vii–xviii; Hannah McCann and Whitney Monaghan, *Queer Theory Now: From Foundations to Futures* (Red Globe Press, 2019). The works of Michel Foucault and Judith Butler are also greatly important in the development of queer theory. See, for instance, Michel Foucault, *The History of Sexuality*, vol. 1, *An Introduction*, trans. Robert Hurley (Vintage Books, 1990); Judith Butler,

Gender Trouble: Feminism and the Subversion of Identity, 10th anniversary ed. (Routledge, 1999).

27 David M. Halperin, *Saint Foucault: Towards a Gay Hagiography* (Oxford University Press, 1997), 62.

28 Visual inspection makes clear that the heart-shaped lock replaced the original, more conventionally shaped lock at some undetermined moment. We thank conservators Marina Kastan and Jennifer Schnitker, Department of Object Conservation, The Metropolitan Museum of Art, New York, for their observations.

29 Karma Lochrie, *Heterosyncracies: Female Sexuality When Normal Wasn't* (University of Minnesota Press, 2005).

30 Roland Betancourt, *Byzantine Intersectionality: Sexuality, Gender, and Race in the Middle Ages* (Princeton University Press, 2020). See also Clovis Maillet, *Les genres fluides: De Jeanne d'Arc aux saintes trans* (Arkhê, 2020).

31 For a more global approach to sex and gender in the Middle Ages, see Bryan C. Keene, "Desires of the Body, Mind, and Soul: Histories of Sexualities in Medieval Europe and the Mediterranean World," in *Companion to Sexuality in the Medieval West*, ed. Michelle M. Sauer and Jenny C. Bledsoe (Arc Humanities Press, forthcoming); Sahar Amer, "Medieval Arab Lesbians and Lesbian-Like Women," *Journal of the History of Sexuality* 18, no. 2 (2009): 215–36.

32 See Diarmaid MacCulloch, *Lower than the Angels: A History of Sex and Christianity* (Allen Lane, 2024).

33 On the relationship between the medieval past and our present as well as community across time, see Carolyn Dinshaw, *Getting Medieval: Sexualities and Communities, Pre- and Postmodern* (Duke University Press, 1999); Leah DeVun and Zeb Tortorici, "Trans, Time, and History," *TSQ: Transgender Studies Quarterly* 5, no. 4 (2018): 518–39; Elizabeth Freeman, *Time Binds: Queer Temporalities, Queer Histories* (Duke University Press, 2010).

BODIES IN FLUX

1 On the tapestry, see Vera K. Ostoia and Nobuko Kajitani, "Two Riddles of the Queen of Sheba," *Metropolitan Museum Journal* 6 (1972): 73–103. Neither end of the tapestry has been cut, and it was likely intended as a wall hanging or cushion cover. In chapter 10 of the Book of Kings, the content of Sheba's questions is not mentioned.

2 The inscriptions are written in Alemannic German. Sheba's scroll reads at right: "Bescheyd mich kuing ob blumen und kind glich an art oder unglich sint." Solomon's reply is on the left-most scroll: "Die bine ein quote blum nit spart das knuwen zoigt die wiplich art."

3 See Sarah Kay and Miri Rubin, eds., *Framing Medieval Bodies* (Manchester University Press, 1994); Caroline Bynum, "Why All the Fuss about the Body? A Medievalist's Perspective," *Critical Inquiry* 22, no. 1 (1995): 27–31; Roy Porter, "History of the Body Reconsidered," in *New Perspectives on Historical Writing*, ed. Peter Burke, 2nd ed. (Penn State University Press, 2001), 233–60; Jean Wirth, *L'image du corps au Moyen Âge* (SISMEL Edizioni del Galluzzo, 2013); Jérôme Bachet, *Corps et âmes: Une histoire de la personne au Moyen Âge* (Flammarion, 2016); Jack Hartnell, *Medieval Bodies: Life, Death, and Art in the Middle Ages* (W. W. Norton & Co., 2019); Wendelien van Welie, *Body Language: The Body in Medieval Art*, exh. cat., Museum Catharijneconvent, Utrecht (nai010, 2020); *begehrt. umsorgt. gemartert. Körper im Mittelalter*, exh. cat., Schweizerisches Nationalmuseum, Zurich (Scheidegger & Spiess, 2023).

4 See Judith Butler, "Performative Acts and Gender Constitution: An Essay in Phenomenology and Feminist Theory," *Theatre Journal* 40, no. 4 (1988): 519–31; Judith Butler, *Who's Afraid of Gender?* (Farrar, Straus and Giroux, 2024).

5 See especially Caroline Walker Bynum, *Metamorphosis and Identity* (Zone Books, 2001).

6 Several scholars have argued this point, most notably Bynum in *Metamorphosis and Identity*. See also Peter Brown, *The Body and Society: Men, Women, and Sexual Renunciation in Early Christianity* (Columbia University Press, 1988), 167.

7 Caroline Walker Bynum, *The Resurrection of the Body in Western Christianity, 200–1336* (Columbia University Press, 1995), 6. See also Caroline Walker Bynum, "Material Continuity, Personal Survival, and the Resurrection of the Body: A Scholastic Discussion in Its Medieval and Modern Contexts," in *Fragmentation and Redemption: Essays on Gender and the Human Body in Medieval Religion* (Zone, 1991), 239–98.

8 Lauren Berlant, *Desire/Love* (Punctum Books, 2012), 64, referencing Elizabeth A. Grosz, *Volatile Bodies: Toward a Corporeal Feminism* (Indiana University Press, 1994).

9 See Berlant, *Desire/Love*, 64, for the notion of "topographical trajectories" of the body.

10 See James A. Brundage, *Law, Sex, and Christian Society in Medieval Europe* (University of Chicago Press, 1987), esp. 517–36. He notes (*Law, Sex, and Christian Society*, 517): "the late fourteenth and fifteenth centuries saw the intrusion of secular law into this domain.... A good many cities adopted local statutes and ordinances providing punishment for adultery, fornication, and other common types of nonmarital sex."

11 See Suzanne Conklin Akbari and Jill Ross, "Introduction: Limits and Teleology: The Many Ends of the Body," in *The Ends of the Body: Identity and Community in Medieval Culture*, ed. Suzanne Conklin Akbari and Jill Ross (University of Toronto Press, 2013), 3–21.

12 For an Old French edition of the text, see Aldobrandino da Siena, *Le Régime du corps...: Texte français du XIIIe siècle, pub.... d'après les manuscrits de la Bibliothèque nationale et de la Bibliothèque de l'arsenal*, ed. Louis Landouzyet and Roger Pépin (Paris: H. Champion, 1911). For an excellent study of the text and its manuscripts, see Jennifer Borland, *Visualizing Household Health: Medieval Women, Art, and Knowledge in the* Régime du corps (Penn State University Press, 2022). On Creation images specifically, see Luís Miguel Campos Ribeiro, "Picturing Medieval Health: Artistic Production and Visual Discourse in *Le Régime du corps* of the Ajuda Library (COD 52-XIII-26)" (master's thesis, Universidade NOVA de Lisboa, 2016).

13 This divine will can be understood as "voluntas" in other parts of the Bible (e.g., Matthew 6:10), but in Genesis (1:3), it manifests through the use of the subjective, e.g., "fiat lux" (let there be light).

14 Jennifer Borland (*Visualizing Household Health*, esp. chap. 2, 61–92) has made the strongest case for the possibility of a female reader. For more on the study of medieval medicine and care of medieval bodies, see Hartnell, *Medieval Bodies*, and Tanja Klemm, *Bild Physiologie: Wahrnehmung und Körper in Mittelalter und Renaissance* (Academie Verlag, 2013). See also Raphaël Cuir, *The Development of the Study of Anatomy from the Renaissance to Cartesianism: Da Carpi, Vesalius, Estienne, Bidloo* (Edwin Mellen Press, 2009).

15 Translation from Aldobrandino da Siena, *Le Régime du corps*, by Joan Ferrante, "Epistolæ, Medieval Women's Latin Letters," https://epistolae.ctl.columbia.edu/letter/501.html.

16 https://epistolae.ctl.columbia.edu/letter/501.html.

17 https://epistolae.ctl.columbia.edu/letter/501.html.

18 Borland, *Visualizing Household Health*, 99.

19 For more on this iconography, its meaning, and the ways that theologians understood Adam and Eve's conjoined bodies, see Leah DeVun, *The Shape of Sex: Nonbinary Gender from Genesis to the Renaissance* (Columbia University Press, 2021), esp. chap. 1, 16–39.

20 See *The Summa Theologiæ of St. Thomas Aquinas*, trans. Fathers of the English Dominican Province, 2nd rev. ed. (1920; online ed., 2017), pt. 1, question 51, "The Angels in Comparison with Bodies," https://www.newadvent.org/summa/1051.htm. On queer readings of medieval angels, see Karl Whittington, "Queer," in "Medieval Art History Today—Critical Terms," special issue, *Studies in Iconography* 33 (2012): 157–68, esp. 164.

21 See Nancy Turner, "'Incarnation' Illuminated: Painting the Flesh in Medieval and Renaissance Manuscripts," in *Colour: The Art and Science of Illuminated Manuscripts*, ed. Stella Panayotova, exh. cat., Fitzwilliam Museum, Cambridge (Harvey Miller, 2016), 270–303; Luke Demaître, *Medieval Medicine: The Art of Healing, from Head to Toe* (Praeger, 2013).

22 See Aldobrandino da Siena, *Le Régime du corps*, "De le coleur clere et rouge," 194.

23 Peter Biller, "Black Women in Medieval Scientific Thought," in *Black Skin in the Middle Ages / La peau noire au Moyen Âge* (SISMEL Edizioni del Galluzzo, 2014), 59–65.

24 Biller ("Black Women in Medieval Scientific Thought," 59) helpfully notes, "While colors deriving from internal matters had subtle variety, those deriving from external matters only had duality, and they dominated, through their geographical-climactic exemplification."

25 The consequences for this transgression are multiple (Genesis 3:7–19). God evicts the first couple from the Garden of Eden and punishes each in gender-specific ways: Eve will "in sorrow... bring forth children" and be theretofore under her "husband's power." Adam, in turn, is cursed to work, or must "labor and toil" in order to have food. The snake, too, is punished for tempting Eve to eat the apple: it must roam the earth on its chest and will be cursed by animals and women (Genesis 3:14–15).

26 See James A. Schultz, *Courtly Love, the Love of Courtliness, and the History of Sexuality* (University of Chicago Press, 2006), esp. 68–69. For late-antique theologian Augustine of Hippo (d. 430), this is the precise moment that Adam and Eve become aware of their sexed bodies and sexually aroused.

27 See Dyan Elliott, *Fallen Bodies: Pollution, Sexuality, and Demonology in the Middle Ages* (University of Pennsylvania Press, 1999).

28 I am grateful to Helen Branch for thought-provoking conversations about this object.

29 Medieval exegetes understood the fruit to be an apple, whose name in Latin was also the word for evil (*malum*). See Jeffrey M. Hoffeld, "Adam's Two Wives," *Metropolitan Museum of Art Bulletin* 26, no. 10 (1968): 430–40, esp. 440.

30 See Hoffeld, "Adam's Two Wives," for more on this argument.

31 Paul Williamson, *Northern Gothic Sculpture: 1200–1450* (Victoria and Albert Museum, 1988), 118, fig. 8. Melanie Holcomb and I are grateful to Michaela Zöschg for allowing us to examine the object with her.

32 Inappropriate love of oneself was strongly associated with same-sex love and sexual desire in medieval thought. Textual and visual narratives of Narcissus, for instance, who fell in love with his own reflection in a fountain, were regularly read in relation to same-gender desire. Christopher T. Richards's recent scholarship on Narcissus further argues that he is a kind of emblem for a group of fourteenth-century manuscript illuminators who are thinking about painting as an "unnatural" or queer art form. See Christopher T. Richards, "Picturing Desire and Desiring Pictures: Ovide moralisé and the Vernacular Manuscript Tradition" (PhD diss., Institute of Fine Arts, New York University, 2024); Christopher T. Richards, "Painting against Nature: A Medieval Queer Theory of Art and the Artist," *Art History* 48, no. 2 (April 2025). I extend my sincere thanks to Richards for sharing a copy of his article with me prior to its publication.

33 Much has been written on this image. See, for instance, Robert Mills, *Seeing Sodomy in the Middle Ages* (University of Chicago Press, 2015), esp. 25–80.

34 Same-sex desire is most often figured obliquely in medieval art, in keeping with the way that many medieval people, particularly members of the Church, spoke about it. James Brundage (*Law, Sex, and Christian Society*, 534) details that a conservative cleric, John Mirc (ca. 1450), "cautioned preachers that they should avoid mentioning sodomy and other sexual sins in their sermons."

35 The term's origins can be traced back to Genesis 19, which recounts the story of the citizens of Sodom and Gomorrah, who wanted to "know" two angels who were guests in the home of Lot.

36 Robert Mills, "Homosexuality: Specters of Sodom," in *A Cultural History of Sexuality in the Middle Ages*, ed. Ruth Evans (Berg, 2011), 57–79, esp. 59, 228n6.

37 James Brundage (*Law, Sex, and Christian Society*, 533–34) also details the way that legal theorists understood sodomy's origins in the "practices of the women" in Sodom and Gomorrah. But despite sodomy's conceptual connection to women, those who policed its practice were far more preoccupied with the risk of sex between men rather than that between women.

38 Brundage, *Law, Sex, and Christian Society*, 1.

39 Mills ("Homosexuality," 64) attributes the impetus to a growing "conflation of sodomites with heretics."

40 We do not know much about the supposed crime, only that "King Rudolph burned Lord Haspisperch for the vice of sodomy." See Louis Crompton, *Homosexuality & Civilization* (Belknap Press of Harvard University Press, 2003), 201n87.

41 Mills, "Homosexuality," 65, 229n27; Helmut Puff, "Female Sodomy: The Trial of Katherina Hetzeldorfer," *Journal of Medieval and Early Modern Studies* 30, no. 1 (2000): 41–51, esp. 48.

42 I have elected to use female pronouns here so as not to impose other pronouns on Katherina, inspired by Leah DeVun's method in "Introduction: Stories and Selves," in *The Shape of Sex*, 1–15.

43 Puff, "Female Sodomy," 46, fol. 13r.

44 In late-medieval Speyer, it was illegal for people with female-sexed bodies to wear men's clothing, and vice versa. See Puff, "Female Sodomy," 50n38; see also Valerie R. Hotchkiss, *Clothes Make the Man: Female Cross-Dressing in Medieval Europe* (Garland Publishing, 1996).

45 In other cities there was a fine for cross-dressing, as there was fear that men would dress as women in order to sit in sections of churches reserved for women and flirt with them. See Brundage, *Law, Sex, and Christian Society*, 536.

46 Francesca Canadé Sautman and Pamela Sheingorn, "Introduction: Charting the Field," in *Same Sex Love and Desire among Women in the Middle Ages*, ed. Francesca Canadé Sautman and Pamela Sheingorn (Palgrave, 2001), 4.

47 For a chart of thirty-four medieval saints who change their gender presentation, see Clovis Maillet, *Les genres fluides: De Jeanne d'Arc aux saintes trans* (Arkhê, 2020), 61–64. See also Roland Betancourt, *Byzantine Intersectionality: Sexuality, Gender, and Race in the Middle Ages* (Princeton University Press, 2020); Alicia Spencer-Hall and Blake Gutt, eds., *Trans and Genderqueer Subjects in Medieval Hagiography* (Amsterdam University Press, 2021); Greta LaFleur, Masha Raskolnikov, and Anna Kłosowska, eds., *Trans Historical: Gender Plurality Before the Modern* (Cornell University Press, 2021).

48 Joan Cadden, *The Meaning of Sex Difference in the Middle Ages: Medicine, Science, and Culture*, 1st pbk. ed. (Cambridge University Press, 1995); Leah DeVun, *The Shape of Sex*, esp. chap. 4, "Sex and Order in Natural Philosophy and Law," 102–33; Betancourt, *Byzantine Intersectionality*, 97, 100n25, where he quotes Philo of Alexandria: "For progress is indeed nothing else than the giving up of the female gender by changing into the male, since the female gender is material, passive, corporeal and sense-perceptible, while the male is active, rational, incorporeal and more akin to mind and thought."

49 See Betancourt, "Where Are All the Trans Women in Byzantium?" in LaFleur et al., *Trans Historical*, 297–315.

50 For more on the representation of Saint Wilgefortis, see Robert Mills, "Recognizing Wilgefortis," in LaFleur et al., *Trans Historical*, 133–59; Hannah Skoda, "St Wilgefortis and Her/Their Beard: The Devotions of Unhappy Wives and Non-Binary People," *History Workshop Journal* 95 (2023): 51–74.

51 See Anne-Françoise Leurquin and Marie-Laure Savoye, "New York Morgan Library and Museum, M.672-675; Mâcon, Bibliothèque municipale, 003," http://jonas.irht.cnrs.fr/manuscrit/73511.

52 On the text and images of Saint Marin(e) (also called Saint Marinos/Marina), see Betancourt, *Byzantine Intersectionality*, 1–18, 89–120; M. W. Bychowski, "The Authentic Lives of Transgender Saints: Imago Dei and imitatio Christi in the Life of Saint Marinos the Monk," in Spencer-Hall and Gutt, *Trans and Genderqueer Subjects*, 245–65.

53 I am grateful to Tommy Myhill for our exchanges about this image.

54 Artists typically depicted the moment in which the saint's female-sexed body is revealed. In the case of Saint Marin(e), see, for instance, Bibliothèque National de France, Paris, MS Français 51, fol. 201v. This manuscript is an illuminated copy of Vincent Beauvais's *Miroir Historial*, trans. Jean de Vignay, https://gallica

.bnf.fr/iiif/ark:/12148/btv1b52506706r/item. See Nancy Thebaut "Gender," in *Handbook of Medieval Ornament*, ed. David Ganz et al. (De Gruyter, forthcoming).

55 The artist's decision to depict Marin(e) as only a monk can be seen as further evidence of what Christopher T. Richards has identified as late-medieval theorizations of manuscript painting as "unnatural" or queer in the ways that they subvert that which is natural. See Christopher T. Richards, "Couverture: Transing the Medieval Manuscript," *Arthuriana: The Journal of Arthurian Studies*, forthcoming. I thank Richards for sharing a copy of this article with me prior to its publication.

56 See the chart in Maillet (*Genres fluides*, 61–64) for the names of saints and the reasons (according to their narrators) they changed their gender presentation.

57 In the thirteenth-century *Roman de Silence*, the protagonist Silence (who, like Marin[e], is also female-sexed, but lives as male) expresses his desire to remain male: "I'm a young man, not a girl. I don't want to lose my high position; I don't want to exchange it for a lesser... I would rather have God strike me dead!"; *Silence: A Thirteenth-Century French Romance*, trans. and ed. Sarah Roche-Mahdi (Michigan State University Press, 1999), 125. See also Richards, "Couverture."

58 Here I take inspiration from Kit Heyam, *Before We Were Trans: A New History of Gender* (Seal Press, 2022).

59 There are a few exceptions, however, including so-called natural eunuchs. See Georges Sidéris, "'Eunuchs of Light': Power, Imperial Ceremonial and Positive Representations of Eunuchs in Byzantium (4th–12th Centuries AD)," in *Eunuchs in Antiquity and Beyond*, ed. Shaun Tougher (Classical Press of Wales, 2002), 161–75. For queer approaches to the study of eunuchs, see Betancourt, *Byzantine Intersectionality*, esp. 161–204; Sean Burke, *Queeering the Ethiopian Eunuch: Strategies of Ambiguity in Acts* (Fortress Press, 2013).

60 Kathryn Ringrose has proposed that eunuchs occupied a "third gender"; Kathryn M. Ringrose, *The Perfect Servant: Eunuchs and the Social Construction of Gender in Byzantium* (University of Chicago Press, 2003). Shaun Tougher has in turn argued that eunuchs could switch between genders depending on the context; Shaun Tougher, *The Eunuch in Byzantine History and Society* (Routledge, 2008). Roland Betancourt (*Byzantine Intersectionality*, 109) writes that they are "embodiments of genderqueer figures."

61 Brown, *The Body and Society*, 169; Betancourt, *Byzantine Intersectionality*, 109, referencing Ringrose, *The Perfect Servant*, 230n73.

62 While the figure is most often referred to by scholars as the Ethiopian eunuch, this language is somewhat imprecise and dehumanizing. Instead, we use the name Simeon Bachos, even though not all medieval exegetes agreed that this was the figure's name. Irenaeus of Lyon (d. 202) calls this person "Simeon" in his book *Adversus haereses* (180), and the Ethiopian Orthodox Church has historically called him "Bachos."

63 See Acts 8:32.

64 On epidermal and hermeneutic race, see Geraldine Heng, *The Invention of Race in the European Middle Ages* (Cambridge University Press, 2018); Pamela A. Patton, "Blackness, Whiteness, and the Idea of Race in Medieval European Art," in *Whose Middle Ages? Teachable Moments for an Ill-Used Past*, ed. Andrew Albin, Mary C. Erler, Thomas O'Donnell, Nicholas L. Paul, and Nina Rowe (Fordham University Press, 2019), 154–65.

65 Suzanne Conklin Akbari, "Where Is Medieval Ethiopia? Mapping Ethiopic Studies within Medieval Studies," in *Toward a Global Middle Ages: Encountering the World through Illuminated Manuscripts*, ed. Bryan C. Keene (J. Paul Getty Museum, 2019), 80–91; Henry Louis Gates Jr., "Introduction: Balthazar's Blackness: Equally Noble, Equally Foreign," in *Balthazar: A Black African King in Medieval and Renaissance Art*, ed. Kristen Collins and Bryan C. Keene (J. Paul Getty Museum, 2023), x–xiii. Akbari ("Where Is Medieval Ethiopia?," 80–91) notes that on medieval maps, the location of "Ethiopia" varies widely; at times it is in India, at others in eastern Africa.

66 These figures mark Ethiopia as "a key reference point in salvation history" as well as a "repeated point of reference, whose essential identity remains the same throughout time"; Akbari, "Where Is Medieval Ethiopia?," 81.

67 Akbari, "Where Is Medieval Ethiopia?," 84. John of Mandeville notes the magus's ties to Ethiopia: "in this land of Ethiopia is the city of Saba, of which one of the three kings that offered to our Lord was king"; quoted in Kristen Collins and Bryan C. Keene, "An African King in Art and Legend," in Collins and Keene, *Balthazar*, 13, 119n7.

68 Elizabeth Ross, *Picturing Experience in the Early Printed Book: Breydenbach's* Peregrinatio *from Venice to Jerusalem* (Penn State University Press, 2014), 74–86. The image of the Ethiopian priest at left corresponds vaguely with the text below, which describes the ways that both "women and men wrap blue veils or bandages around their heads and go barefoot"; Ross, *Picturing Experience in the Early Printed Book*, 84. The text that describes their practice of Christianity is tinged with judgment, but there is obvious curiosity in the Ethiopic language, Ge'ez, of which Breydenbach prints the alphabet.

69 Sam Kennerly, "Ethiopian Christians in Rome, c. 1400–c.1700," in *A Companion to Religious Minorities in Early Modern Rome*, ed. Matthew Coneys Wainwright and Emily Michelson (Brill, 2020), 142–68, esp. 165.

70 See Kristen Collins and Bryan C. Keene, "Black Africans and the Paradox of the Renaissance," in Collins and Keene, *Balthazar*, 83.

71 On late-medieval images of the Fountain of Youth and its connection to actual bathing practices, see Christiane Klapisch-Zuber, "La Fontaine de Jouvence: Bain et jeunesse entre XIVe et XVIe siècle," *Clio: Femmes, Genre, Histoire* 42 (2015): 181–90.

72 Henry Louis Gates, Jr., "Did a Black Man Discover the Fountain of Youth?," *The Root*, December 23, 2013, https://www.theroot.com/did-a-black-man-discover-the-fountain-of-youth-1790899464.

73 Andreas Capellanus, *The Art of Courtly Love*, trans. and ed. John Jay Parry (Columbia University Press, 1960), 32.

74 Capellanus, *The Art of Courtly Love*, 32.

75 Michael Camille, *The Medieval Art of Love: Objects and Subjects of Desire* (Abrams, 1998), 58; Peter Dronke, *Medieval Latin and the Rise of European Love-Lyric*, vol. 2, *Medieval Latin Love Poetry* (Clarendon Press, 1966), 485.

76 Capellanus, *The Art of Courtly Love*, 185.

77 James Schultz argues this point throughout *Courtly Love*.

78 Kristen Collins and Bryan C. Keene, "An African King in Art and Legend," in Collins and Keene, *Balthazar*, 17. Saba was understood as Arabia, Ethiopia, or India.

79 Betancourt (*Byzantine Intersectionality*, 182) considers a similar line of thinking.

80 Guillaume de Lorris and Jean de Meun, *The Romance of the Rose*, trans. Frances Horgan (Oxford University Press, 2009), 246. I thank Christopher Richards for speaking with me about medieval ideas of Nature and Nurture in relation to this tapestry. For more on Nature in the *Roman de la Rose*, see Richards, "Painting against Nature."

81 De Lorris and de Meun, *The Romance of the Rose*, 248.

82 Nature and Nurture also engage in a heated debate in the *Roman de Silence*. When Nature learns that Silence is living as male, she is furious. Nurture responds: "Nature, leave my nursling alone... I have completely dis-natured her [Silence]. She will always resist you.... I have succeeded very well in turning a noble child into a defective male. I will undo all your work. Nature, begone in disgrace!"; Roche-Mahdi, *Silence*, 123.

83 Barbara Newman, *God and the Goddesses: Vision, Poetry, and Belief in the Middle Ages* (University of Pennsylvania Press, 2003), 136.

84 See Judith Butler, *Bodies That Matter: On the Discursive Limits of Sex* (Routledge, 1993).

85 On visibility as a trap, see Michel Foucault, *Discipline and Punish: The Birth of the Prison*, trans. Alan Sheridan, 2nd ed. (Vintage Books, 1995), 200; Chris E. Vargas, "Welcome to MOTHA," *Trans Hirstory in 99 Objects*, ed. David Evans Frantz, Christina Linden, and Chris E. Vargas (Hirmer, 2024), 10–14.

MEDIEVAL EROTICA

1 Peter Dronke, *Medieval Latin and the Rise of European Love-Lyric*, vol. 2, *Medieval Latin Love-Poetry* (Clarendon Press, 1966), 478–79. See his remarks on the gender of the writer and recipient, *Medieval Latin*, 2:482. See also Peter Dronke, "Women's Love Letters from Tegernsee," in *Medieval Letters: Between Fiction and Document*, ed. Christian Høgel and Elisabetta Bartoli (Brepols, 2015), 215–45, esp. 227–28.

2 Carolyn Dinshaw, *How Soon Is Now?: Medieval Texts, Amateur Readers, and the Queerness of Time* (Duke University Press, 2012), 4.

3 Jack Halberstam, *In a Queer Time and Place: Transgender Bodies, Subcultural Lives* (New York University Press, 2005), 6. See also Lee Edelman, *No Future: Queer Theory and the Death Drive* (Duke University Press, 2004); Tom Boellstorff, "When Marriage Falls: Queer Coincidences in Straight Time," *GLQ: A Journal of Lesbian and Gay Studies* 13, nos. 2–3 (2007): 227–48; Leah DeVun and Zeb Tortorici, "Trans, Time, and History," *TSQ: Transgender Studies Quarterly* 5, no. 4 (2018): 518–39.

4 So troubling is this lack of resolution to modern eyes that one scholar proposed that the lid had been replaced. See Laila Gross, cat. 16, in Carmen Gómez-Moreno, assisted by Charles E. von Nostitz, *Medieval Images: A Glimpse into the Symbolism and Reality of the Middle Ages*, exh. cat. (Katonah Gallery, 1978). Physical examination shows that the lid and box fit together and stylistically seem to derive from the same second-tier workshop. The carving of the lid is slightly askew, which prevents the bands used for metal strapping to align with those on the box's front face. Crucially, however, the bands match up perfectly with those on the back face, which is where the box and lid would have been hinged together. In a letter to Jean Campbell (see note 5), dated June 17, 1992, curator Charles Little also noted the stylistic similarity between the lid and the sides, remarking that if the top was not original to the work, it was replaced "at a very early date and perhaps by the same ivory workshop"; Object Files, Department of Medieval Art, The Metropolitan Museum, New York.

5 C. Jean Campbell, "Courting, Harlotry and the Art of Gothic Ivory Carving," *Gesta* 34, no. 1 (1995): 11–19.

6 "What is the difference between erotica and pornography?," undated question posted in the series Notes and Queries, https://www.theguardian.com/notesandqueries/query/0,,-2224,00.html.

7 Martha Easton, "'Was It Good For You, Too?': Medieval Erotic Art and Its Audiences," *Different Visions: New Perspectives on Medieval Art* 1 (2008), https://doi.org/10.61302/BUIO3522; Sarah Salih, "Erotica," in *A Cultural History of Sexuality in the Middle Ages*, ed. Ruth Evans (Berg, 2011), 181–212; Madeline H. Caviness, "Erotic Iconography," in *The Routledge Companion to Medieval Iconography*, ed. Colum Hourihane (Routledge, 2017), 267–82.

8 Among the groundbreaking works in this area are Michael Camille, *The Medieval Art of Love: Objects and Subjects of Desire* (Abrams, 1998); Michael Camille, "'For Our Devotion and Pleasure': The Sexual Objects of Jean, Duc de Berry," *Art History* 24, no. 2 (April 2001): 169–94; Alexa Sand, "The Fairest of Them All: Reflections on Some Fourteenth-Century Mirrors," in *Push Me, Pull You: Imaginative, Emotional, Physical, and Spatial Interaction in Late Medieval and Renaissance Art*, ed. Sarah Blick and Laura D. Gelfand (Brill, 2011), 529–59; Diane Wolfthal, "The Sexuality of the Medieval Comb," in *Thresholds of Medieval Visual Culture: Liminal Spaces*, ed. Elina Gertsman and Jill Stevenson (Boydell Press, 2012), 176–94.

9 *The Book of Vices and Virtues: A Fourteenth Century English Translation of the Somme le Roi of Lorens D'Orleans*, ed. W. Nelson Francis (published for the Early English Text Society by H. Milford, Oxford University Press, 1942), 44.

10 As quoted in Michael Baxandall, *The Limewood Sculptors of Renaissance Germany* (Yale University Press, 1980), 88–89.

11 *Andreas Capellanus on Love*, ed. and trans. P. G. Walsh (Duckworth, 1982), 33. The term Andreas uses is "immoderata cogitatione." On the multisensory nature of pleasure, see Michael Camille, "Editor's Introduction," in Michael Camille and Adrian Rifkin, eds., *Other Objects of Desire: Collectors and Collecting Queerly* (Blackwell, 2001), 2.

12 C. Stephen Jaeger, *Ennobling Love: In Search of a Lost Sensibility* (University of Pennsylvania Press, 1999), 11–26.

13 Karma Lochrie, *Heterosyncrasies: Female Sexuality When Normal Wasn't* (University of Minnesota Press, 2005), xviii–xix.

14 Karma Lochrie and Usha Vishnuvajjala, eds., *Women's Friendship in Medieval Literature* (Ohio State University Press, 2022).

15 For instance, the *Prose Lancelot* by Marie de France, and *Sir Gawain and the Green Knight*. See Albert B. Friedman and Richard H. Osberg, "Gawain's Girdle as Traditional Symbol," *Journal of American Folklore* 90, no. 357 (1977): 301–15. The best discussion of the use and form of medieval belts is Ronald W. Lightbown, *Mediaeval European Jewellery: With a Catalogue of the Collection in the Victoria & Albert Museum* (Victoria & Albert Museum, 1992), 306–41.

16 Benjamin Linley Wild, "A Gift Inventory from the Reign of Henry III," *English Historical Review* 125, no. 514 (2010): 529–69, esp. 545–47.

17 Wild, "A Gift Inventory from the Reign of Henry III," 532–33.

18 Wild, "A Gift Inventory from the Reign of Henry III," 544–45.

19 Bernard Prost and Henri Prost, eds., *Inventaires mobiliers et extraits des comptes des ducs de Bourgogne de la maison de Valois (1363–1477)*, 2 vols. (Paris: Ernest Leroux, 1902–13). For examples of servants, see Prost and Prost, *Inventairs mobiliers*, 2:50, no. 322; 2:92, no. 543; 2:100, no. 576. For Philip's brothers on New Year's Day, see Prost and Prost, *Inventairs mobiliers*, 2:180–82, no. 1194.

20 Prost and Prost, *Inventairs mobiliers*, 1:75 no. 510, 2:75 no. 447; Danielle Gaborit-Chopin, ed., *L'inventaire du trésor du dauphin futur Charles V, 1363: Les débuts d'un grand collectionneur* (Société de l'Histoire de l'Art Français, 1996), 66 no. 532.

21 Jaeger, *Ennobling Love*; Carol M. Chattaway, *The Order of the Golden Tree: The Gift-Giving Objectives of Duke Philip the Bold of Burgundy* (Brepols, 2006); Brigitte Buettner, "Past Presents: New Year's Gifts at the Valois Courts, ca. 1400," *Art Bulletin* 83, no. 4 (December 2001): 598–625.

22 Dietrich von der Glezze, "The Belt," in *Erotic Tales of Medieval Germany*, ed. and trans. Albrecht Classen (ACMRS [Arizona Center for Medieval and Renaissance Studies], 2007), 19–28.

23 Von der Glezze, "The Belt," 47.

24 See Wolfthal, "The Sexuality of the Medieval Comb"; Emma Le Pouésard, "Contested Sites of Feminine Agency: Ivory Grooming Implements in Late Medieval Europe" (PhD diss., Columbia University, 2024), esp. 58–119.

25 *Andreas Capellanus on Love*, 268–69.

26 Cited in Wolfthal, "The Sexuality of the Medieval Comb," 186–87.

27 I thank Julia Perratore for this reference. Emmanuel Le Roy Ladurie, *Montaillou: Cathars and Catholics in a French Village, 1294–1324*, trans. Barbara Bray (Folio Society, 2005), 165.

28 Roberta Milliken, *Ambiguous Locks : An Iconology of Hair in Medieval Art and Literature* (McFarland & Company, Inc., 2012).

29 Though relatively early, Luitprand of Cremona's no-holds-barred insult of the Byzantine emperor Nicephorus effectively encapsulates the western European attitude toward excessive hair: "you burnt-out coal, you fool; old woman in your walk, wood-devil in your look; you peasant, you frequenter of foul places, you goatfoot, you horn-head, you double-limbed one; bristly, unruly, countrified, barbarian, harsh, hairy, a rebel, a Cappadocian!"; "Luitprand of Cremona: Report of His Mission to Constantinople," *Internet Medieval Sourcebook*, ed. Paul Halsall, https://sourcebooks.fordham.edu/source/liudprand1.asp. See also Kim M. Phillips, "Race and Ethnicity: Hair and Medieval Ethnic Identities," in *A Cultural History of Hair in the Middle Ages*, ed. Roberta Milliken (Bloomsbury Academic, 2022), 125–36.

30 Florent Pouvreau, *Du poil et de la bête: Iconographie du corps sauvage en Occident à la fin du Moyen Âge, XIIIe–XVIe siècle* (Comité des Travaux Historiques et Scientifiques, 2014).

31 Prost and Prost, *Inventaires mobiliers,* 2:248, no. 1501 (December 7, 1386); 2:328–29, no. 1819 (June 1387); 2:320, no. 1787 (December 1387); 2:395, no. 2577 (February 26, 1388); 2:452, no. 3014 (December 9, 1388). Philip's nephew Louis also owned several Desgrez ivory combs as did Louis's brother King Charles VI. Ducal patronage of Desgrez combs continued well into the fifteenth century. See "Peigne" in Victor Gay and Henri Stein, *Glossaire archéologique du Moyen Age et de la Renaissance* (Paris: Librairie de la Société Bibliographique, 1887–1928), 2:217–18.

32 Aldobrandino da Siena, *Le Régime du corps…: Texte français du XIIIe siècle, pub.… d'après les manuscrits de la Bibliothèque nationale* et de *la Bibliothèque de l'arsenal*, ed. Louis Landouzyet and Roger Pépin (Paris : H. Champion, 1911), 85–89. See also Jennifer Borland, *Visualizing Household Health: Medieval Women, Art, and Knowledge in the* Régime du corps (Penn State University Press, 2022).

33 Michel Foucault, *The History of Sexuality*, vol. 1, *An Introduction*, ed. Frédéric Gros, trans. Robert Hurley (Vintage Books, 1980), 103.

34 Morgan Library and Museum, New York (MS M. 133, fol. 57v), https://www.themorgan.org/collection/berry-apocalypse/62; Wolfthal, "The Sexuality of the Medieval Comb," 188–89, fig. 1.2.

35 For example, the comb mentioned in the 1360 inventory of Jeanne de Boulogne; Louis Douët d'Arcq, "Inventaire des meubles de la reine Jeanne de Boulogne, seconde femme du roi Jean (1360)," *Bibliothèque de l'École des Chartes* 40 (1879): 559, no. 129.

36 Illustrated in *The Secular Spirit: Life and Art at the End of the Middle Ages*, exh. cat., The Metropolitan Museum of Art, New York (Dutton, 1975), 94–95, cat. 107b. The comb was sold at auction in 1979; its current whereabouts are unknown. I thank Christine Brennan for her help in trying to track down this work.

37 While scholars regularly assert that the fine teeth of medieval combs were especially designed to remove lice, I can find no evidence to support that claim. One medieval image of delousing in the *Hortus Sanitatis* (Mainz: Jacob Meydenbach, 1491, bk. 2, chap. 119) in fact shows a brush; see, for example, Cambridge University Library, Inc.3.A.8[37], fol. 287v, https://cudl.lib.cam.ac.uk/view/PR-INC- 00003-A-00001-00008-00037/578.

That fine teeth were used for precision styling instead we might surmise from a reference in a fourteenth-century French royal account, which mentions small ivory combs used specifically for hair at the temples; Louis Douët-d'Arcq, *Comptes de l'argenterie des rois de France au XIVe siècle* (Paris: Jules Renouard et Cie, 1851), 396.

38 Elisabeth Lalou, "Inventaire des tablettes médiévales et présentatio générale," in *Les tablettes à écrire de l'antiquité à l'époque moderne: Actes du colloque international du Centre National de la Recherche Scientifique, Paris, Institut de France, 10–11 octobre 1990*, ed. Elisabeth Lalou (Brepols, 1993), 233–88; Michelle P. Brown, "The Role of the Wax Tablet in Medieval Literacy: A Reconsideration in Light of a Find from York," *British Library Journal* 20, no. 1 (1994): 1–16; Svea Janzen, "Notes from the Past: Ivory Writing Tablets and their Users," in *Gothic Ivories between Luxury and Crisis*, ed. Manuela Studer-Karlen (Schwabe Verlag, 2024), 75–99.

39 M. T. Clanchy, *From Memory to Written Record, England 1066–1307* (Blackwell, 1993), 118–25.

40 Bernard Bousmanne, "A propos d'un carnet à écrire en ivoire du 14e siècle conservé à la Bibliothèque Royale de Belgique," in *Als Ich Can: Liber Amicorum in Memory of Professor Dr. Maurits Smeyers*, ed. Bert Cardon et al. (Peeters, 2002), 1:165–202; Catherine Yvard, "Gothic Ivories Unhinged," in *Illuminating the Middle Ages: Tributes to Prof. John Lowden from His Students, Friends and Colleagues*, ed. Laura Cleaver, Alixe Bovey, and Lucy Donkin (Brill, 2020), 326–40.

41 See Brown, "The Role of the Wax Tablet," 10.

42 See Brown, "The Role of the Wax Tablet," 8.

43 Barbara Newman, ed. and trans., *Making Love in the Twelfth Century: "Letters of Two Lovers" in Context* (University of Pennsylvania Press, 2016); Myra Stokes and Ad Putter, *Medieval Love Letters: A Critical Anthology* (Cambridge University Press, 2025), 100 (letter 14), 168 (letter 66).

44 Jacques Toussaint, ed., *Dialogue avec l'invisible: L'art aux sources de l'Europe: Œuvres d'exception issues de la communauté française de Belgique (VIIIe–XVIIe siècle)*, exh. cat. (Société Archéologique de Namur, 2010), 316–21, cat. 42.

45 Diana Webb, *Privacy and Solitude in the Middle Ages* (Hambledon Continuum, 2007); Karma Lochrie, *Covert Operations: The Medieval Uses of Secrecy* (University of Pennsylvania Press, 1999); Philippe Ariès et al., eds., *A History of Private Life*, vol. 2, *Revelations of the Medieval World*, ed. Georges Duby, trans. Arthur Goldhammer (Belknap Press of Harvard University Press, 1988).

46 Giles Constable, *Letters and Letter-Collections*, Typologie des sources du Moyen Age occidental, fasc. 17 (Brepols, 1976); Newman, *Making Love in the Twelfth Century*; Stokes and Putter, *Medieval Love Letters*.

47 Dronke, "Women's Love Letters from Tegernsee."

48 As quoted in Dronke, "Women's Love Letters from Tegernsee," 232–33.

49 Dronke, "Women's Love Letters from Tegernsee," 217–26.

50 Peter Dronke, *Medieval Latin and the Rise of European Love-Lyric*, vol. 1, *Problems and Interpretations* (Clarendon Press, 1965), 221–29; Dronke, *Medieval Latin*, 2:422–47; Newman, *Making Love in the Twelfth Century*, 257–78.

51 Emma Le Pouésard, "Fighter, Player, Hunter: Queer Women and Female Agents on Secular Gothic Ivories," *Medieval Feminist Forum: A Journal of Gender and Sexuality* 59, no. 1 (2023): 5.

52 As quoted in Dronke, *Medieval Latin*, 2:481–82. See also E. Ann Matter, "My Sister, My Spouse: Woman-Identified Women in Medieval Christianity," *Journal of Feminist Studies in Religion* 2, no. 2 (1986): 81–93.

53 Karma Lochrie, "Between Women," in *The Cambridge Companion to Medieval Women's Writing*, ed. Carolyn Dinshaw and David Wallace (Cambridge University Press, 2003), 70–88; Lochrie and Vishnuvajjala, *Women's Friendship in Medieval Literature*.

54 Camille, *The Medieval Art of Love*, 31–32.

55 Robert W. Scheller, *Exemplum: Model-Book Drawings and the Practice of Artistic Transmission in the Middle Ages (ca. 900–ca. 1470)*, trans. Michael Hoyle (Amsterdam University Press, 1995).

56 Maria Schierling, *"Das Kloster der Minne": Edition und Untersuchung; Anhang, vier weitere Minnereden der Donaueschinger Liedersaal-Handschrift* (Kümmerle, 1980). See also Ludger Lieb, "Seeing Love in the World of Lovers: Late Medieval Love Literature as a Fulfillment of Gottfried's *Tristan*," in *Visuality and Materiality in the Story of Tristan and Isolde*, ed. Jutta Eming, Ann Marie Rasmussen, and Kathryn Starkey (University of Notre Dame Press, 2012), 83–104, esp. 95–100.

57 Paula Mae Carns, "*Compilatio* in Ivory: The Composite Casket in the Metropolitan Museum," *Gesta* 44, no. 2 (2005): 69–88. On these types of boxes in general, see Sarah M. Guérin, "Notes on a Scandal: Secular Ivories and Their Social Contexts," in Studer-Karlen, *Gothic Ivories between Luxury and Crisis*, 149–80.

58 *Andreas Capellanus on Love*, 33. See also James A. Schultz, *Courtly Love, the Love of Courtliness, and the History of Sexuality* (University of Chicago Press, 2006), 71–75.

59 On armor as an object of mockery, see Le Pouésard, "Fighter, Player, Hunter," 13.

60 On the various versions of the story, see Susan L. Smith, *The Power of Women: A "Topos" in Medieval Art and Literature* (University of Pennsylvania Press, 2016), 66–102.

61 Smith, *The Power of Women*, esp. 103–36; Marilynn Desmond, *Ovid's Art and the Wife of Bath: The Ethics of Erotic Violence* (Cornell University Press, 2006), 11–34.

62 The story also offered an amusing variant of the many tales of chivalric masochism found in the corpus of courtly romance. The classic discussion is in Slavoj Žižek, *The Metastases of Enjoyment: Six Essays on Woman and Causality* (Verso, 1994).

63 Ruth Mazo Karras and Katherine E. Pierpont, *Sexuality in Medieval Europe: Doing unto Others*, 4th ed. (Routledge, 2023), 27.

64 Kathryn Gravdal, *Ravishing Maidens: Writing Rape in Medieval French Literature and Law* (University of Pennsylvania Press, 1991).

65 Martha Easton, "Roses and Resistance: The Iconography of Courtly Love in the #MeToo Moment," in *Art, Power, and Resistance in the Middle Ages*, ed. Pamela A. Patton (Penn State University Press, 2025), 189–214; Sarah Baechle, Carissa M. Harris, and Elizaveta Strakhov, eds., *Rape Culture and Female Resistance in Late Medieval Literature: With an Edition of Middle English and Middle Scots Pastourelles* (Penn State University Press, 2022); Diane Wolfthal, *Images of Rape: The "Heroic" Tradition and Its Alternatives* (Cambridge University Press, 1999), among many others.

66 Karmen MacKendrick, *Counterpleasures* (State University of New York Press, 1999); Anita Phillips, *A Defence of Masochism* (Faber and Faber, 1998).

67 Sarah Salih, "Unpleasures of the Flesh: Medieval Marriage, Masochism, and the History of Heterosexuality," *Studies in the Age of Chaucer* 33 (2011): 125–47.

68 Martha Easton, "Saint Agatha and the Sanctification of Sexual Violence," *Studies in Iconography* 16 (1994): 83–118.

69 Elizabeth Robertson, "Response: A Telling Difference; Sexual Violence, Consent, and Literary Form," in Baechle et al., *Rape Culture and Female Resistance in Late Medieval Literature*, 167–80.

70 Juliana Dresvina, "'I Am Not Having What She's Having': Female Sexual (Un)Pleasure Medieval and Modern," in *Painful Pleasures: Sadomasochism in Medieval Cultures*, ed. Christopher Vaccaro (Manchester University Press, 2022), 209–34. See also Sherry C. M. Lindquist, "Visualizing Female Sexuality in Medieval Cultures," *Different Visions: New Perspectives on Medieval Art* 1, no. 5 (2014), https://doi.org/10.61302/MGSJ2504; Sarah Salih, "The Trouble with 'Female Sexuality,'" *Different Visions: New Perspectives on Medieval Art* 1, no. 5 (2014), https://doi.org/10.61302/IRRS2726.

71 The same theme is treated on an ivory tablet of inferior craftsmanship in the British Museum, London (1856,0623.97).

72 Jan M. Ziolkowski and Michael C. J. Putnam, eds., *The Virgilian Tradition: The First Fifteen Hundred Years* (Yale University Press, 2008), 874–90.

73 Michael Camille, *Image on the Edge: The Margins of Medieval Art* (Harvard University Press, 1992), 36–46; E. Jane Burns, "Knowing Women: Female Orifices in Old French Farce and Fabliau," *Exemplaria* 4, no. 1 (1992): 81–104.

74 On class distinctions in the explicit depiction of sexuality, see Salih, "Erotica," 200.

75 Though *sadomasochism* is a nineteenth-century term, the concept has proven useful in investigating the various forms of erotized violence found in medieval contexts. See Vaccaro, *Painful Pleasures*.

76 On the ways in which sadism and masochism are *not* complementary states, see Phillips, *A Defence of Masochism*, 11–13.

77 That readers and viewers differed in their understanding of the meaning of the story is evident in illustrations in other contexts. There is no standard iconography and the story is rarely presented with humorous intent. See Gesine Mierke, *Riskante Ordnungen: Von der Kaiserchronik zu Jans von Wien* (Akademie Verlag, 2014), 114–26; Cristelle L. Baskins, *Cassone Painting, Humanism, and Gender in Early Modern Italy* (Cambridge University Press, 1998), 70–72. I thank Nina Rowe for directing me to the German iterations of this theme.

78 Qualitative differences in the many extant medieval ivories indicate that their use extended beyond the courtly class. See Nina Rowe, "Pocket Crucifixions: Jesus, Jews, and Ownership in Fourteenth-Century Ivories," *Studies in Iconography* 32 (2011): 81–120.

79 The Burgundian dukes famously collected precious objects for their own enjoyment. The 1469 accounts of Queen Charlotte of Savoy mention payment to a Paris merchant for a wide selection of ivory objects including two daggers, two boxes, and three hair-parters, all purchased "pour . . . fair son plaisir"; "Ivoire, ivorier," in Gay and Stein, *Glossaire archéologique du Moyen Age et de la Renaissance*, 2:51.

80 The concept of Saint Valentine's Day as a day for lovers appears to have originated among courtly circles in this period. Chaucer's poem "Parliament of Fowls," likely written to honor the 1382 marriage of King Richard II to Anne of Bohemia, is one of the first poems to connect the saint's feast day with romantic love. Jack B. Oruch, "St. Valentine, Chaucer, and Spring in February," *Speculum* 56, no. 3 (1981): 534–65.

81 Prost and Prost, *Inventaires mobiliers*, 2:387, no. 2550.

82 Zita Eva Rohr, *Yolande of Aragon (1381–1442) Family and Power: The Reverse of the Tapestry* (Palgrave Macmillan, 2016), 17–18.

83 Michael Curschmann, "From Myth to Emblem to Panorama," in Eming et al., *Visuality and Materiality in the Story of Tristan and Isolde*, 116.

MARITAL AND MYSTICAL UNIONS

1 Susan L'Engle, "The Illumination of Legal Manuscripts in Bologna, 1250–1350: Production and Iconography" (PhD diss., New York University, 2000). See Susan L'Engle and Robert Gibbs, *Illuminating the Law: Legal Manuscripts in Cambridge Collections*, exh. cat., Fitzwilliam Museum, Cambridge (Harvey Miller, 2001).

2 For an English translation of the *Decretals* of Gregory IX, see *Marriage Canons from the Decretum of Gratian and the Decretals, Sext, Clementines and Extravagantes*, trans. John T. Noonan, Jr., 1993, http://legalhistorysources.com/Canon%20Law/MARRIAGELAW.htm.

3 Some useful discussions of marriage iconography in the Middle Ages include Edwin Hall, *The Arnolfini Betrothal: Medieval Marriage and the Enigma of Van Eyck's Double Portrait* (University of California Press, 1994); Virginia Brilliant, "Art and Love in the Middle Ages," in *A Feast for the Senses: Art and Experience in Medieval Europe*, ed. Martina Bagnoli, exh. cat. (Walters Art Museum, 2016), 117–31; Harriet M. Sonne De Torrens, "Representations of Marriage: Iconographical Origins and Trends," in *A Cultural History of Marriage*, vol. 2, *A Cultural History of Marriage in the Medieval Age*, ed. Joanne Marie Ferraro and Frederik Pedersen (Bloomsbury Academic, 2020), 147–65; Jessica Barker, *Stone Fidelity: Marriage and Emotion in Medieval Tomb Sculpture* (Boydell Press, 2020); Jérôme Baschet, "Matrimonio," in *Enciclopedia dell'arte medievale* (Istituto della Enciclopedia Italiana, 1991–2002), 8:264–70; Jörg Wettlaufer, "Visual Representations of Weddings in the Middle Ages: Reflections of Legal, Religious, and Cultural Aspects," *Religions* 15, no. 8 (2024): 1011, https://doi.org/10.3390/rel15081011.

4 "Great delectation": Barry Windeatt, ed., *The Book of Margery Kempe: Annotated Edition* (Brewer, 2004), bk. 1, chap. 3, 62–63; "happy drunkenness" (*felix inebriatio*): Bonaventure, *Soliloquium de quatuor mentalibus exercitiis*, quoted in Latin in Jeffrey F. Hamburger, *The Rothschild Canticles: Art and Mysticism in Flanders and the Rhineland circa 1300* (Yale University Press, 1990), 280n46.

5 Interview with Michel Foucault (*Le Gai Pied*, April 1981), "Friendship as a Way of Life," in *Ethics: Subjectivity and Truth*, vol. 1 of *The Essential Works of Michel Foucault, 1954–1984*, ed. Paul Rabinow, trans. Robert Hurley et al. (New Press, 1997), 135–40.

6 John T. Noonan, "Marriage in the Middle Ages: 1. The Power to Choose," *Viator* 4 (1973): 419–34. See also Philip L. Reynolds, *How Marriage Became One of the Sacraments: The Sacramental Theology of Marriage from Its Medieval Origins to the Council of Trent* (Cambridge University Press, 2016), chap. 5, "Betrothal and Consent," 157–208.

7 The foundations of the notion of conjugal or marital debt can be found in Paul's First Letter to the Corinthians 7:4–5.

8 Anna Boeles Rowland, "'With this rynge': The Materiality and Meaning of the Late Medieval Marriage Ring," in *Gift-Giving and Materiality in Europe, 1300–1600: Gifts as Objects*, ed. Lars Kjaer and Gustavs Strenga (Bloomsbury Academic, 2022), 17–42.

9 Kathleen M. Ashley and Pamela Sheingorn, eds., *Interpreting Cultural Symbols: Saint Anne in Late Medieval Society* (University of Georgia Press, 1991).

10 Mirella Levi D'Ancona, *The Iconography of the Immaculate Conception in the Middle Ages and Early Renaissance* (College Art Association of America in conjunction wth the Art Bulletin, 1957).

11 See Hall, *The Arnolfini Betrothal*, p. 18, for more on the history of this rite, as well as Bernhard Kötting, "Dextrarum iunctio," *Reallexikon für Antike und Christentum* 3 (1957): 881–88; Reynolds, *How Marriage Became One of the Sacraments,* 88–98.

12 For the medieval marriage rite and its objects, see Brilliant, "Art and Love in the Middle Ages," 117–31; Hall, *The Arnolfini Betrothal*, esp. 13–47; Ronald W. Lightbown, *Mediaeval European Jewellery: With a Catalogue of the Collection in the Victoria & Albert Museum* (Victoria & Albert Museum, 1992), esp. 67–73; Edith Benkov, "Courtship and Ritual," in *A Cultural History of Marriage in the Medieval Age*, vol. 2 of *A Cultural History of Marriage*, ed. Joanne M. Ferraro and Frederik Pedersen (Bloomsbury Academic, 2021), 21–36.

13 In southern Europe, the placement of a ring on the bride's finger could mark the beginning of the marriage itself rather than the promise to marry. See Hall, *The Arnolfini Betrothal,* 34–36; Rowland, "With this rynge," 18–19. See also Marian Campbell, *Medieval Jewellery in Europe 1100–1500* (V&A Publishing, 2009), 92–97.

14 Rowland, "With this rynge," 29–30. See also *Andreas Capellanus on Love*, ed. and trans. P. G. Walsh (Duckworth, 1982), 268–71.

15 "CORTA PORT[A] AMOR," which appears on the outside of the band, can be translated as "courtship leads to love" or "the heart brings love to you." Sandra Hindman with Scott Miller, *Take This Ring: Medieval and Renaissance Rings from the Griffin Collection* (Les Enluminures in association with Brepols, 2015), 198.

16 Hindman and Miller, *Take This Ring*, 193.

17 Diane Wolfthal, *In and Out of the Marital Bed: Seeing Sex in Renaissance Europe* (Yale University Press, 2010), 166–85; Hindman and Miller, *Take This Ring*, 68.

18 Virág Somogyvári, "The Art of Love in Late Medieval Bone Saddles" (master's thesis, Central European University, 2017); Virág Somogyvári, "'Laugh, My Love, Laugh': Mottos, Proverbs and Love Inscriptions on Late Medieval Bone Saddles," *Annual of Medieval Studies at CEU*, Central European University, Budapest 24 (2018): 113–28; Emma Le Pouésard, "Contested Sites of Feminine Agency: Ivory Grooming Implements in Late Medieval Europe" (PhD diss., Columbia University, 2024), 207–10; Maria Schröder, *Die Beinsättel des 13. bis 17. Jahrhunderts: Reitzeuge als Sinnbilder ritterlich-höfischer Ideale* (Deutscher Verlag für Kunstwissenschaft, 2024).

19 Stephen V. Grancsay, "A Mediaeval Sculptured Saddle," *Metropolitan Museum of Art Bulletin* 36, no. 3 (1941): 73–76.

20 Such is the case with Middle English and Middle High German, the languages of the inscriptions on numerous bone saddles. See "riden" and "priken" in the Middle English Compendium: Middle English Dictionary, https://quod.lib.umich.edu/m/middle-english-dictionary/dictionary. See "reiten" in the Deutsches Wörterbuch von Jacob Grimm and Wilhelm Grimm, https://woerterbuchnetz.de/?sigle=DWB&lemid=R04288. Interestingly, J. N. Adams in *The Latin Sexual Vocabulary* (Johns Hopkins University Press, 1982, 165–66) suggests that riding metaphors in pre-medieval Latin were primarily pejorative descriptors for sex acts in which a woman (or a man with another man) assumed the dominant role. "Reiten" (MHG) or "riden" (ME) could also carry the gendered connotation of nagging or hounding. We thank Shirin Fozi and Steven Rozenski for their observations and help with the visual and linguistic dimensions of this object.

21 The story of Patient Griselda likely survives in earlier oral traditions (prior to Bocaccio's *Decameron*). For more on the origins of the story, see Dudley David Griffiths, *The Origin of the Griselda Story* (1931; Folcroft Library Edition, 1973). For variations of her story, see Madeline Rüegg, *The Patient Griselda Myth: Looking at Medieval and Early Modern European Literature* (De Gruyter, 2019). The most thorough treatment of the purse is in Nancy Gardner Feldman, "Towards a New Reading of Aumônières: The Term 'Aumônière Sarazinoise' and the Role of Alms Purses in Images of Late Medieval French Marriage Ceremonies" (PhD diss., University of Chicago, 2012).

22 According to one account of the alms rite in fourteenth-century France, the priest blessed thirteen coins (one for Christ, twelve for the apostles) and then handed them to the groom, who would in turn given them to the bride. She would then place them in her purse. Immediately following or during the nuptial mass, she either gave the coins to the priest to distribute to those in need or handed them out during the offertory. See Feldman, "Towards a New Reading of Aumônières," 145.

23 See Glen D. Burger, *Conduct Becoming: Good Wives and Husbands in the Later Middle Ages* (University of Pennsylvania Press, 2017), esp. chap. 4, "Affecting Conduct: Feeling Steadfast with Griselda," 141–90.

24 All quotations from Bocaccio's *Decameron* are from *The Decameron of Giovanni Boccaccio*, trans. J. M. Rigg (London: A. H. Bullen, 1903), which is widely recognized as a translation that adheres closely to the original Italian. The entire text can be found on Brown University's Decameron Web, https://www.brown.edu/Departments/Italian_Studies/dweb/texts/DecIndex.php?lang=eng.

25 Brown University Decameron Web, X, 10, [004], https://www.brown.edu/Departments/Italian_Studies/dweb/texts/DecShowText.php?myID=nov1010&lang=eng.

26 See Christiane Klapisch Zuber, "Le complexe de Griselda: Dot et dons de marriage au quattrocento," *Mélanges de l'École Française de Rome: Moyen-Age, Temps Modernes* 94, no. 1 (1982): 7–43.

27 We are grateful to Daisy Delogu, Sarah-Grace Heller, and Jacqueline Victor for their help parsing the ambiguities of this iconography; it is also possible that the images represent scenes from *Erec and Enide* by Chrétien de Troyes (ca. 1170); neither story is a perfect fit. Nancy Feldman has also underscored the indeterminacy of the bag's iconography; Feldman, "Towards a New Reading of Aumônières," 194–205.

28 Brown University Decameron Web, X, 10, [061], https://www.brown.edu/Departments/Italian_Studies/dweb/texts/DecShowText.php?myID=nov1010&lang=eng. For more on the ways that teaching one's spouse was considered a form of marital affection worthy of practice, see Burger, *Conduct Becoming*, 19.

29 Philippe de Mézières, *Le livre de la vertu sacrement: Ed. from Paris, Bibl. nat., MS fr. 1175*, ed. Joan B. Williamson (Catholic University of America Press, 1993). See also Burger, *Conduct Becoming*, 170.

30 De Mézières's reading of Griselda's story was not universal: several medieval authors also expressed discomfort with Gualtieri's cruelty, incredulity at Griselda's constancy, and even humor in the ways that the marital contract is pushed to an extreme. Bocaccio, Chaucer, and Christine de Pisan all express concern for the excess suffering she endured and condemn Gualtieri's actions. Even Griselda herself acknowledges the abuse Gualtieri has put her through just before his second wedding (in Bocaccio's account): "I entreat you, that you spare her those tribulations which you did once inflict upon another that was yours, for I scarce think she would be able to bear them"; Brown University Decameron Web, X, 10, [059], https://www.brown.edu/Departments/Italian_Studies/dweb/texts/DecShowText.php?myID=nov1010&lang=eng.

31 See Jessie McNab, cat. 26, in Andrea Bayer, ed., *Art and Love in Renaissance Italy*, exh. cat. (The Metropolitan Museum of Art, 2008), 93–94; Jesse McNab, "European Sculpture and Decorative Arts," in "*Ars Vitraria*: Glass in The Metropolitan Museum of Art," special issue, *Metropolitan Museum of Art Bulletin*, n.s. 59, no. 1 (2001): 45–50, esp. 46; Inês Coutinho, Luís C. Alves, and Teresa Medici, "The Broken Piece of a Larger Picture: A Renaissance Enameled Glass Fragment Depicting a Triumphal Procession," *Journal of Glass Studies* 61 (2019): 87–96, esp. 90.

32 John Webster Spargo's reading is emblematic of a scholarly tradition that refers to the iconographic type as Virgil's revenge in a disturbing erasure of Febilla and the sexual violence she endures. See John Webster Spargo, *Virgil the Necromancer: Studies in the Virgilian Legends* (Harvard University Press, 1934), chap. 6, "The Mage's Revenge," 199–206.

33 On Febilla in the Renaissance context, see Cristelle Louise Baskins, *Cassone Painting,*

Humanism, and Gender in Early Modern Italy (Cambridge University Press, 1998), 70–73.

34 In Bayer, *Art and Love in Renaissance Italy*, McNab (cat. 26, 93–94) offers a more positive reading: "Febilla, who preserved her virginity, saved Rome by accepting her fate, becoming a heroic figure, whereas Virgil, isolated and impotent to inflict further harm, derived no benefit from his humiliation of the princess."

35 For exceptions to this rule, see, for instance, Michael Camille, *The Medieval Art of Love: Objects and Subjects of Desire* (Abrams, 1998), 140–44 ("Doing it"); and Wolfthal, *In and Out of the Marital Bed*, 13–42 ("The Bed").

36 See Jennifer Borland, *Visualizing Household Health: Medieval Women, Art, and Knowledge in the* Régime du corps (Penn State University Press, 2022); Michael Camille, "Manuscript Illumination and the Art of Copulation," in *Constructing Medieval Sexuality*, ed. Karma Lochrie, Peggy MacCracken, and James A. Schultz (University of Minnesota Press, 1997), 58–90; Camille, *The Medieval Art of Love*, 140–44.

37 For more on the regulation of sexual acts and positions, see "Bodies in Flux" in this catalogue.

38 These actions are in keeping with medieval understandings of sex as a transitive act, or something that someone does to someone else. See discussion below. See also Danielle Jacquart and Claude Thomasset, *Sexuality and Medicine in the Middle Ages*, trans. Matthew Adamson (Princeton University Press, 1988); Joan Cadden, *The Meanings of Sex Difference in the Middle Ages: Medicine, Science, and Culture* (Cambridge University Press, 1993); Katharine Park, *Secrets of Women: Gender, Generation, and the Origins of Human Dissection* (Zone Books, 2006); Karl Whittington, "The Cruciform Womb: Process, Symbol, and Salvation in Bodleian Library MS. Ashmole 399," *Different Visions: A Journal of New Perspectives on Medieval Art* 1 (2008), https://doi.org/10.61302/GLRT6998.

39 Aldobrandino da Siena, *Le Régime du corps…: Texte français du XIIIe siècle, pub.… d'après les manuscrits de la Bibliothèque nationale et de la Bibliothèque de l'arsenal*, ed. Louis Landouzyet and Roger Pépin (Paris: H. Champion, 1911), 28–30. See also the partial translation of these passages in Camille, *The Medieval Art of Love*, 142. Borland (*Visualizing Household Health*, 61–92) has argued that the principal readers of *Le Régime du corps* were women.

40 Aldobrandino da Siena, *Le Régime du corps*, 28–30.

41 Aldobrandino da Siena, *Le Régime du corps*, 28–30.

42 Laila Gross argues that the upper body of the man was removed at some point in the box's history. See Laila Gross, cat. 16, in Carmen Gómez-Moreno, assisted by Charles E. von Nostitz, *Medieval Images: A Glimpse into the Symbolism and Reality of the Middle Ages*, exh. cat. (Katonah Gallery, 1978). The scene is clumsily carved, but under magnification there is no obvious evidence of missing elements.

43 Sherry C. M. Lindquist, "Introduction," in *The Meanings of Nudity in Medieval Art*, ed. Sherry C. M. Lindquist (Ashgate, 2012), 1–45, esp. 22–23; Brigitte Buettner, "Profane Illuminations, Secular Illusions: Manuscripts in Late Medieval Courtly Society," *Art Bulletin* 74, no. 1 (1992): 75–90, esp. 86–87.

44 See James A. Brundage, *Law, Sex, and Christian Society in Medieval Europe* (1987; pbk. ed., University of Chicago Press, 1990), 6. Many theologians, including Augustine, noted that using genitalia in ways that go "against nature" is "abominable," an idea adopted by the canonist Gratian; discussed in Karras and Pierpont, *Sexuality in Medieval Europe*, 107, 162. There are a few literary references to oral sex, including by the poet Oswald von Wolkenstein (1337–1445); see Karras and Pierpont, *Sexuality in Medieval Europe*, 163.

45 On this manuscript, see especially Hamburger, *The Rothschild Canticles*; Barbara Newman, "Contemplating the Trinity: Text, Image, and the Origins of the Rothschild Canticles," *Gesta* 52, no. 2 (2013): 133–59; Sherry C. M. Lindquist, "Gender," in "Medieval Art History Today—Critical Terms," special issue, *Studies in Iconography* 33 (2012): 113–30.

46 On potential male identification with the depiction of the soul in the manuscript, see Sarah Bromberg, "Gendered and Ungendered Readings of the Rothschild Canticles," *Different Visions: New Perspectives on Medieval Art* 1 (2008), https://doi.org/10.61302/PMSR4045; Pamela Sheingorn, "Reviews: Jeffrey F. Hamburger, *The Rothschild Canticles…*," *Art Bulletin* 74, no. 4 (1992): 679–81; Robert Mills, "Ecce Homo," in *Gender and Holiness: Men, Women, and Saints in Late Medieval Europe*, ed. Samantha J. E. Riches and Sarah Salih (Routledge, 2002), 152–73.

47 Augustine of Hippo, "The Excellence of Marriage: III, Marriage as a Remedy for Sensuality," in *Love, Sex, & Marriage in the Middle Ages: A Sourcebook*, ed. Conor McCarthy, 2nd ed. (Routledge, 2022), p. 35.

48 See Sarah Salih, *Versions of Virginity in Late Medieval England* (D. S. Brewer, 2001), esp. chap. 2, "Perpetual Incorruption in Corruptible Flesh: Towards a Theory of Virginity," 16–41; Anke Bernau, Ruth Evans, and Sarah Salih, eds., *Medieval Virginities* (University of Toronto Press, 2003), esp. Sarah Salih, Anke Bernau, and Ruth Evans, "Introduction: Virginities and Virginity Studies," 1–13.

49 For the significance of the bed in scenes of the Annunciation, see Laurent Bolard, "*Thalamus Virginis*: Images de la *Devotio moderna* dans la peinture italienne du XVe siècle," *Revue de l'Histoire des Réligions* 216, no. 1 (1999): 87–110; José María Salvador-González, "The Symbol of Bed (*Thalamus*) in Images of the Annunciation of the 14th–15th Centuries in the Light of Latin Patristics," *International Journal of History and Cultural Studies* 5, no. 4 (2019): 49–70.

50 For an overview of the theology of her miraculous impregnation, see Anthony Maas, "Virgin Birth of Christ," *The Catholic Encyclopedia* (Appleton, 1912), vol. 15, as transcribed in http://www.newadvent.org/cathen/15448a.htm.

51 On the linguistics and legal definitions of penetration, see Karras and Pierpont, *Sexuality in Medieval Europe*, 5 and passim.

52 Barbara Drake Boehm, "A Blessing of Unicorns: The Paris and Cloisters Tapestries," special issue, *Metropolitan Museum of Art Bulletin* 28, no. 1 (2020): 31–33.

53 Richard de Fournival, *Master Richard's Bestiary of Love and Response*, trans. Jeanette Beer (Purdue University Press, 2000), 15.

54 On the male-to-male address in the story, see Chimène Bateman, "Gender and Sexuality in the *Rose* I: Theory and Discourse," in *Approaches to Teaching the Romance of the Rose*, ed. Daisy Delogu and Anne-Hélène Miller (Modern Language Association of America, 2023), 85–100, esp. 89–90. On Bel Accueil as a male allegorical figure, see Simon Gaunt, "Bel Acueil and the Improper Allegory of the *Romance of the Rose*," in *New Medieval Literatures: Vol. 2*, ed. Rita Copeland, David Lawton, and Wendy Scase (Clarendon Press, 1998), 65–93. For more on male embraces in the *Roman de la Rose*, see Camille, *The Medieval Art of Love*, 139–40.

55 Guillaume de Lorris and Jean de Meun, *The Romance of the Rose*, trans. Charles Dahlberg, 3rd ed. (Princeton University Press, 1995); Guillaume de Lorris and Jean de Meun, *Le Roman de la Rose*, ed. Armand Strubel (Le Livre de Poche, 1992), 1681–1925.

56 Caroline Walker Bynum, *Holy Feast and Holy Fast: The Religious Significance of Food to Medieval Women* (University of California Press, 1987), 246–50; Karma Lochrie, "Mystical Acts, Queer Tendencies," in Lochrie et al., *Constructing Medieval Sexuality*, 180–200; Sarah Salih, "Performances of Suffering: Secular and Devotional Eros in Late Medieval Writing," in *The Cambridge Companion to Erotic Literature*, ed. Bradford K. Mudge (Cambridge University Press, 2017), 34–46.

57 As quoted in Hamburger, *The Rothschild Canticles*, 74.

58 As quoted in Hamburger, *The Rothschild Canticles*, 74.

59 As quoted in Annette Volfing, *The Daughter Zion Allegory in Medieval German Religious Writing* (Routledge, 2017), 111.

60 "The Mystical Vine," in *The Works of Bonaventure: Cardinal, Seraphic Doctor and Saint*, vol. 1, *Mystical Opuscula*, trans. José de Vinck (St. Anthony Guild Press, 1960), 203–4.

61 James A. Schultz, *Courtly Love, the Love of*

Courtliness, and the History of Sexuality* (University of Chicago Press, 2006), 41.

62 Schultz, *Courtly Love*, 31.

63 Ann W. Astell, *The Song of Songs in the Middle Ages* (Cornell University Press, 1990); E. Ann Matter, *The Voice of My Beloved: The Song of Songs in Western Medieval Christianity* (University of Pennsylvania Press, 1990).

64 Matter, *The Voice of My Beloved*, 6.

65 Hamburger, *The Rothschild Canticles*, 2. This paragraph hews to his discussion of the Song of Songs cycle in the miniatures; Hamburger, *The Rothschild Canticles*, 70–87.

66 David S. Areford, "Printing the Side Wound of Christ," in *The Viewer and the Printed Image in Late Medieval Europe, Visual Culture in Early Modernity* (Ashgate, 2010), 228–67; Vibeke Olson, "Penetrating the Void: Picturing the Wound in Christ's Side as a Performative Space," in *Wounds and Wound Repair in Medieval Culture*, ed. Larissa Tracy and Kelly DeVries (Brill, 2015), 313–39.

67 Annette Lermack, "Spiritual Pilgrimage in the Psalter of Bonne of Luxembourg," in *The Art, Science, and Technology of Medieval Travel*, ed. Robert Bork and Andrea Kann (Ashgate, 2008), 97–111.

68 Lochrie, "Mystical Acts, Queer Tendencies," in Lochrie et al., *Constructing Medieval Sexuality*, 180–200; Martha Easton, "The Wound of Christ, the Mouth of Hell: Appropriations and Inversions of Female Anatomy in the Later Middle Ages," in *Tributes to Jonathan J. G. Alexander: The Making and Meaning of Illuminated Medieval & Renaissance Manuscripts, Art & Architecture*, ed. Susan L'Engle and Gerald B. Guest (Harvey Miller, 2006), 395–409, esp. 397. See also Flora Lewis, "The Wound in Christ's Side and the Instruments of the Passion: Gendered Experience and Response," in *Women and the Book: Assessing the Visual Evidence*, ed. Lesley Smith and Jane H. M. Taylor (British Library; University of Toronto Press, 1997), 204–29.

69 Foucault, "Friendship as a Way of Life," 135–37.

70 Foucault, "Friendship as a Way of Life," 137.

71 Peter Barnet, "A Recently Acquired Christ Child at The Metropolitan Museum of Art and Sculptures for Medieval Nuns," in *A Reservoir of Ideas: Essays in Honour of Paul Williamson*, ed. Glyn Davies and Eleanor Townsend (Paul Holberton Publishing in association with V&A Publishing, 2017), 204–14, figs. 1, 2. The statue is one of many late-medieval sculptures of the infant Christ that are frequently referred to as dolls (*Kindli*). See Frank Matthias Kammel, ed., *Im Zeichen des Christkinds: Privates Bild und Frömmigket im Spätmittelalter: Ergebnisse der Ausstellung Spiegel der Seligkeit* (Verlag de Germanischen Nationalmuseums, 2003); Natalia Keller, "'Pick Him up and Hold Him in your arms': The Function of the Holy Dolls in the Convent Life of the Late Middle Ages," in *Dolls, Puppets, Sculptures and Living Images from the Middle Ages to the End of the 18th Century*, ed. Kamil Kopania (Aleksander Zelwerowicz National Academy of Dramatic Art in Warsaw, Department of Puppetry Art in Białystok, 2017), 76–93; Christine Klapisch-Zuber, "Holy Dolls: Play and Piety in Florence in the Quattrocento," in *Women, Family, and Ritual in Renaissance Italy*, trans. Lydia G. Cochrane (University of Chicago Press, 1985), 310–29; Ulinka Rublack, "Female Spirituality and the Infant Jesus in Late Medieval Dominican Convents," *Gender & History* 6, no. 1 (1994): 37–57; Patricia Simons, "'Kiss the Feet of the Infant Jesus': The Emotional Efficacy of Early Christ Child Sculptures in Europe and Beyond," in *Emotions, Art, and Christianity in the Trans-atlantic World, 1450–1800*, ed. Heather Graham and Lauren Kilroy-Ewbank (Brill, 2021), 247–79.

72 For several monastic visions such as that of the nun Mehthilt von Torlikon, see Gertrud Jaron Lewis, *By Women, for Women, about Women: The Sister-Books of Fourteenth-Century Germany* (Pontifical Institute of Mediaeval Studies, 1996), 102.

73 James A. Schultz, "Parzival's Penis: A Brief History," in *Courtly Love*, 3–16, esp. 4 ("manly valor"), 10 ("penis of love").

74 *Margaret Ebner: Major Works*, trans. and ed. Leonard P. Hindsley (Paulist Press, 1993), 58. See Rosemary Drage Hale, "Rocking the Cradle: Margaretha Ebner (Be)Holds the Divine," in *Performance and Transformation: New Approaches to Late Medieval Spirituality*, ed. Mary A. Suydam and Joanna E. Ziegler (St. Martin's Press, 1999), 211–39; Hans Wenzel, "Eine Wiener Christkindwiege in München und das Jesuskind der Margaretha Ebner," *Pantheon* 18, no. 6 (1960): 276–83. See also Jeffrey Hamburger, "The Visual and the Visionary: The Image in Late Medieval Monastic Devotions," *Viator* 20 (1989): 161–82; Ulinka Rublack, "Female Spirituality and the Infant Jesus in Late Medieval Dominican Convents," *Gender & History* 6, no. 1 (1994): 49.

75 As quoted in Rublack, "Female Spirituality and the Infant Jesus," 44.

76 Lewis, *By Women, for Women, about Women*, 101–2.

77 Lewis, *By Women, for Women, about Women*, 100–105.

78 Jeffrey F. Hamburger, "On the Little Bed of Jesus: The Image in Late Medieval Monastic Devotions," in *The Visual and the Visionary: Art and Female Spirituality in Late Medieval Germany* (Zone Books; MIT Press, 1998), 383–426, esp. 390.

79 Andrea Pearson, *Gardens of Love and the Limits of Morality in Early Netherlandish Art* (Brill, 2019). She cites Christina of Markyate, who begs Christ "to be freed from temptation. Even in solitude she unwillingly endured lustful urges." The infant Christ then visits her, and she takes him "in her hands, gave thanks and pressed him to her bosom.... From that moment, the fire of lust was so completely extinguished [in her] that never again could it be revived"; Pearson, *Gardens of Love and the Limits of Morality*, 220–21n53.

80 As quoted in Rublack, "Female Spirituality and the Infant Jesus," 42.

81 As quoted in Hamburger, *The Rothschild Canticles*, 109.

82 For the complete, edited text of Friedrich Sunder's biography, see Siegfried Ringler, *Viten- und Offenbarungsliteratur in Frauenklöstern des Mittelalters: Quellen und Studien* (Artemis Verlag, 1980), 391–444. See also Leonard P. Hindsley, "The Gnaden-Vita of Friedrich Sunder, Chaplain of Engelthal," in *The Mystics of Engelthal*, 83–109; Meri Heinonen, "Friedrich Sunder and the Boundaries of Gender," *Journal of Medieval History* 41, no. 4 (2015): 466–83; Annette Volfing, "Male Brides of Christ: Friedrich Sunder and Heinrich Seuse," in *The Daughter Zion Allegory*, 104–30.

83 Pearson, *Gardens of Love and the Limits of Morality*, 17, 224. Less than a century after the statue was made, theologian Johannes Molanus (d. 1585) spoke out against images of the naked Christ Child, writing, "For what sort of edification can there be in this nakedness? All one can hope is that children are not endangered by this or little ones brought to harm." See David Freedberg, "Johannes Molanus on Provocative Paintings: *De Historia Sanctarum Imaginum et Picturarum*, Book II, Chapter 42," *Journal of the Warburg and Courtauld Institutes* 34 (1971): 238–39, quoting and translating Johannes Molanus, *De Historia Sanctarum Imaginum et Picturarum* (1570; rev. and enl., Louvain, 1594), chap. 42, "In picturis cavendum esse quidquid ad libidinem provocat."

84 Pearson, *Gardens of Love and the Limits of Morality*, 225.

85 See Carolyn S. Jirousek, "*Christ and St. John the Evangelist* as a Model of Medieval Mysticism," *Cleveland Studies in the History of Art* 6 (2001): 6–27. For a list of the known sculptures, some of which have been lost, see Justin Lang, *Herzens Anliegen: Die Mystik mittelalterlicher Christus-Johannes-Gruppen* (Schwabenverlag, 1994), 96–98.

86 Though several of these sculptures are indisputably associated with Swabian convents, this work is said to come from an unspecified chapel in Württemberg; Jirousek, "*Christ and St. John the Evangelist*," 24n4. On the local manuscript and handbook tradition, see Jeffrey F. Hamburger, *St. John the Divine: The Deified Evangelist in Medieval Art and Theology* (University of California Press, 2002), esp. 95–164; Annette Volfing, *John the Evangelist and Medieval German Writing: Imitating the Inimitable* (Oxford University Press, 2001), esp. 101–62.

87 Both ideas are expressed in John 19:26–27: "When Jesus therefore had seen his mother and the disciple standing whom he loved, he saith to his mother: Woman, behold thy son. After that, he saith to the disciple: Behold thy mother. And from that hour, the disciple took her to his own."

88 Carolyn Diskant Muir, *Saintly Brides and Bridegrooms: The Mystic Marriage in Northern Renaissance Art* (Harvey Miller, 2012), 67–90.

89 For example, John Scotus Eriugena. See Volfing, *John the Evangelist,* 109.

90 By the sixteenth century, religious authorities no longer tolerated this seemingly contradictory stance. Hamburger, *St. John the Divine,* 160.

91 Jeffrey F. Hamburger, "The Body and Blood of Christ: Mary's Adopted Son," in *St. John the Divine*, 165–78. Volfing (*John the Evangelist*, 148–53) discusses this idea as it was presented in certain German handbooks for nuns as a corrective to what was perceived as excessive devotion to the bridal relationship.

92 Volfing, *John the Evangelist*, 134. Other religious women who identified with John include the Beguine Agnes Blannbekin (Volfing, *John the Evangelist*, 134); Berta von Herten (Jacqueline E. Jung, "Crystalline Wombs and Pregnant Hearts: The Exuberant Bodies of the Katharinenthal Visitation Group," in *History in the Comic Mode: Medieval Communities and the Matter of Person*, ed. Rachel Fulton and Bruce W. Holsinger [Columbia University Press, 2007], 223–37, esp. 232–33); Gertrude the Great and Adelheid Langmann (Muir, *Saintly Brides and Bridegrooms,* 86). For spiritual friendship, see Henrike Lähnemann and Eva Schlotheuber, *The Life of Nuns: Love, Politics, and Religion in Medieval German Convents* (Open Book Publishers, 2024).

93 The sculpture, attributed to Master Heinrich of Constance, is now in the Museum Mayer van den Bergh, Antwerp; Jirousek, "*Christ and St. John the Evangelist*," 20; Muir, *Saintly Brides and Bridegrooms,* 80.

94 Muir, *Saintly Brides and Bridegrooms,* 81. The Mechthild von Eschenz reference is cited in Jung, "Crystalline Wombs and Pregnant Hearts," 231–32.

95 Much has been written on the sculpture. See especially Jung, "Crystalline Wombs and Pregnant Hearts"; and Frances Lilliston, "'As Clear as Crystal': Transparency in the Katharinenthal Visitation Group and Sister Book," *Lapis* 3 (August 2021), https://wp.nyu.edu/lapis/frances-lilliston-katharinenthal-visitation-group/.

96 Physical examination underneath the crystals indicates they were added after the sculpture was made but certainly while the sculpture was still at the convent. Originally, there seems to have been a painted or sculpted element used to suggest their pregnant state.

97 On the last possibility, see Robert Mills, "Gender, Sodomy, Friendship and the Medieval Anchorhold," *Journal of Medieval Religious Cultures* 36, no. 1 (2010): 1–27; E. Ann Matter, "My Sister, My Spouse: Woman-Identified Women in Medieval Christianity," *Journal of Feminist Studies in Religion* 2, no. 2 (1986): 81–93.

98 As quoted in Jung, "Crystalline Wombs and Pregnant Hearts," 237, 362n60.

99 Salih, "Performances of Suffering," 38.

TOUCHING SAINT SEBASTIAN

1 See James M. Saslow, "The Tenderest Lover: Saint Sebastian in Renaissance Painting: A Proposed Homoerotic Iconology of North Italian Art 1450–1500," *Gay Academic Union Journal: Gai saber* 1, no. 1 (1977): 58–66; Richard A. Kaye, "Losing His Religion: Saint Sebastian as Contemporary Gay Martyr," in *Outlooks: Lesbian and Gay Sexualities and Visual Cultures,* ed. Peter Horne and Reina Lewis (Routledge, 1996), 86–105; Rachel Wall, "Saint Sebastian in the Renaissance: The Classicization and Homoeroticization of a Saint," *Art Journal* 1, no. 2 (2012): 11–23; James M. Saslow, "The Desiring Eye: Gender, Sexuality, and the Visual Arts," in *A Companion to Renaissance and Baroque Art*, ed. Babette Bohn and James M. Saslow (Wiley-Blackwell, 2013), 127–48; Jason James Hartford, *Sexuality, Iconography, and Fiction in French: Queering the Martyr* (Palgrave Macmillan, 2018); Tomás Miguel Cabrera Mimbrera, "Saint Sebastian: An Iconographic Study: From Painting to Film," *UcoArte: Revista de Teoría e Historia del Arte* 11 (2022): 223–45.

2 Giorgio Vasari, *Lives of the Artists*, trans. George Bull (Penguin, 1987), 2:123.

3 See Patricia Simons, "Prayer and Presence in a Small Italian Devotional Panel of Saint Sebastian (ca. 1500)," *Source: Notes in the History of Art* 38, no. 2 (2019), 77–87, esp. 82; Wall, "Saint Sebastian in the Renaissance," 13.

4 Kaye, "Losing His Religion," 90.

5 Recent conservation of the sculpture by Lucretia Kargère, conservator for medieval sculptures at The Met, confirms the originality of much of the polychromy. She estimates that approximately 60 percent of the paint is original, with the face being particularly well-preserved. The analysis also confirms that the cracks visible in the sculpture, particularly on the figure's right hand, were present soon after its creation. Strips of fabric in several places under the original paint make clear that the outer edges of the trunk were beginning to crack even as the piece was being made.

6 Adrian Randolph, citing concepts developed by Whitney Davis, argues for a similar formal disagreement between the front and rear sides of Donatello's bronze *David* (ca. 1440; Museo Nazionale de Bargello, Florence). See Adrian W. B. Randolph, "Homosocial Desire and Donatello's Bronze David," in *Engaging Symbols: Gender, Politics, and Public Art in Fifteenth-Century Florence* (Yale University Press, 2002), 139–92.

7 See Karl Whittington, "The Cluny Adam: Queering a Sculptor's Touch in the Shadow of Notre-Dame," in "Visualizing Gender and Sexuality in the Middle Ages," special issue, *Different Visions: A Journal of New Perspectives on Medieval Art* 8 (2022), https://doi.org/10.61302/YCIG9401. See also Karl Whittington, *Queer Making: Artists and Desire in Medieval Europe* (Penn State University Press, 2025).

FLIRTATION, VIOLENCE, AND DOMINATION ON AN IVORY CASKET

1 Alexandra Gajewski, "Attack on the Castle of Love: Flower Power or 'Traffic in Women'? An Allegorical Representation in Ivory Analysed from the Perspective of War and Gender," in *Gewalt, Krieg und Geschlecht im Mittelalter*, ed. Amalie Fößel (Peter Lang, 2020), 381–414. See also E. Jane Burns, *Courtly Love Undressed: Reading through Clothes in Medieval French Culture* (University of Pennsylvania Press, 2002), 140–41; James A. Schultz, *Courtly Love, the Love of Courtliness, and the History of Sexuality* (University of Chicago Press, 2006), 23–47.

2 Katherine Sedovic, "Materially Different, Visually Similar: Collaborative Production Processes Among Arthurian Manuscripts and Ivories in Fourteenth-Century Paris," in *Outils et pratiques des artisans du livre au Moyen-Âge*, ed. Jean-Luc Deuffic (Brepols, 2017), 181. And see Paula Mae Carns, "A Curious Collection in Ivory: The Lord Gort Casket," in *Collections in Context: The Organization of Knowledge and Community in Europe*, ed. Karen L. Fresco and Anne D. Hedeman (Ohio State University Press, 2011), 248; C. Jean Campbell, "Courting, Harlotry and the Art of Gothic Ivory Carving," *Gesta* 34, no. 1 (1995): 11.

3 See Sarah M. Guérin, "Meaningful Spectacles: Gothic Ivories Staging the Divine," *Art Bulletin* 95, no. 1 (2013): 53–77; Martha Easton, "Feminist Art History and Medieval Iconography," in *The Routledge Companion to Medieval Iconography*, ed. Colum Hourihane (Routledge, 2017), 430.

4 Joyce E. Salisbury, *The Beast Within: Animals in the Middle Ages*, 2nd ed. (Routledge, 2011), 62, 134–38.

5 Salisbury, *The Beast Within*, 119.

6 Emma Le Pouésard, "Fighter, Player, Hunter: Queer Women and Female Agents on Secular Gothic Ivories," *Medieval Feminist Forum: A Journal of Gender and Sexuality* 59, no. 1 (2023): 1–31.

QUEER CONNECTIONS WITH CHRIST'S BODY

1 For the visual traditions of the Man of Sorrows, *Imago pietatis*, and *Ecce homo* across Byzantium and Western Europe, see Robert Mills, "Ecce Homo," in *Gender and Holiness: Men, Women, and Saints in Late Medieval Europe*, ed. Samantha J. E. Riches and Sarah Salih (Routledge, 2002), 152–73. I am grateful to Melanie Holcumb and Nancy Thebaut for generously inviting me to contribute to this volume.

2 For themes of the body in writings about Saint Francis, see Kittredge Cherry, "Francis of Assisi: Queer Side Revealed for Saint who Loved Creation, Peace, and the Poor," *Q Spirit* (October 2017), https://qspirit.net/francis-assisi-queer/.

3 For definitions and discussions of seductive and sensual dimensions of Man of Sorrows imagery, see Michael Camille, "Seductions of the Flesh: Meister Francke's Female 'Man' of Sorrows," in *Frömmigkeit im Mittelalter: Politisch-soziale Kontexte, visuelle Praxis, körperliche Ausdrucksformen*, ed. Klaus Schreiner and Marc Müntz (Fink, 2002), 243–70; Thomas Kren, "Christian Imagery and the Development of the Nude in Europe," in *The Renaissance Nude*, ed. Thomas Kren with Jill Burke and Stephen J. Campbell, exh. cat. (J. Paul Getty Museum, 2018), 17–33. I thank Karl Whittington for our discussions on this topic.

4 For Giambono's three Man of Sorrows panels and two smaller versions on liturgical vestments worn by figures in larger paintings, as well as one *Vera Icon* of Christ's face imprinted on the sacred cloth, see William L. Barcham, "Six Panels by Michele Giambono, 'pictor Sancti Marci,'" in *New Perspectives on the Man of Sorrows*, ed. Catherine R. Puglisi and William L. Barcham (Medieval Institute Publications, 2013), 191–218. The seventh picture, another *Vera Icon*, was offered for sale as lot 118 at the Hôtel des Ventes de Poitiers Boissinot & Tailliez, May 22, 2021; see https://www.gazette-drouot.com/lots/15044204-michele-giambono-documente---.

5 Quoted in Amy Neff, "Byzantium Westernized, Byzantium Marginalized: Two Icons in the *Supplicationes variae*," *Gesta* 38, no. 1 (1999): 91.

6 Bonaventure, "Vitis mystica, " in *The Works of Bonaventure: Cardinal, Seraphic Doctor, and Saint*, trans. José de Vinck, vol. 1, *Mystical Opuscula* (St. Anthony Guild Press, 1960), 203–4.

7 Martha Easton, "The Wound of Christ, the Mouth of Hell: Appropriations and Inversions of Female Anatomy in the Later Middle Ages," in *Tributes to Jonathan J. G. Alexander: The Making and Meaning of Illuminated Medieval & Renaissance Manuscripts, Art, & Architecture*, ed. Susan L'Engle and Gerald B. Guest (Harvey Miller, 2006), 395–414; Martha Easton, "'Was It Good for You Too?': Medieval Erotic Art and Its Audiences," *Different Visions: A Journal of New Perspectives on Medieval Art* 1 (2008), https://doi.org/10.61302/BUIO3522.

8 Richard Hoffman Reinhardt, "Francis of Assisi's Perfect Jouissance: Theorizing Conversion through Objects and Affects in Early Franciscan Fragments," *Material Religion: The Journal of Objects, Art, and Belief* 18, no. 2 (2022): 228–49.

9 Franco Mormando, "'Nudus Nudum Christum Sequi': The Franciscans and Differing Interpretations of Male Nakedness in Fifteenth-Century Italy," in *Fifteenth-Century Studies*, vol. 33, ed. Edelgard E. DuBruck, Barbara I. Gusick, and William C. McDonald (Boydell and Brewer, 2008), 171–97; Sarah Salih, "Erotica," in *A Cultural History of Sexuality in the Middle Ages*, ed. Ruth Evans (Berg, 2011), 191. In the Middle Ages and the Renaissance, "sodomy" could refer to individuals of any gender identity or expression and include any non-procreative sexual act; see Robert Mills, *Seeing Sodomy in the Middle Ages* (University of Chicago Press, 2015).

10 Amy Neff, "'Palma Dabit Palmam': Franciscan Themes in a Devotional Manuscript," *Journal of the Warburg and Courtauld Institutes* 65 (2002): 22–66; Emanuele Lugli, *The Making of Measure and the Promise of Sameness* (University of Chicago Press, 2019), 145–52.

11 E. James Mundy, "*Franciscus alter Christus*: The Intercessory Function of a Late Quattrocento Panel," *Record of the Art Museum, Princeton University* 36, no. 2 (1977): 4–15.

12 Lars R. Jones, "*Visio divina?* Donor Figures and Representations of Imagistic Devotion: The Copy of the 'Virgin of Bagnolo' in the Museo dell'Opera del Duomo, Florence," in *Italian Panel Painting of the Duecento and Trecento*, ed. Victor M. Schmidt (National Gallery of Art, 2002), 30–55. I thank Sarah Kozlowski for sharing this source with me.

13 Caroline Walker Bynum, *Jesus as Mother: Studies in the Spirituality of the High Middle Ages* (University of California Press, 1982); Camille, "Seductions of the Flesh." See also Leo Steinberg, *The Sexuality of Christ in Renaissance Art and in Modern Oblivion* (MIT Press for the Institute for Architecture and Urban Studies, 1983); with a response from Caroline Walker Bynum about "feminine" Christ in "The Body of Christ in the Later Middle Ages: A Reply to Leo Steinberg," *Renaissance Quarterly* 39, no. 3 (1986): 399–439.

14 Penny Howell Jelly, "Pubics and Privates: Body Hair in Late Medieval Art," in *The Meanings of Nudity in Medieval Art*, ed. Sherry C. M. Lindquist (Ashgate, 2012), 183–206.

15 Jesse Dorris, "Catherine Opie Fixes Her Lens on the Vatican," *Surface*, February 20, 2024, https://www.surfacemag.com/articles/catherine-opie-fixes-her-lens-on-the-vatican/; "Catherine Opie: Walls, Windows, and Blood," press release for the exhibition at Lehmann Maupin, New York, February 8, 2024, https://www.lehmannmaupin.com/exhibitions/catherine-opie8/press-release.

16 See press release for "Catherine Opie." I am grateful to Mark, Alexander, and Éowyn Keene for discussing Opie's photographs with me.

MASCULINITIES AND TRANSGENDER EXPRESSION IN *THE BELLES HEURES* OF JEAN DE FRANCE, DUC DE BERRY

1 "Mortuo autem liberio papa ieronimis dignus summo / sacerdocio ab omnibus acclamatur sed derisus turpiter / a quibusdam vestem muliebrem per sua induit et ad ma- / tutinum derisus ab eis tante insanie locum dedit"; Limbourg Brothers, *The Belles Heures* of Jean de France, duc de Berry, 1405–1408/1409 (The Metropolitan Museum of Art, New York; The Cloisters Collection [54.1.1a, b]), fol. 184v.

2 Robert Mills, *Seeing Sodomy in the Middle Ages* (University of Chicago Press, 2015), 1–3.

3 Françoise Autrand, *Jean de Berry: L'art et le pouvoir* (Fayard, 2000), 434–35.

4 Odile Blanc, *Parades et parures: L'invention du corps de mode à la fin du Moyen Âge* (Gallimard, 1997), 9.

5 Georges Sidéris, "Bassianos: Les monastères de Bassianou et de Matrônès (Ve–VIe siècle)," in *Le saint, le moine et le paysan: Mélanges d'histoire byzantine offerts à Michel Kaplan*, ed. Olivier Delouis, Sophie Métivier, and Paule Pagès (Publications de la Sorbonne, 2016), 631–56.

6 Peter Brown, *The Body and Society: Men, Women and Sexual Renunciation in Early Christianity* (Columbia University Press, 1988), 366–86.

7 "Sin autem Christo magis voluerit servire quam sæculo, mulier esse cessabit, et dicetur vir, quia omnes in perfectum virum cupimus occurrere"; Jerome, "Commentariorum in Epistolan ad Ephesios, bk. 3, col. 533 (Eph. 5:28), in J.-P. Migne, ed., *Patrologiae cursus completus . . . : Series latina*, vol. 26 (Paris: Garnier frères, 1844).

8 Inès Villela-Petit, "Les frères Limbourg," *Dictionnaire d'histoire de l'art du Moyen Âge occidental* (Robert Laffont, 2009), 527–28.

9 Martha Easton, "Uncovering the Meanings of Nudity in the *Belles Heures* of Jean, Duke of Berry," in *The Meanings of Nudity in Medieval Art*, ed. Sherry C. M. Lindquist (Ashgate, 2012), 149–81.

LOVE IN MORTAL TIME

1 Deborah Youngs, *The Life Cycle in Western Europe, c. 1300–c. 1500* (Manchester University Press, 2006), 98–99.

2 Youngs, *The Life Cycle in Western Europe*, 102.

3 Margaret B. Freeman, *The Unicorn Tapestries* (The Metropolitan Museum of Art, 1976), 135.

4 Susan Crane, *The Performance of Self: Ritual, Clothing, and Identity During the Hundred Years War* (University of Pennsylvania Press, 2002), 20.

5 Crane, *The Performance of Self*, 52–53, 47.

6 See Elina Gertsman and Barbara H. Rosenwein, *The Middle Ages in 50 Objects* (Cambridge University Press, 2018), 200–203; Michael Camille, *The Medieval Art of Love: Objects and Subjects of Desire* (Abrams, 1998), 160.

7 Youngs, *The Life Cycle in Western Europe*, 102.

8 Geoffrey Chaucer, "The Wife of Bath's Prologue," in *The Canterbury Tales*, lines 706–10, https://chaucer.fas.harvard.edu/pages/wife-baths-prologue-and-tale-0.

9 Christine de Pisan, *The Book of the City of the Ladies*, trans. Rosalind Brown-Grant (Penguin Books, 1999), 18–19.

FURTHER READING

Bernau, Anke, Ruth Evans, and Sarah Salih, eds. *Medieval Virginities*. University of Toronto Press, 2003.

Betancourt, Roland. *Byzantine Intersectionality: Sexuality, Gender, and Race in the Middle Ages*. Princeton University Press, 2020.

Boswell, John. *Christianity, Social Tolerance, and Homosexuality: Gay People in Western Europe from the Beginning of the Christian Era to the Fourteenth Century*. 1980; University of Chicago Press, 2015.

Bullough, Vern L., and James A. Brundage, eds. *Handbook of Medieval Sexuality*. Garland Publishing, 1996.

Bynum, Caroline Walker. *Jesus as Mother: Studies in the Spirituality of the High Middle Ages*. University of California Press, 1982.

Camille, Michael. "'For Our Devotion and Pleasure': The Sexual Objects of Jean, Duc de Berry." *Art History* 24, no. 2 (2001): 169–94.

Camille, Michael. *The Medieval Art of Love: Objects and Subjects of Desire*. Abrams, 1998.

Campbell, Emma, and Robert Mills, eds. *Troubled Vision: Gender, Sexuality, and Sight in Medieval Text and Image*. Palgrave Macmillan, 2004.

Caviness, Madeline H. "Patron or Matron? A Capetian Bride and a Vade Mecum for Her Marriage Bed." *Speculum* 68, no. 2 (1993): 333–62.

DeVun, Leah. *The Shape of Sex: Nonbinary Gender from Genesis to the Renaissance*. Columbia University Press, 2021.

Dinshaw, Carolyn. *Getting Medieval: Sexualities and Communities, Pre- and Postmodern*. Duke University Press, 1999.

Easton, Martha. "'Was It Good For You, Too?': Medieval Erotic Art and Its Audiences." *Different Visions: New Perspectives on Medieval Art* 1 (2008). https://doi.org/10.61302/BUIO3522.

Easton, Martha. "The Wound of Christ, the Mouth of Hell: Appropriations and Inversions of Female Anatomy in the Later Middle Ages." In *Tributes to Jonathan J. G. Alexander: The Making and Meaning of Illuminated Medieval & Renaissance Manuscripts, Art & Architecture*, edited by Susan L'Engle and Gerald B. Guest, 395–409. Harvey Miller, 2006.

Evans, Ruth, ed. *A Cultural History of Sexuality in the Middle Ages*. Berg, 2011.

Halberstam, Jack. *In a Queer Time and Place: Transgender Bodies, Subcultural Lives*. New York University Press, 2005.

Hamburger, Jeffrey F. *The Visual and the Visionary: Art and Female Spirituality in Late Medieval Germany*. Zone Books; MIT Press, 1998.

Jaeger, C. Stephen. *Ennobling Love: In Search of a Lost Sensibility*. University of Pennsylvania Press, 1999.

Karras, Ruth Mazo, and Katherine E. Pierpont. *Sexuality in Medieval Europe: Doing unto Others*. 4th ed. Routledge, 2023.

Keene, Bryan C. "An Unmentionable History: The Stigma of Sodomy and Images of Violence Toward Queer and Trans Peoples in Premodern Europe." In *Gender Violence, Art, and the Viewer: An Intervention*, edited by Ellen C. Caldwell, Cynthia S. Colburn, and Ella J. Gonzalez, 50–61. Penn State University Press, 2024.

Le Pouésard, Emma. "Fighter, Player, Hunter: Queer Women and Female Agents on Secular Gothic Ivories." *Medieval Feminist Forum: A Journal of Gender and Sexuality* 59, no. 1 (2023): 1–31.

Lindquist, Sherry C. M. "Gender." In "Medieval Art History Today—Critical Terms." Special issue, *Studies in Iconography* 33 (2012): 113–30.

Lochrie, Karma. *Heterosyncrasies: Female Sexuality When Normal Wasn't*. University of Minnesota Press, 2005.

Lochrie, Karma, Peggy McCracken, and James A. Schultz, eds. *Constructing Medieval Sexuality*. University of Minnesota Press, 1997.

McCarthy, Conor, ed. *Love, Sex & Marriage in the Middle Ages: A Sourcebook*. 2nd ed. Routledge, 2022.

McClanan, Anne L., and Karen Rosoff Encarnación, eds. *The Material Culture of Sex, Procreation, and Marriage in Premodern Europe*. Palgrave, 2002.

Mills, Robert. *Seeing Sodomy in the Middle Ages.* University of Chicago Press, 2015.

Muir, Carolyn Diskant. *Saintly Brides and Bridegrooms: The Mystic Marriage in Northern Renaissance Art.* Harvey Miller, 2012.

Schultz, James A. *Courtly Love, the Love of Courtliness, and the History of Sexuality*. University of Chicago Press, 2006.

Spencer-Hall, Alicia, and Blake Gutt eds. *Trans and Genderqueer Subjects in Medieval Hagiography*. Amsterdam University Press, 2021.

Vaccaro, Christopher, ed. *Painful Pleasures: Sadomasochism in Medieval Cultures*. Manchester University Press, 2022.

Whittington, Karl. "Queer." In "Medieval Art History Today—Critical Terms." Special issue, *Studies in Iconography* 33 (2012): 157–68.

Wolfthal, Diane. "'A Hue and a Cry': Medieval Rape Imagery and Its Transformation." *Art Bulletin* 75, no. 1 (1993): 39–64.

Wolfthal, Diane. *In and Out of the Marital Bed: Seeing Sex in Renaissance Europe*. Yale University Press, 2010.

INDEX

Page numbers in *italics* refer to illustrations.

PHOTOGRAPHY CREDITS

Courtesy of Beinecke Rare Book & Manuscript Library, Yale University: pls. 34, 39; Photo: © By permission of the British Library: fig. 1; Brussels, FWB-Plan Pep's/Atelier de l'imagier: figs. 14, 15; Photo © Cleveland Museum of Art / Bridgeman Images: pls. 4, 43; Cleveland Museum of Art, OH, USA/Delia E. Holden and L. E. Holden Funds/Bridgeman Images: pl. 48; fig. 36; Image © The Metropolitan Museum of Art: frontispiece, pp. 8, 44; pls. 1, 12, 16, 19, 23, 26, 30, 31A,B, 32, 35–37, 42, 44, 46, 47; figs. 8, 20–22, 32, 33; Image © The Metropolitan Museum of Art, photo by Katherine Dahab: pl. 25; fig. 19; Image © The Metropolitan Museum of Art, photo by Paul Lachenauer: pl. 18; Image © The Metropolitan Museum of Art, photo by Mark Morosse: pl. 40; Image © The Metropolitan Museum of Art, photo by Bruce Schwarz: p. 6, pls. 2, 14, 29; figs. 9, 10, 13, 23, 24; Image © The Metropolitan Museum of Art, photo by Hyla Skopitz: pl. 6; Image © The Metropolitan Museum of Art, photo by Juan Trujillo: p. 70, pls. 3, 15; figs. 4, 11, 12; Image © The Metropolitan Museum of Art, photo by Peter Zeray: front cover, back cover, p. 26; pls. 5, 8, 13, 22, 27, 28, 41, 45; figs. 16, 17, 25, 27–31; Courtesy of The Morgan Library & Museum, New York: pls. 7, 10, 11, 17, 20, 21, 33, 38; fig. 3; Photo Musées de Strasbourg, M. Bertola: fig. 37; © Catherine Opie, Courtesy Regen Projects, Los Angeles; Lehmann Maupin, New York, Hong Kong, London, and Seoul; Thomas Dane Gallery, London and Naples; and Peder Lund, Oslo: fig. 34; Courtesy of Princeton University Library: pl. 9; ©RMN-Grand Palais (domaine de Chantilly) / Michel Urtado: fig. 35; © The Trustees of the British Museum: fig. 7; Courtesy of University Library, Basel: fig. 26; Courtesy of Van Beuningen Family Collection: fig. 2; © Victoria and Albert Museum, London: fig. 5; Courtesy of Vienna National Library: fig. 6; Courtesy of The Walters Art Museum, Baltimore: pl. 24; Courtesy of Wellcome Collection: fig. 18

This catalogue is published in conjunction with
SPECTRUM OF DESIRE:
LOVE, SEX, AND GENDER IN THE MIDDLE AGES
on view at The Met Cloisters, New York
from October 17, 2025, through March 29, 2026.

The exhibition is made possible by the Michel David-Weill Fund and Kathryn A. Ploss.

The catalogue is made possible by the Michel David-Weill Fund and Nellie and Robert Gipson.

Additional support is provided by Wendy A. Stein and Bart Friedman.

Published by The Metropolitan Museum of Art, New York
Mark Polizzotti, Publisher and Editor in Chief
Peter Antony, Associate Publisher for Production
Michael Sittenfeld, Associate Publisher for Editorial

Edited by Elizabeth L. Block
Production by Christina Grillo
Designed by Beverly Joel, pulp, ink.
Bibliographic editing by Margaret Aspinwall
Image acquisitions and permissions by Jenn Sherman

Photographs of works in The Met collection are by Peter Zeray, Imaging department, The Metropolitan Museum of Art, unless otherwise noted.

Additional photography credits appear on page 143.

Typeset in Roman Grotesque and AT Realm
Printed on Perigord 150 gsm
Separated, printed, and bound by Trifolio S.r.l., Verona, Italy

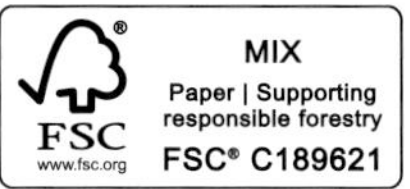

Cover illustrations: front, Saint Sebastian, late 15th century (detail, PL. 45); back, Plaque with the Fountain of Youth, ca. 1320–40 (detail, PL. 13)

Page 2: The Visitation, ca. 1310–20 (detail, PL. 44); page 6: Back cover of a writing tablet showing flirtatious lovers (detail, FIG. 13); page 8: The Limbourg Brothers, Saint Jerome in a woman's dress from *The Belles Heures* of Jean de France, duc de Berry, 1405–1408/1409 (detail, PL. 47)

Every effort has been made to track object provenances as thoroughly and accurately as possible based on available scholarship, traceable transactions, and the existing archaeological record. Despite best efforts, there is often an absence of provenance information. Provenances of objects in The Met collection are updated as additional research comes to light. Readers are encouraged to visit metmuseum.org and to search by an object's accession number for its most up-to-date information.

The Metropolitan Museum of Art
1000 Fifth Avenue
New York, New York 10028
metmuseum.org

Distributed by
Yale University Press, New Haven and London
yalebooks.com/art
yalebooks.co.uk

Authorized Representative in the EU: Easy Access System Europe, Mustamäe tee 50, 10621 Tallin, Estonia, gpsr.requests@easproject.com

Cataloguing-in-Publication Data is available from the Library of Congress.
ISBN 978-1-58839-805-5